D1172752

The Remembered Gate

A Deep South Book

The Remembered Gate

Memoirs by Alabama Writers

Edited by
Jay Lamar and Jeanie Thompson

The University of Alabama Press
Tuscaloosa and London

Writing and editing of this book was made possible through grants from the Alabama Civil Justice Foundation and the Alabama Corporate Foundation for Children.

9 8 7 6 5 4 3 2 1   09 08 07 06 05 04 03 02

Designer: Michele Myatt Quinn; Typeface: Caslon

Patricia Foster, "What Do You Do for the Place?" first appeared in the *Virginia Quarterly Review* 76, no. 4 (2000).

Portions of Frye Gaillard's "The Heart of Dixie" appeared in *Close to Home: Revelations and Reminiscences by North Carolina Authors* (Winston-Salem, N.C.: John F. Blair, 1996) and in a different form in *Lessons from the Big House* (Asheboro, N.C.: Down Home Press, 1994).

A version of Andrew Hudgins's "Alabama Breakdown" first appeared in *New England Review* (winter 1999).

Rodney Jones's "A Half Mile of Road in North Alabama" first appeared in *Oxford American* 37 (January/February 2001).

C. Eric Lincoln's "Coming through the Fire" first appeared as "The Fire in Alabama," in *Coming Through the Fire: Surviving Race and Place in America* (Durham, N.C.: Duke University Press, 1996). Copyright 1996, Duke University Press. All rights reserved. Reprinted with permission.

Albert Murray's "Regional Particulars and Universal Implications" first appeared in *Blue Devils of Nada: A Contemporary American Approach to Aesthetic Statement* (New York: Pantheon Books, 1996). Copyright 1996, Albert Murray. All rights reserved. Reprinted with permission.

∞
The paper on which this book is printed meets the minimum requirements of American National Standard for Information Science—Permanence of Paper for Printed Library Materials, ANSI Z39.48–1984.

Library of Congress Cataloging-in-Publication Data

The remembered gate: memoirs by Alabama writers / edited by Jay Lamar andd Jeanie Thompson.
    p. cm. — (Deep South books)
ISBN 0-8173-1123-8 (cloth: alk. paper)
1. Authors, American—Alabama—Biography. 2. Alabama—Biography. I. Lamar, Jay, 1956–
II. Thompson, Jeanie. III. Series.
PS266.A5 R46 2002
810.9'9761–dc21   2001003753

British Library Cataloguing-in-Publication Data available

Photo of Patricia Foster by Jon Van Allen; photo of Mary Ward Brown by Jerry Siegel; photo of James Haskins by Bill Horne; photo of Andrew Glaze by Adriana Glaze; photo of Helen Norris by Robertson Photography; photo of Wayne Greenhaw by Sally Greenhaw; photo of Andrew Hudgins by Joanna Eldredge Morrissey; photo of Phyllis Alesia Perry by M. Shawn Dowdell; photo of Rodney Jones by Gloria Jones; photo of William Cobb by Amy Cunliffe; photo of Frye Gaillard by Amy Rogers; photo of Sena Jeter Naslund by Sigrid Estrada; photo of Charles Gaines by Michael Marzelli; photo of Judith Hillman Paterson by Dennis Cauchon; photo of Albert Murray by Jeanie Thompson

This collection is dedicated
to the memory of Dr. C. Eric Lincoln,
1924–2000.

Contents

Preface

JAY LAMAR

JEANIE THOMPSON

Place once whispered something unimpeachable and anomalous
about a human being, and it still does, but it is damned odd.
—Rodney Jones, "A Half Mile of Road in North Alabama"

Nineteen writers who claim Alabama kin have contributed essays
to *The Remembered Gate: Memoirs by Alabama Writers.* Each one
approaches the journey back with opened-eye frankness. We are
invited to observe what is sometimes a harrowing experience, sometimes a playful, even wistful look back. However, in every one of
these essays, we learn how an individual artist has come to understand her- or himself as a developing writer within a changing
Alabama landscape.

Whether from the perspective of a black boy beaten for his pre-
sumption that he deserved to be paid for his work or the point of
view of a white woman floundering with her unresolved relationship
with her family's former maid, these personal renderings are intensely realized visions of a writer's sense of being a writer. Further,
there seems to be no way to separate these writers' sense of themselves from their awareness of the place that shaped them. Perhaps
the South is unique in this regard. Perhaps not. Still, the evidence
here is clear: people, landscape, and cultural perspectives have made
these writers who they are, and their work what it is.

To the general question, "How did growing up in Alabama, or
spending formative years in the state, shape you as a writer?" we

received nineteen variations on a theme of self-awareness and self-discovery. This collection blends into a complex, richly textured portrait of men and women struggling with, and within, Alabama's economic and cultural evolution in the twentieth century. Some of the writers' lives began as early as the 1910s, and thus we witness the pre–civil rights era from both black and white perspectives. Others enter the scene in the 1950s, or as late as the 1960s, yet Alabama looms large as the main character, an ephemeral but overarching presence, in each tale. For some, the character just won't go away, nagging like a late-summer mosquito.

C. Eric Lincoln begins "Coming through the Fire" with these seemingly innocent sentences: "I shall always be sentimental about Alabama. It used to be my home." But the reader must be wary. No one reading about Lincoln's struggle with the "fire" of racism can read this essay unaffected by the cruel physicality of hate, and its scars. The issues of race, the Wallace era, and Alabama's transformation from rural to urban economies permeate all of these essays in one way or another. Lincoln directly addresses this in relation to his experience as a black writer who had to leave the South to do his work. Frye Galliard tells how bitter racial arguments with his white elders in south Alabama were the catalyst for his becoming a journalist. For writers Patricia Foster and Phyllis Alesia Perry, however, race is backdrop, not foreground, to self-examination. "Who am I?" is the overwhelming question.

For others here, the southern way of life might be translated to any small American town where treasure-laden homes, literate parents, and dedicated teachers shape a budding writer's imagination. James Haskins memorializes a generation who believed in self-reliance and personal responsibility and who nurtured in him a cultural identity in spite of racism and segregation. Robert Inman tours his grandmother's attic and tells lovingly of his discovery of books, trunks of World War II artifacts, and the beginnings of imaginative ruminations. Sena Jeter Naslund paints a portrait of Birmingham in the 1950s and 1960s as a city that boasted a fine children's library and good public schools where she and her brothers began to "narrate their adventures" at an early age, developing a sense of character, panorama, and scene that she later applied to fiction. For Wayne Greenhaw learning to swim was literal—with a one-legged black man during a boyhood summer—*and* figurative, as he moved through the nutrient-rich waters of older writers' guidance, in particular that of Tuscaloosa writers Borden and Babs Deal and Hudson Strode.

In his energetic "Alabama Breakdown," Andrew Hudgins remembers being introduced as an exhibit of "Southern Culture" to a gathering in Mississippi. Examining how he did or did not fit into this ready-made formula shapes Hudgins's self-portrait about coming of age in a city where racism collided publicly with aspects of his personal life. One element of that formula to which Hudgins submits himself is southern "cussedness" and its cousin, the southern "grotesque," which also appears as the diabolical Cletus Hickey in William Cobb's essay on personal demons and the redemptive power of love and work. Traveling with lesser demons, Nanci Kincaid brings us from Florida into Alabama, riding the wake of her father's compulsive returning and surveying the disappearing scene from the back dash of the family Chevy. The ties that bind make long stitches in the fabric of her young universe, where she is deeply attentive to truth and appearance and the critical content of point of view. Perhaps the staunchest supporter of Alabama's uncanny ability to form writers comes from Fannie Flagg, who asserts that Alabamians have a bond that exceeds all others. This fierce sense of self shapes Flagg's own characters, she tells us, and her love of the people of Alabama—and her desire to set the record straight about them—fuel her writing.

Three senior writers in this volume allow us a look back at Alabama's urban and rural past. Mary Ward Brown's evocative "Swing Low: A Memoir" tells a story that will never be repeated in Alabama. The devotion of a black man, one of the "household help," to her mother, which extends to her deathbed, may be unfathomable today, yet it was the reality in which Brown grew up and which shapes her fiction. For Helen Norris, her young life in pre-urban Montgomery provides us with a picture of life when children could discover a gradual unfolding of events and "a keen awareness of the hereness of things." Norris convinces us that as a child she "always felt around [her] the land, its living presence, its every contour, as if [her] body were laid upon it." Andrew Glaze addresses head-on the difficult terrain of an overweening father as the continuing theme of "Growing Up a Poet in Alabama." In this painful look at how a poet's sensibility develops within and despite battering from an insensitive adult's point of view, Glaze evokes Birmingham of the 1930s through the 1960s. Though he could've grown up a poet in any state, and probably would have, his story is Alabama-flavored in every way.

Undeniably, the thread of how stories are made, how language is shaped, how an ear is tuned and an eye trained for detail is part of the fabric of any writer's life. In his lyrical musing about a half mile of road in rural Morgan County, Alabama, Rodney Jones tells how "whatever consciousness I possess spreads outwards from there in a tentative, grappling wonder"; before electricity carried the messages and lighted the landscape, story was the current, and currency, of human discourse. And how one learns to tell one's story is inextricably tied to place and family. Witness Charles Gaines's playful, postmodern "Growing Up in Alabama: A Meal in Four Courses, Beginning with Dessert" and Judith Hillman Paterson's essay, which concludes that she's closest not to Thomas Wolfe's dictum about home, but to T. S. Eliot's concise description of the learning process: "The end of all our exploring / Will be to arrive where we started / And know the place for the first time."

As epilogue to the journey back home, Albert Murray's "Regional Particulars and Universal Implications" gives us perspective on the "representative anecdote" that is the essence of all life-writing. Murray reminds us that what is universal is also *always* particular to a place. He delineates his "down-home source," "the fully orchestrated blues statement," as a survival strategy for one black writer from Alabama bent on trumpeting his particular tale.

Perhaps as Rodney Jones says, the "paradox of region is that it is too large to create great art." But the work of each of these writers makes a serious creative counterargument. In Alabama, people often begin a sentence, "I'm proud. . . ." We are proud to have asked these men and women to consider a fundamental question: What has Alabama meant to you as a writer?

The Remembered Gate

C. Eric Lincoln

Coming through the Fire

Alabama: The Tender Years

I shall always be sentimental about Alabama. It used to be my
home. There were cotton fields and clay pits, and an abandoned
limestone quarry where we swam in the summertime. And there
were dusty roads like velvet to the tough soles of our bare feet. And
creeks full of perch. And peach orchards to rob. And snakes not to
step on. And county fairs once a year. And on Sunday mornings
there was the wonderful smell of frying chicken—to be ready with
lots of rice and turnip greens when the preacher came by to eat dinner after service. And there was the procession to the Sunday school
that began at Miss Katie's house and grew by ones and twos and
threes all the way to Village View Methodist Church on the corner
of Hines Street and Plato Jones Dirt Road.

It was just a little town in north Alabama. So small that when anybody left to go to Nashville or Chicago, everybody missed him before the train had whistled on past the county line. Athens wasn't much of a town, but that's where I was born, and there is a part of me still there, left over from those tender years.

The first consciousness of race comes early. It is not something you learn in the same way you learn about stinging caterpillars or poison ivy. You do not have to learn it from some overt experience. It is a pervasive awareness, an insidious thing that seeps into the soil of consciousness, sending its toxic tendrils deep into the walls of the mind. It is like a mold, a blight. If you scrape it away here, you find it mockingly virulent there. Once the concept of race takes root in the mind, it is there to stay. You cannot run away from it because it is *inside* you. You cannot close your eyes to it because it is an idée fixe that never leaves the retina of awareness. You may cover it with an intellectual tarpaulin as you would cover a weed patch on an otherwise perfect lawn with a sheet of black plastic. But the landscape is marred by the patchwork, and when it is removed, the weeds you thought were dead come springing back to life.

In the South, where I was raised, the pervasive awareness of race was helped along by a series of "lessons" learned in the process of growing up. These lessons were sometimes impromptu, and often impersonal, but they were never unplanned or unintended. They were always there in the arsenal of race and place waiting for the most effective moment for inculcation. Their sources were varied, and as might be expected some of the most traumatic derived from everyday personal relations with white people. But others were carefully taught at home or in the informal councils of the elders as the fundamentals of black survival. Some were taught in more stressful settings by the local police or by night riders as constant reminders of the inevitability of the status quo, white over black, now and forever. And no nonsense about it. Depending upon the source and cause of such "instruction," the lessons were often accompanied by loss of employment, foreclosure, loss of credit or credibility, intimidation, personal assault, jail time, a "bad name," or any combination of these. Repeated failure to learn meant long-term incarceration or permanent exile. Peremptory challenge meant death.

A First Lesson

The summer when I was nine years old I went to the county health office in the basement of the county courthouse to be immunized against some childhood disease. As I stood in a long line of children, waiting for my turn at the needle, I became aware that some of the boys and girls were not required to wait in line. These favored children, who were taken as soon as they came into the room, were all "white." I was vaguely aware, of course, that they were somehow different beyond the fact of their whiteness, for this uncanny, unexplained awareness is the first bitter fruit of acculturation. But I had, as yet, no appreciation of the deadly meaning of that difference. I had swum and fished and fought and filched and played with anybody who would play, white or black. What did it matter, if you could hit the ball and run the bases? As often as not my playmates and fellow adventurers had been white, for these were the children who owned the baseballs, the bicycles, the air rifles, and all the other toys and paraphernalia that enhanced the fun and adventure to which every boy seemed somehow entitled. Most of the time white boys and black boys played together without incident. The major problem for black children was managing to escape from the ever-escalating chores of the household, not the acceptance of the white children waiting to play with them. My grandmother cooked for a white family, and I had always felt at ease anywhere in the town. People knew her because she "cooked for the Martins." And I guess I expected to be known and accepted by extension. How, then, could I have known that I was about to challenge one of the fundamental privileges of white identity when I presented myself unbidden to be serviced? *I was nine years old:* How could I have known that this instance of tending two races at the same time in the same place was itself an extraordinary concession to expediency in protecting the town from some sort of epidemic? How could I have known that had we been adults instead of children such a breach of convention could not have happened if the whole town had been dying of cholera or whatever, expediency notwithstanding?

I could not have known any of this, so in my childish determination to enter into the spirit of the game the white kids seemed to be playing, I stepped forward with some newly arrived white children and offered my arm without being specifically bidden to do so. The very next second I learned my first lesson in race relations. The nurse grabbed my outstretched arm and flung me brutally back against the wall. "Boy!" she scowled threateningly, "Get back in line! *Get all the way back there! All you niggers have to wait!*" It was brutal, it was direct. And it was perplexing. As I stood against the wall rubbing my arm, I soon came to realize that it was not my arm that was hurting, it was my soul. There was a sort of numbness, a *dead* feeling. The pain was *inside* me and I would never be able to rub it away. Over and over I repeated the words: *Get all the way back there! All niggers have to wait! All niggers have to wait! All niggers have to wait! All niggers have to wait! Wait! Wait! Wait! Nigger, wait!*

My first lesson was a difficult one, for it offered no explanation, no rationale, just, *"All niggers have to wait."* Why? For what? I did not know that the why had already been answered, and that I was supposed to know the answer. It was presumed to be innate in my being. Ultimately, the answer was inured in the color of my skin. That was *why,* and I was supposed to know that. The question *for what?* was endless in application: for an education, for a job, for a place to live, for a ride on the bus, for a space on the elevator, for a place to go to school, for buying a loaf of bread, for ginning a load of cotton, for a chance to vote, for justice in the courts, and even for a chance to fight for the homeland. I was supposed to know that too. *All niggers have to wait!* and since I was obviously a nigger in the mind of the nurse, I was charged with knowing all that by the ripe old age of nine.

The next lesson in race relations came close on the heels of the first, and this time it was learned not in the strange, unpredictable world of the white man but from the lips of my own grandmother.

It was a curious lesson indeed, and one I was not to fully understand until succeeding years unlocked the remarkable esoterics of history and economics that structured the South in confusing paradox. It happened this way:

I lived with my grandparents on the edge of town in a frame house on Westview Street. It wasn't much of a street, really, and when it rained too hard it was impassable to all except the most determined pedestrian traffic. Yet we were only two blocks from the edge of the white community—"where the sidewalk begins"—and scarcely eight or ten blocks from Courthouse Square, the center of the town itself. Horses and wagons were still common in the town, and indeed they remain so in gardening and small-scale farming to this day.

One rainy Saturday morning a white man knocked at our door and asked to borrow a singletree. He explained that his wagon, loaded with firewood, was stuck in the mud a little way down the street, and he had broken his singletree in his efforts to dislodge it. My grandfather had a horse and wagon which he used for odd jobs of gardening and hauling about town, and for "farming" his three acres of cotton. As he was sick in bed, I offered to fetch the "tree," whereupon Grandma ordered me into the house and directed the white man to the barn to find the piece for himself. Then she immediately dispatched me behind him to make certain that he made no unauthorized acquisitions. When the man brought the singletree back half an hour later, he again knocked at the front door. However, Grandma refused to answer the door, and a "look" from her conveyed perfectly the message that I had better not answer it either.

A few minutes later the white man went around the house and knocked on the back door. Ma Matt immediately got out of her rocking chair, smoothed out her apron, and went to open the kitchen door.

"Yes?" she said.

"I brought back your tree," the man said. "I got my wagon out of that mudhole, and A'nty, I'm much obliged to you."

My grandmother was not a black-skinned woman, but at that
moment her face darkened so that I became a little frightened. I had
never seen her so angry.

"What did you say?" she demanded. "Didn't you call me 'A'nty'?"
She shook the heavy singletree at the man, who retreated rapidly
across the back porch and down the low steps to the ground. "Well,
I ain't your A'nty!" she declared. "And if you don't know your manners no better than that, then you get on out of this yard right now!"
With that she threw the "tree" at the man and he hurried out of the
yard and down the street to his wagon. Had not Grandpa appeared
at the door to see what the commotion was about, I'm certain she
would have chased that white man all the way to the pavement!

When Mama Matt had had a chance to cool off a little, I asked
her why she had become so angry.

"Didn't you hear that white man call me 'A'nty'?" she asked dis-
dainfully. Her face was starting to darken up again.

"Yes ma'am," I answered hastily. Then, with well-calculated innocence I ventured: "But the people you work for, Miss Lidie and Mr.
Martin, they call you 'A'nty'?"

"Yes!" she said sharply, "but *he* ain't Miss Lidie and he ain't Mr.
Dubbie Gee. He ain't nothing but a po' white cracker, and ain't no
po' white trash gon' come up in my yard and call me no 'A'nty!' *Po'
white trash don't count for nothin'!*"

This was indeed a strange world, and it was growing increasingly
complex by the day. I had hardly learned that there are important
distinctions between white people and people who are not white
before I was required to learn a second lesson—that not all white
people are the same. *Po' white trash don't count!* They could be
required to come to the back door, just like colored people had to go
to the back doors of the "quality" white folks downtown. And you
could say "yes" to them, though to "real" white folks you had to say
"Yes, sir!" and "Yes, ma'am!" You could even chase them away from
your house if they insulted you by calling you "A'nty," which was
considered an honorific if used by *quality* white people. Later I was
to hear Mr. Martin refer to poor white folks like the woodman as

"pore-assed peckerwoods"; and many times I heard him tell Grandpa that "one good nigger is worth half a dozen of them redneck crackers spitting 'round Courthouse Square on Saturday." Later, I was to hear him elaborate on just what a "good nigger" was, and that would be another lesson in the race relations everybody was supposed to understand.

Counting Cotton Money

The town in which I lived did not afford a public high school that black people could attend. There were two public high schools for white youngsters, but as far as the city fathers and the county administration were concerned, education for black children should not exceed the sixth grade, especially if higher education for blacks meant scaled-down appropriations for white schools. And of course, for black and white children to attend the same school was a notion beyond the possibility of conception in the Alabama of that era.

There was, however, a private high school for blacks in the town. It was a missionary school, established by the New England–based American Missionary Association shortly after the Civil War. And it was a better school than any the city might have provided had it had a mind to do so. Very possibly it was the best school in north Alabama. It was run as a missionary expression of the Congregational Church, and its interracial faculty was disproportionately blessed with dedicated Christian women from Massachusetts and Connecticut.

Tuition at Trinity High School was twenty-seven dollars a year, but since no one ever had twenty-seven dollars to pay in a lump sum, tuition was computed at three dollars a month. Even this sum was difficult to come by, so more than half of the student body were either working for the school or were on scholarships provided by New England philanthropy. As for myself, I first started earning my tuition when I reached the third grade by hauling horse manure from Grandpa's stable to spread on the school garden at fifteen cents per wheelbarrow load. Then, when I was thirteen, our home burned to the ground; Grandpa was sick again; there was no money in the house. Mama Matt and I went out into the nearby fields where the cotton had been harvested, and after several hours of effort managed to "glean" a large sackful of cotton "lint." School was open . . . and I had to have books. And books cost money if you went to a black school.

Early next morning I put the sack of cotton on a wheelbarrow and pushed it into town to the gin. The manager of the gin was a tall red-faced man who always wore a cigar stub plugged into the corner of his mouth. I had seen him before when I had gone there with Grandpa, but I had never spoken to him. I did not know his name, but he was standing in the doorway of his office as I pushed the wheelbarrow upon the platform.

"What you got there, boy?" he asked as he wobbled the cigar stub from corner to corner of his small, tobacco-stained mouth.

"I've got some cotton I'd like to sell," I said.

"You steal it, nigger?" he demanded. When I assured him I did not, he ordered me to "put it on the scales."

I hung the bag on the long iron balance that is a symbol of cotton country all over the South. The white man adjusted the pea, and when the balance was struck I could see that the bag of cotton weighed exactly forty-one pounds. Cotton lint was selling at nine cents a pound. Allowing a pound for the bag, I made the calculation that I would receive three dollars and sixty cents. I would use part of the money to buy something to take home for breakfast. The rest would go for books and tuition. My musings were interrupted by the white man's order to dump the cotton into a bin he pointed out to me. I did so. When I emptied the bag, I rolled it carefully and followed the white man upstairs into his office to be paid. I was very proud to be taking home some money so that my family could eat again. Suddenly, I was the man of the house. Ma Matt would be mighty proud of me.

The white man sat down behind a battered old desk and busied himself with some papers. I waited with a carefully controlled impatience, for I wanted very much to be able to get on home in time to go to the store for Mama Matt before going to school. At last the man looked up as if he was surprised to see anyone standing there. He seemed very annoyed, and the cigar stump wobbled back and forth around his mouth like a bottle stopper on a trotline.

"What'cha want, boy?" he asked in the suspicious, measured tones of someone about to make trouble.

I told him that I was waiting to be paid for my cotton. "What you mean you waitin' to get your money?" he rasped. "Boy, I thought I done paid you." His cold blue eyes glinted in the early morning light. When I showed no sign of leaving, he felt around in his pocket and flipped a coin in my direction. Instinctively, I caught it. It was a quarter. The white man again busied himself among the papers on his desk. He was as oblivious of my presence as he was of Tutankamen. I was standing there in front of him—close enough to touch him—but suddenly I felt as though I did not exist at all. And at that moment I did not want to exist. I wanted to disintegrate, to wither away into the nothingness he communicated that I was. I was ashamed. Humiliated. And I was afraid. Somehow I knew that I had unwittingly stepped across a boundary. I tried to move. Perhaps if I could move my feet I could somehow pass into the nothingness I coveted to save me from the awesome sense of developing catastrophe. Finally I stumbled out of the office on leaden feet, but by the time I had reached the ground, my feet wouldn't go any further. I turned and forced myself back up the stairs and into the office.

"Excuse me, sir," I said without waiting to see if anybody was listening. "Excuse me, but I think you made a mistake. I had forty pounds of cotton and that was just a quarter you gave me." Suddenly, there was an awesome silence, a dreadful eternity in which there was absolutely no sound at all. Anywhere. The world had simply stopped moving, stopped existing! And then just as suddenly, I could hear again.

"Jist wait a minute, nigger," the gin man said very slowly and carefully. "Jist a minute." He got up and slouched to the door of his office and bolted it. Then he came and planted himself in front of me like some glowering colossus from Hell. "Now, nigger," he demanded with the greasy unction of an executioner, "what's that you said? I done made a mistake? That's what you said? Well I'll jist be goddamned and a sonofabitch to boot! Nigger done come ra'chere in my office an' done called me a liera' chere to my face!"

The truth is that I had no intention of such a gross breach of manners as calling an adult, *any* adult, a liar. Grandma would not have stood for that even if I survived it. At the moment I was only thinking about the books I needed to get back in school, and of something for Mama Matt and Papa to eat until Mama Matt got her wash money on the weekend. But because it was true that I was proud to have a quick mind with figures, I think that somehow I had actually expected the gin man to be pleased I was able to help him settle the matter so quickly. Now, as it turned out, that "quick mind" my teachers applauded and my grandmother expected was about to cost me my life. Nor was my premonition of impending catastrophe merely the excess of boyish imagination. The precedents were all around me as elements of daily experience, and a fleeting recollection of a prayer in a poem by Langston Hughes fluttered into my consciousness:

> O Lord if you can save me from this man
> Don't let him make a pulp out of me
> But the Lord, He was not quick
> And the man raised up his stick. . . .
> And he beat the living hell out of me.[1]

The angry white man stood looking down at me, his red, bony fists tightly balled and hanging tensed at his side. He was tall, the tallest man I ever saw, and I felt so very small at thirteen years old. "Now, nigger, I want you to tell me one more time what you said to me so's I can be shore I done got it right."

I wanted desperately to apologize, or to at least find some more acceptable words to tell the man what he owed me. But no other words would come. There were no other words, and so I heard myself explaining: "You see sir, I had forty pounds of cotton, not counting the croker sack I brought it in. I see on the wall there that your price is nine cents a pound. That comes to $3.60 for the forty pounds, sir, but you only gave me a quarter."

"And you say I done made a mistake? Near as I can figger it, you done called me a liera'!" The man flushed red to the base of his neck. He spat out the cigar stub and his lips jerked and sputtered wordlessly, tobacco juice oozing from the corner of his mouth. Suddenly I saw his red, bony fist coming up at me, but I was too paralyzed with fear to move. His first blow to my chin lifted me off the floor and crumpled me at his feet. Then he began to rhythmically stomp my head and kick me in the face and stomach with his heavy brogans. Each kick was punctuated with an oath. "A goddamned nigger!" he complained, "Acomin' in here gon' teach me how to count cotton money! A goddamned, black-assed nigger gon' tell me I done made a mistake! Iggerant-assed nigger gon' try to count behind a white man! Boy you listen and you listen good: *Ain't no nigger can count behind a white man!* God ain't made no such-a nigger yet, and God ain't gon' never make no such-a nigger because ain't no such-a nigger can be made! And don't you never forget it!"

That lesson in racial etiquette cost me a tooth, a bloated, bloody face, a ruptured stomach, and a mouth full of scar tissue. The lesson was indelible: *Ain't no nigger can count behind a white man!* The lesson was explicit, and though I have never been impressed by the credibility of its source, I have never forgotten it. Nevertheless, it was always a confusing proposition. If the white man's figures on cotton money are not ever to be challenged, is all white thinking beyond debate? Theology? Ethics? Law? Art? Politics? It was a disturbing prospect that I thought left all civilization a little more vulnerable to the arbitrariness of racially selective perception than seems warranted by what we know of human fallibility.

By the time I was in high school I had internalized all the learnings I needed to cope with coming through the fire of race and place in Alabama. I knew the boundaries. There was a white world and a black world, and they were not the same. They touched or they abutted, occasionally they collided, and sometimes they overlapped, but they never merged. In Athens there was a college for girls, but not for the girls who graduated from my school. *They* went to work in the kitchens of the white folks. There was a park, but black kids could not play in it. It too was for whites only. There was a swimming pool. We were not allowed to use it—not even one day a week. We swam in the creek. So did the town's sewage. The railroad depot, the Greyhound bus station, the restrooms in the courthouse all had "White" and "Colored" signs. You couldn't sit at the counter in the five-and-ten-cent store to drink a Coke or eat a hotdog. If you went to the Ritz Theatre to see a Western you had to enter through the alley and sit way, way upstairs in the gallery called "nigger heaven." The only place where black and white people could meet with any semblance of mutual dignity was at Trinity School, and this was possible only because there was a grudging, uncertain toleration of an enclave of Old Maid Yankees set on ruining the colored help with education they didn't understand and couldn't ever use. There was an occasion when even this tiny oasis of human civility would be challenged.

A visiting college choir was presenting a concert at Trinity. The principal invited "our white friends" from downtown to "come and share with us the rich experience" of that event as a gesture of goodwill and political cultivation. In compliance with local tradition, "special" seating in the auditorium was arranged for these white friends. To this I took exception, and as editor of the *Campus Chronicle* I denounced the overture as "an unconscionable desecration of the only island of probity in the whole state of Alabama." But islands of probity are not always sacrosanct, and when the faculty adviser to the paper refused to permit my editorial to be run, "the Three Charleses,"[2] as we were known thereafter by people less sensitive to such issues, went to press that night on our own. We mimeographed the forbidden article and plastered it around the campus and the adjacent community. The furor it created the next day had consequences somewhat larger than we had anticipated, and I lost my part-time job with some of the choicest language from Mr. Martin that southern biliousness could afford. It was an ungracious parting, but a timely one for me, for it was the first overt fracture of the symbols of my bondage. Thereafter, my days in Alabama would be numbered from one sunrise to the next.

Nothing on the Program

There were six or eight black churches in Athens, almost all of them Methodist or Baptist. Grandma and I went to Village View Methodist, Rev. L. G. Fields, pastor. Ma Matt was very proud of being a Methodist. It was one of the ways in which she punctuated her identity, and she paid twenty-five cents "dues" every week for the privilege. Often that quarter she kept knotted in the corner of her dress handkerchief was the only money there was in the house, but she never sacrificed it to personal exigence. It belonged to the Lord. Papa didn't have anything to do with the church. Everybody, black and white, said he was as good a man as you were likely to find in Alabama, but he just didn't have anything to do with the church. I guess I wondered why, but I never did ask anybody. I just went on with Ma Matt every Sunday the Lord sent, and sometimes on Wednesday night too. I felt secure in the church. God and Ma Matt were there.

The white churches were different, although I didn't know exactly why. I always wondered whether God was in them, too, since Ma Matt was not. They seemed so imposing, so imperious. Maybe white churches didn't really need God. I wondered a lot about that. During the Christmas season of the last year I was to spend in Alabama, Charles Wesley Tisdale and I were walking in the downtown area in the vicinity of a large, awe-inspiring church. As we strolled along we could hear the magnificent crescendos of a pipe organ in tandem with what must have been a very large mass choir of mixed voices. It was the Hallelujah Chorus of Handel's *Messiah*. We stopped near the church to listen. Such music we had never heard before except on records or over the radio. Nor had either of us ever been close to a pipe organ. The music was so compelling that we permitted ourselves to be lost for a moment, enraptured by the magnificence of it all. But in that moment of spiritual ecstasy we wandered too close to the doors of the church. Suddenly we were thrust back into earthly reality by a white man who met us on the broad concrete steps outside the sanctuary. He was extremely agitated, although he must have known that we had no intention of trying to come into a white church. Panting and flushed with consternation, he cried out: "Get away from here! Get away from here! You niggers can't be standing on these steps! They'll be coming out of there any minute now, and there ain't a-going to be no niggers straggling around out here when they do!" Frantically, he waved us away from the church and into the street.

"Mister, we didn't mean no harm," I protested. "We just wanted to hear the organ and the singing."

"Boy, it don't make no difference what you want," he said. "Not one bit of difference. This here is a white church, and *there ain't nothing on the program for no niggers! Not a blessed thing!*" His flailing right arm etched an imaginary X on the air for emphasis. "Nothing!" he repeated. "Now y'all git on back over yonder where you belong and don't be hanging 'round the doors of this church ever no more. Ain't a thing in there for you!"

As the deacon, or whatever he was, opened the ornate door to go back into the church, a final snatch of Handel wrenched through, but the music didn't seem to soar any more.

Alabama had taught me my final lesson in race and place: *There ain't nothing on the program for no niggers. Not a thing in the world!*

Alabama Postscript

A few months later I left Alabama to see what the "program" was like in the rest of America. My hopes were high. Outside the South, I had heard it said, those beautiful words of Robert Burns—"A man's a man for a' that"—had real meaning. I headed for Chicago to experience it for myself.

I had scarcely installed myself in the Thirty-eighth Street YMCA on the Chicago South Side when I was invited by Dr. Jay T.

Wright to spend a weekend with him in his parents' home in Green Bay, Wisconsin. Dr. Wright was the new headmaster at Trinity School, succeeding the venerable Louise H. Allyn, who had held that post for more than thirty years. Green Bay was to be my first real encounter with the world of white folks outside the state of Alabama. I looked forward to that new experience. But my initial encounter with that other world proved somewhat dismaying, or at least it got off to an unanticipated launching. Living next door to the Wrights was an Irish family that included a beautiful red-haired teenager about my own age, named Gloria. She came out to the backyard fence where Jay and I were enjoying a game of catch.

"Hi!" she said, extending her hand across the palings. "My name is Gloria. What's yours? Would you please smile so that I can see your pretty white teeth? Tell me, why do the Negro people in the South carry razors and eat—what is it, 'possums all the time? I've never been to the South except to Chicago, but I don't think I'd like to live there. It's a dreadful place, don't you think? I hope you'll stay up here where it's nice." Just then, I didn't know quite *what* to hope.

After that introduction to Green Bay, on the following day Jay and I drove to Appleton, Wisconsin, to visit his married sister. On the way Jay told me a little about Appleton: It was the home of Sen. Joe McCarthy, the dubious scourge of crypto-communism, he said. And no colored people lived there as far as he knew. Well, perhaps not, but I was soon to find out that whether they lived there or not, there was a structure in place for dealing with them. I was given the guest bedroom at Jay's sister's house, and when I awoke the next morning I was vaguely aware that I was not alone. As a matter of fact, I had apparently been sleeping before an extensive audience of curious little urchins from all over the neighborhood. For how long, I had no way of knowing, but when I opened my eyes my incredulous blinks met the steady stares of Barbara, aged six, and seven or eight of her playmates. Barbara was the daughter of my hosts, and on this particular morning she was surely the unchallenged impresario of the neighborhood. There was a show going on, and I was Exhibit 1.

"You see there?" Barbara was saying as my consciousness caught up with my vision. "You see there? I told you we had a brown man at our house, and there he is, *right there!*" The motley passel of little urchins edged a bit closer and peered more intently. "My Uncle Jay brought him from Chicago," Barbara declared, "and he's ours. We're going to keep him *right here!* Now go on and say 'Good morning' to him. My mother says you have to do it."

One by one several of the timid little company trotted by the bed mouthing a muffled "Goo' Morning, Brown Man!" and so on out the door to less stressful encounters. That is, until one little blue-eyed, towheaded maverick ambled up to the bedside, planted his feet, and pointed an accusatory finger: "That," he declared pontifically, "ain't neither no 'brown man.' That there ain't nothing but a great big ole nigger, and *don't nobody have to say nothing to him!*" With that, he stuck out his tongue at me in gleeful derision, made a "whooshing" noise, waved his fingers in his ears, and pattered on out of my bedroom. There was a look of triumph on his cherubic-impish countenance, but my hopes for a place on "the program" "up north" were already lying shattered at the foot of my borrowed bed. *Don't nobody have to say nothing to a nigger.* A nigger is a nonentity by definition. Damn!

I turned over and tried to go back to sleep. I had to come all the way to Wisconsin to find out what I had already learned in Alabama.

Five months later—Sunday, December 7, 1941, it was—I rounded up my little clutch of buddies at the Thirty-eighth Street "Y" and we all went to the naval recruiting office in downtown Chicago to join the U.S. Navy. Pearl Harbor had been attacked, and we were at war. There were seven of us, mostly from the South, and one or two underage, but all of us ready to fight and die for our country.

The salty old bosun's mate handling the recruiting traffic turned us aside at the door, shaking his grizzled old head and waving his hash marks and sounding very much like he was reading from a script: "You boys g'won back home," he said. "We ain't taking no niggers in the Navy today. Just fightin' men." *No niggers, just fightin' men!* That's what he said. He then waved a group of white boys forward, signifying that our interview was concluded. "You men get on up there to the counter and sign up," he said to the white volunteers. "Step lively now, we got to go kill ourselves some Japs!"

The war went on, and in due course I received an official-looking letter from the president of the United States. "Greetings!" it said. The next thing I knew I was a "fightin' man" in a navy uniform, but I hadn't changed my color to any perceptible degree. The president said that we were fighting for four freedoms: Freedom from Fear, Freedom from Want, Freedom of Religion, and Freedom of Conscience. I wished that he had added a fifth freedom: Freedom from the *Fire* I mistakenly thought I had left behind me in Alabama when I made it to Chicago. But those were the salad days of my innocence, and little did I dream that it would take considerably more than a global war for four massive freedoms abroad to establish one small freedom at home.

Notes

1. Langston Hughes, "Who but the Lord," in *The Panther and the Lash* (New York: Alfred A. Knopf, 1974).

2. William Charles Mason, Charles Wesley Tisdale, and Charles Eric Lincoln. Charles Mason was a casualty of World War II. Charles Tisdale publishes the bullet-scarred, award-winning *Jackson Advocate* in Jackson, Mississippi.

PATRICIA FOSTER

What Do You Do for the Place?

"There was a time I was pushed to the river and didn't intend to jump,"
Ora says, pressing her hands tight together, then dropping them flat to her
lap. "It was that gas man who did it. Came 'round here every week to
check our meters, then started showing his privates, trying to get in the
house at my girls."

Ora looks beyond me at a wall of pictures, little black girls in pigtails
with snaggle-toothed grins, their faces open and trusting, white peter-
pan collars circling soft, sloping necks.

"He kept trying to get in, but my girls locked him out. They just sat
real still and didn't say a word till I got home."

Ora sighs, telling me she was at work at Miz E's, cleaning for the
family, doing the kitchen, the laundry, changing all the beds, pushing
away all those cats. "When I got home they told me the story and next
morning I told Miz E, told her I'd been pushed to the river and didn't

intend to jump. Miz E went right to the phone, called her husband and the po-lice, and it was taken care of." Ora straightens in her chair, her starched blue-denim skirt crackling as she leans forward. "But I bought me a rifle, Pat. I wasn't gonna have nobody hurt my girls." She gazes beyond me at the pictures on the wall, shudders, then closes her eyes. "But he didn't come 'round no more. Miz E took care of it. I knew she wouldn't stand for that kind of behavior. She always stood up and said what she wanted. But I kept the rifle. Used it too."

I settle back into my seat, staring at Ora, then at Jesus on the cross two feet from my chair. An evangelist is shouting on the radio, then crooning in a soft, southern voice, "With Goooodddd, everything is possible. Everything, my friend."

I think of the rifle. I think of Jesus. I think of Ora sitting as prim and proper as any antebellum lady, and I feel a jangling of the nerves, a ripple of excitement. I'm back in the South. Back with the women I love.

It's 1997 and I'm driving down a dusty blacktop, past miles and miles of weedy pasture, blackberries and kudzu growing from ditches wide enough to build a house in. A spread of light cuts through my window, warming the length of my thigh. I look from side to side, waiting for something, anything, a bird, a possum, a movement in the trees. Then I see it, a burned-out house, its tin roof sliding quietly, effortlessly, into the dirt. A gust of fear prickles my shoulders. Abandoned houses. Ditches. Shanties. I'm out in nowhere, in a place I don't belong. I'm going to Ora's house in what we used to call "colored town."

"You come on," Ora said when I called earlier this morning. "I be here all day, so you come on."

Though it's been over forty years, I still see Ora sitting in the backseat of our Cadillac in 1956, a sack of greens in her lap, her head turned toward the window, her face moody, distracted as if she's burdened with thoughts so distant from mine there's no way in. Her eyes flicker at the ditches like a horse ready to bolt. I watch her furtively, curiously, her body so rigid I dare not touch it though I sit right beside her, my knee wedged up against one of her sacks.

And yet there's something I want from her, something that has to do with the right questions and the complicated answers, not the easy, paint-by-number kind. The questions I know how to ask go something like this: Why do they live here, Mama? Why doesn't Ora have a nice house? And why are black people so courteous and respectful to us?

Mother looks away, frowning at the evening sun. "It isn't fair the way it is," she sighs, glancing toward me, singling out the permissible question, "but Ora doesn't make enough money to live in a nice house. You have to go to college and make a good living if you want nice things. That's just the way the world is." I try to put Ora and college in the same thought—Ora strolling across the green lawns of a college campus with books in her arms—but she slips silently, effortlessly out of my grasp. This, of course, is the simple answer, ignoring the facts of the color line, implying that this is just "their condition," something intrinsic, inevitable, unremarkable, just the way things are, the way things have always been.

But I know it isn't so. I know as Mother drives Ora down the dirt road past the familiar shotgun shacks, past houses covered in fake brick siding, past Folger's coffee cans blooming with gladiolas and petunias, past the smell of collard greens and wood smoke, that whatever poses for reality is a big fat lie; later I'll understand that the underclass is politically determined, a ready workforce of cultural pariahs, sustained by custom and primed for obedience, but as a child, I know this only through feeling. *Ora shouldn't have to live in that house.*

It would be foolish to pretend that I've figured out the questions as I drive this morning toward Ora's house or that I understand precisely the anxiety of my position. The only thing I'm certain about is that my discomfort also resides in me, a woman who's had a hard time claiming a southern identity, a woman who's drowned too often in the quicksand of her own failures, flailing and squirming, sometimes begging for help. And yet I've always had the choice to pursue these failures, to wander aimlessly or tenaciously down my desired path. Now as I buzz down the highway to visit a woman who's had few choices, my own life looks plump and privileged by comparison. For a moment I think of myself that way: I roll down the electric windows, peer through the windshield of my fully paid for car, and smell the dust as it rises from the sides of the road. Cotton plants thrust their thick white blooms into the air. A cow turns its mournful head toward me and moos in dismay as if the sky might fall. In the thick heat of the day I'm released from my anxieties; I am going to visit Ora, and I wonder what she will tell me about her life.

When Ora emerges from her house, she's slumped, a little shrunken, her grizzled hair smoothed back in a pageboy. She hugs me to her thin, spry body, neat and prim in a blue-denim skirt and blouse, her feet in white tennis shoes laced up tight. I pull back, looking in the clear darkness of her eyes. She drops her gaze and says, "You Pat, you came all this way from Iowa." But before I can answer she's staring beyond me, her face alert, expectant. "Where's Miz Foster? Didn't she come with you?"

I tell her Mother stepped on a nail yesterday. "Wearing those thin-soled shoes and it went right through the ball of her foot." I can see Mother hobbling around the kitchen, pouring boiling water into the pitcher of tea, her face flushed, her foot in a pink terrycloth slipper, the kind she wouldn't be caught dead in outside the house.

"A shame," Ora says. "I was thinking I'd get to see her. I always like to see Miz Foster, but you come in." I follow her through the porch where the plastic screens are torn and flapping. A humid wind blows through the cracks; flies buzz indolently above my head in a halo of motion. I smell mildew and must, and automatically breathe shallowly, anxious to get inside. In the living room, there are two chairs, easy chairs draped in white sheets with an end table in between. Above us a tiny Jesus slumps on a peeling gold cross beside a curtained door. There is little furniture in this room, only a couch, a TV, and two chairs, all lined up in a row, facing the sagging porch. I look out the door at the empty fields, at the hazy sun and blazing strip of road, imagining hordes of mosquitoes rising out of the ditch at dusk, floating in waves toward this house, vigilant as bombers; revulsion shudders inside me and I look quickly at Ora's face, but she's gazing beyond me at Jesus, whose head bows down toward his bloody chest.

Then she sniffs, blows her nose on a white paper napkin. "Allergies," she says, stuffing the napkin into her pocket. "It's this heat make you sick."

I nod, feeling the sweat trickle down my collar as we talk about the usual things, about the weather and family, flying through the dailiness of the present until there's a lull in the conversation, when impulsively I ask how she came to work for us in the late fifties. I can still see Ora getting out of our car, hefting up that sack of leftovers while we turn around in her dirt drive, leaving her in the sweltering heat while we race back to our air-conditioned house with its wood floors and carpets, its chandeliers and antiques, its washing machine and dishwasher, all the comforts of middle-class life. Glancing up, I notice a cheap chandelier hanging cheerfully in this desolate room, its plastic prisms cascading in a waterfall of yellow light, sprinkling the floor with patterns that shift when a sudden gust of wind breezes through the flapping plastic of the screens. It's one of the ugliest chandeliers I've ever seen.

"That's a long story," Ora says, following my gaze. She stares at me with hooded eyes, and for a split second I think she's reading my mind, and I'm ashamed that I've come here as much out of curiosity as friendship, but then her face softens as she knots and unknots her hands, worrying her paper napkin. "I can't remember things like I used to." She closes her eyes as if she's thinking about where her mind has gone, where all that stuff really does go. "But I'll try to tell you, Pat. Yes, there's some things I can tell you. You was just a girl, you know, when I come to work for Miz Foster, but it starts before that. It starts . . . well, I guess it starts after my divorce, when I had to choose between the bottle and Jesus."

The bottle or Jesus. I lean forward, staring into the stillness of the air like a little girl waiting for a story. A fly buzzes against the screen door, worrying its wings as Ora begins telling me about her divorce, how afraid she was, afraid of being alone, afraid of raising her two girls, afraid of not having enough money, afraid of all the heart pain of leaving her husband. "After I left him, I had me a hard time, Pat." Ora looks at me with silent knowing and I nod, thinking of my own divorce, how crazy I was, ricocheting from room to room, Quaaludes squeezed tight in one hand, a bottle of tequila in the other as I drifted through my shadowless world. I try to imagine Ora in her early thirties alone in a shack with two little girls, but my imagination falters, for in my mind she's ageless, always sitting in the backseat of our car. I look up at the ugly chandelier and see a bare bulb, fly-speckled, dangling from the ceiling, or maybe a paper shade covering its rawness.

"I didn't drink much," Ora continues, shifting her gaze and looking at me with sudden gravity, "maybe a beer or two every now and then. But I *liked* it, you know. And sometimes I went to this colored club in Mobile where you could dance and drink. I'd go there and *forget*." She frowns, sucks in her breath, sends out a little whistling sigh. "This one Saturday night I sat with my friend, had me some beer and I started telling him my worries. Told him how the beer just eased my troubles, and he looked quick at me and said just as solemn as you please, 'Well now, Ora, you can go out on weekends and drink all you want, but come Monday morning your troubles be on your doorstep just waiting for you.'"

Ora pauses, glancing up at Jesus on the cross. "And that just made sense."

I want to look at Jesus, wondering if he's happy for such a convert, but Ora holds my attention, saying insistently, "I didn't know if I could make it, Pat, 'cause the bottle can be awfully sweet. But I said to myself, 'You gotta give Jesus a chance.'" Again I nod, for I know the psychology of choosing Jesus over the bottle is the choice of self-preservation in a small southern town that depends on "good women" to bring up their children and "do right." Black women weren't exempt from such customs, their lives as scrutinized as white women's. *I'm not going to help you with that car loan if you're still hanging around with Luster Hadley. Now he's no good and you know he's no good! He's just feeding off you, doing what you know isn't right.* If black women didn't "behave" they wouldn't find work, wouldn't be given the extra little privileges a white employer might bestow.

"And Jesus took me in," Ora nods. "He did."

For a moment I grow quiet, sad. Everyone, I imagine, comes eventually to this crossroads, this split in their lives where the choices are elemental, primal, downright hard. I see myself at age twenty-four after my divorce, slipping a Quaalude in my mouth, waiting for the dreamy softness of surrender, my mind sap-sweet with hope, my body's tension drifting above me, scattering like dandelion fluff in the air. I'd waltz around the kitchen in my pajamas, getting a little dizzy, everything blurring to romantic confusion, my body as light as a feather. I'd linger at the stove. Why, it looked *wonderful,* the shiny aluminum eyes locked behind each black barred grill, the illuminated clock a brilliant emerald green, the nicks on the dials as bumpy as Braille. Why hadn't I noticed that before? It amazed me that the world could feel so good when inside I was locked in a shameful battle with myself.

"Jesus said come home," Ora whispers, staring not at me, but through me as if she's seeing into the beyond where desires come unraveled and lie loose and sweaty as old clothes.

I sink back into myself. Unlike Ora, I didn't wake up that fast, didn't hear anything that "just made sense," but when the Quaaludes finally wore off, I too had a choice: to lie down or keep going, to follow the old life or begin a new one. But there was no Jesus to save me, no choir group singing sweet gospels in my ear; in the segregated South, Jesus redeemed the poor, the afflicted, the disinherited, while the middle and upper classes sought salvation through ambition, affairs, another round of education. Instead of religion, I chose education with its sanction of upward mobility and intellectualization, the only transcendence I believed in.

Ora pauses, still staring beyond me, smiling with another memory. "And it was a few years later that I came to work for your mama." She taps my hand and I'm startled back to the present. "Remember?"

And as suddenly I'm that nine-year-old girl again, moving to our newly built house, racing from room to room, sitting on all three of the toilets in the new bathrooms with a burst of pride (we'd never had more than two), then watching Mother rush around the house, talking with gardeners and seamstresses and plumbers, measuring the paisley armchair, the width of the sofa for Mrs. Mayberry, the upholsterer who'll come with her carload of cats to pick up the material. Mother was always in motion and we were right behind her, trying to claim her attention. *"Mother!"* we'd yell, running down the long hallway, anxious and excited until she appeared at the doorway, a pile of clean clothes in her arms. "What?" she'd ask, but immediately she was distracted, the phone ringing, the doorbell chiming, until we simply followed her around.

"What I always remember about your mama," Ora continues, still holding my gaze, "is that she never scolded you children. Never raised her voice or said no harsh word and that made an impression on me." Ora sighs, glancing up at the pictures of Ernestina and Willomena in grammar school, their faces close together in family pictures. Willomena, I know, has recently died of cancer, but as a little girl she worked with her sister in the fields picking beans and cotton, earning money for clothes and books while my sister and I rode our bikes around the neighborhood, read books, and took swimming lessons and music lessons and tennis. I never once thought about earning money as a child. Perhaps it's absurd to make this comparison between our lives, but it's the only way I can see the emergence of a southern identity, which was always a class identity, always a secret bullying by the haves of the have-nots to accept their lot as individual and self-determined, never cultural and political. "A hard worker" was the only praise black people ever got, rarely a pay raise, only a compliment denoting willful self-sacrifice. We were raised not to *see* black people, not to think of them as people but as shadows, servants, laborers with no interior lives. The interior lives were ours. *We* felt tragedy and joy, *we* burst into the kitchen in a rage because our clothes weren't ready or our feelings were hurt, but Ora kept her feelings hidden behind silent eyes, masks of duty.

Whatever emotions she had were kept from us. As for black children, they were invisible to the white community, cloaked by the apartheid of segregated schools and churches. I never saw Ernestina or Willomena except when they peeked out the door when we brought Ora home. "Bye-bye," I'd sometimes wave to their darting shadows behind the screen.

"I wanted to be like that," Ora says bluntly, staring not at me, but just beyond me to where Jesus hangs on the wall. "I wanted to be like Miz Foster, but seems like I had the *tension* in me when I got home from work, a pressure I carried with me all the time." Ora is frowning now, her face knotted with remembering as if she's trying to diagnose just what that pressure really was. "It's like I just didn't have no more energy to be nice."

I think of Ora walking into her kitchen, where there's a busted screen, tree roaches scurrying through the widened mesh, their hard brown shells glittering in the overhead light. Flies buzz above the sink and gnats swim in shallow pools of light. I try to imagine Ora fixing supper, washing dishes, washing clothes in the sink, knowing the next day will be just like this one. All my life I've been taught to worship the future, to dream about tomorrow with its bright lights and possibility, never to be pessimistic, never to assume that failure or difficulty might prevail. Education and self-discipline, I was taught, opened the road to success, but in the fifties and sixties success wasn't an equal opportunity endeavor.

As if Ora can read my thoughts, she says, "They didn't hire us at the factories or the sheds around here." She's looking again at her hands, which are work-worn and wrinkled, the knuckles knotted with arthritis. "So all we had was maid work. 'Course we only made four dollars a day, and it wasn't much, even back then."

I have the sudden disquieting image of those four dollars laid out on the bed while Ora stares intently at them, trying to figure out how to make four dollars a day, twenty dollars a week, eighty dollars a month equal rent, food, clothing, heat, and medical bills for three people. Forget about Christmas, Easter, birthdays, roast beef, movies, and a hairdo. But what I see instead of the money is the

Christmas dress I bought when I was sixteen, how the gold *peau de soie* fabric was tucked in tiny pleats over the bodice, giving my breasts the added "lift," how the skirt flounced out from the waist, hemmed just a little bit shorter than the other girls'. "Why don't you buy a cheaper dress and give the money to Ora?" I imagine someone asking. Now my mouth goes dry as I think how quickly I might have protested, "But I *love* this dress!"

Ora straightens in her seat, presses her hands into her starched denim skirt. "I didn't make much money, but I made sure my girls always had something to eat," she says, sounding as prideful as my mother, who often said she'd do anything—clean toilets and scrub floors all day long—for her children, but being white and middle class, she never had to. "I never let them go to bed hungry no matter how poor we was, and when there wasn't enough to eat, I just prayed one of them left me some scraps." Ora smiles, a flash of white teeth, and leans forward. "You know, I was always a praying person, Pat, and usually they left me a little bit." I laugh too at Ora's joke, aware that I've never gone to bed hungry, never had to pray for food, but as quickly Ora's face turns serious, her mouth set in a determined way. "You know, Pat, everything I have come from these two hands." She looks down at her hands, then her head snaps up and I see a strident victory blooming in her face. "These two hands."

It's the tone of her voice that startles me, makes me glance away, staring into the hazy light as if a veil has been lifted from my eyes. *Why, Ora sounds just like my mother.* They both have "the tension," both have indentured themselves to the next generation, professing no bitterness over their lot, tough, brooding women, relentless in their sacrifice. Is it because they're products of a more stoical generation, one that depended on Jesus and community to air their grievances, rather than activists and therapists? Did they learn early not to expect gratification other than for a job well done, no matter how menial? Did they agree to sacrifice everything for good children? I don't know. Maybe I'll never know. But what I realize is that my mother and Ora might have changed places had their skin color been different. My mother escaped poverty by going to college on a scholarship at age sixteen from a small mining town in northern Alabama. Education and a white skin saved her from a dreary life in a mining camp, but had fate been different, Ora might have had the same possibility.

Again, I glance up at the chandelier, trying to imagine Ora buying it, wondering if it gives her pleasure: the gold fixture beams brightly, shiny in its cheapness. I remember the day Mother bought our chandelier, the one that hangs in the dining room with crystal prisms and ropes of crystal chains, elegant and baroque in its aesthetic complexity. While the workmen put it up, Mother stood inside the door, frown lines furrowing her forehead until it was fully in place, swaying gracefully over the dining room table, set with Royal Worcester china, Saint Louis crystal, and pale linen napkins.

Then I imagine Ora standing on a kitchen chair on some hazeless, almost airless day, her firm hands screwing in the tiny bolts, fingers caressing the falling crystals. Sneaking looks at Ora's chandelier, I see both women tense and anxious for this symbol of "the good life," and I can't help but wonder if it gave either of them a moment of joy. I try to imagine Ora smiling with pleasure, but what I see is Ora coming out of our house in her white maid's uniform, her face private, opaque, unreadable, and instead, I ask what I really want to know. "Were you angry back then?"

Ora's expression doesn't change, but she sits straighter in her chair, her legs sticking out of her skirt like brown stalks, veined and knobby. She clears her throat, sniffs, takes out her paper napkin. "You know, Pat, during segregation there was lots of things we couldn't do. Lots of things I didn't imagine doing. But one thing that got to me was the way we couldn't eat inside a restaurant. Now that bothered me. There was this place, Bill's, and they had a window where the colored could come by and order food and take it home. But I never stopped at that window. I told myself, 'If I can't go in, then my money won't go in.'"

Ora smiles at this, and I smile with her. "Good for you," I say, but what do I really know about such courage? I've never been denied food, shelter, or medical attention, never had to "be careful" of my tone and bearing, never had to do more than rage and fret over the indignities of my life.

"But I felt hate, too," Ora says, frowning, her mouth tight, her eyes darkening. "During the bad times of integration, white boys used to come through here at night shooting their guns. All we could do was turn out the lights and sit in the dark, waiting. We knew we weren't going to get no help. Who could we call?" She looks at me with a quick, penetrating gaze and I nod. "One night some boys come by and we heard them yelling and shooting. Must have had some old car because it rattled and squeaked when they stopped. I'd parked my car in the drive like I always do and I heard that car stop somewhere outside. I'd turned out all the lamps and I just sat in my chair, holding my rifle in my lap. It was kinda heavy but that night it felt light as a spoon. I heard them talking, you know, then rip-rip, a shot goes off—*like to scared me to death!*—then sounds like something breaking, smashing against the car, so I pointed my rifle at the door." Ora stops and sniffs into her napkin. "I could hear them laughing, Pat. I didn't know what to do, didn't know if they'd try to get in. I'd never shot that rifle before," Ora shakes her head, "and there I was just waiting for what would happen next. Seems like I could hear the moon turn over. Sure could hear the faucet drip." She smiles. "Finally I hear that old car start up, rattle, rattle, rattle, but I didn't dare move. I didn't turn on no lights. Almost forgot to breathe. Just sat there a good long time. When I could breathe right I stepped out on my porch, saw they'd shot off my side mirror. I looked at it all broken on the ground and that did something to me. I lifted my rifle and fired straight up at the sky."

Heat swirls around us and I see a spider making its slow crawl up the corner wall. Little fans of dust twirl in the air as a white Oldsmobile speeds down the road, then vanishes around the corner. The evangelist sings, *"Hallelujah! . . . God is goooood . . . he is soooo gooood."*

Hate. That word sits uncomfortably at the bottom of my spine.

It's 1968 and I'm walking along the Mississippi River, holding hands with my new husband, looking at the wild, surging water, gray-brown and fast moving, the tugboats passing under the Memphis–West Memphis bridge. We've just gotten married, are settling down to night classes and work, and I'm surprised when he pauses on the patchy bank, looking down at the grassy slopes, saying sudden, stinging words that stop my heart. "My parents got a letter," he mumbles, "from someone in your town." There's a stutter to his voice, a tightening of his mouth. He looks frightened, uneasy, and relaxes his grip on my hand. "He said I shouldn't marry you. Probably some crank"—his eyes widen in boyish concern—"he didn't give a name."

"What?" My voice rises up into empty air, the life force sucked out of me as I drop his hand to clutch my own. A storm of weeping shakes me, and I crouch to the ground, my brain bristling, screaming, then darkening inside. Who could hate me so much he'd write an anonymous note branding me as unfit for marriage? And why? What had I done? Was it because I was moody and quiet, not cheerful and optimistic like a well-bred southern girl? Was it because I wore short skirts and hot pants like the models in *Mademoiselle*? Was it because I resisted the requirements of my class—to be gracious and subordinate, insisting that others go first while I lingered in the shadows? I stare into my open hands, feel the simmer of violence creep into my palms, and in that instant all wholeness shatters. The only thing I know is that I'm hated, and this knowledge changes me, shows me how arbitrary approval is, how—regardless of my conduct—someone in the world will find me repulsive, despicable, unworthy. Now I'll spend my life trying to pull the fragments together, covering up the raw spots, using all my psychic energy to protect myself, building an external shell, hard and resistant, to cover up the softness.

I've been pushed to the river.

I don't look at my husband, but stare out at the Mississippi, knowing its secret, deadly currents can pull a body deep into the water, holding it fast against its mud-soiled bottom.

Though I remember this incident as a turning point in my life, undeserved cruelty was an anomaly for me while for Ora it wove its threads through the scratchy fabric of her life. She was denied the basic courtesy of human decency, the right of agency. That's a torment I can't hold firm in my imagination, though as a child I used to wonder "how can Ora stand it?" Now, as an adult, I know that human beings are amazingly resilient and can stand almost anything, though the mental and psychological exhaustion takes its toll. Rejection becomes a "tension," sucking hope and desire out of your skull, leaving only the dry ashes of duty. Duty, I think, can't heal souls.

"Do you hate the South?" I ask, knowing that Ora also worked in New Jersey and Michigan and Ohio, places where the politics of race were more liberal than in Alabama. Earlier in the day, Ora told me about going to Teaneck, New Jersey—"way up there!"—for a year as a live-in maid with her own room in the family house, then going to Michigan to pick cherries and apples. "They treated me good," she said, "in both places. Treated me like a white person."

But now she surprises me. "I always come back to Alabama," she says, looking out the window at the empty fields and fading sun where glimmers of light torch the dying weeds. "It was something inside me, I guess. Something that kept me. I was from here and I said to myself it ain't what the place do for you, but what you do for the place."

And I smile, pleased at what she's said, pleased that she prefers the South, as I do, not because it's a better place (in so many ways, it's absurdly anachronistic) but because it feeds something primal, a longing, maybe, that's inarticulate and necessary, the way sleep is necessary. Or perhaps it's only *longing* I understand. I think of the day in 1995 when I stood at the bend in the Magnolia River to watch the stillness of the water beneath a new growth of banana trees. It could have been 1955—the enduring silence of the place, fall leaves floating on the surface of the water like the open petals of flowers, a few boats docked under rusty tin sheds. Weeds grew up next to the shore. The air smelled of pine needles and mold. But most important there was no one around, only an occasional car thundering across the bridge, then roaring out of sight. Silence. A flight of birds. I'd forgotten the porousness of the soil, the ant beds that clung like smushed hats to the sides of trees and spilled voluptuously onto the ground. I'd forgotten the oaks and pines and palms all crowded together on a bed of soft pine. I stared at the river, breathing in the quiet. And for a moment I forgot myself.

And yet I didn't come to this love easily. For years I couldn't decide if I wanted to claim the South, to be southern, to try to untangle its knotted ideas about race and class. During my twenties, I hated its political and social conservatism, obstinately resented its parentage, longing only to get away, to be free of its lineage. When I left at age twenty-six, I imagined myself saying, "I'm *from* here, but not *of* here." And always I've asked myself what the South has created in me, whether that creation is a monster or a blessing, or something suspicious in between.

Perhaps every question has its moment, its season in the sun. Mine came not on that first visit to Ora, but almost a year later in early spring when the harsh weather of Iowa sends me scrambling once again to Alabama. In Iowa, I walk haltingly through the snow, looking up at the bare frosted trees into a hazy sky, longing for a golden sun. When I arrive in Alabama, leaves are sprouting, flowers blooming, grass turning a luxuriant shade of green. I throw my backpack on the sofa of my parents' house and go outdoors, finally able to breathe deeply, to feel the comfort of soft air. That afternoon, I call Ora, asking if I can visit.

"Come on," she says once again. "My great-granddaughter's living with me now, and I pick her up every day after school. Then I be here."

We set a time for later in the afternoon when Ora will be home, and I rush off to another appointment, a visit with my old music teacher, Mama Dot, who's just had a pig valve put in her heart. She's ailing and wants to talk, so we sit in her sun-drenched living room with the baby grand and the sprouts of cotton near the fireplace, taking up where we left off years ago. When I try to leave, Mama

Dot starts another interesting story, keeping me pinned to my seat, intrigued and yet anxious. I want to hear what she has to say, but I also have to meet Ora. When I finally pull my car from her driveway, the air's turned gummy, thick, the sky a gray blanket of clouds. As I race down Highway 98—the AC on high—I know it'll take me twenty-five minutes to get to Miller's Corner, but this isn't my only worry; I've borrowed my mother's car, and she hates being stranded, so I decide to check in with her before I rush to Ora's. I'll call Ora from Mother's house, telling her why I'm late, hoping she'll still have time to see me.

But the signals are already crossed, the path split, the day once crisp turning limp and stale. When I arrive at home, my parents are furious at each other—my father huffed and muttering in the den, my mother silent and seething as she strings celery in the kitchen. Coming into the midst of their boiling energy, I forget to call Ora. When I remember, it's five o'clock in the afternoon and I get the buzz of a busy signal. That night, trying again, the line crackles with static.

It isn't until I'm at home in Iowa City that I talk to Ora. It's a dark, bitterly cold evening and I'm wrapped in several sweaters, my feet in socks and fluffy slippers. I dial slowly. When Ora answers, I apologize profusely, describing what happened, my rush home and the family argument. But we both know there's been four days' lapse between that afternoon and this call.

Ora allows it—I can hear her soft breathing on the other end of the line—then subtly scolds me, telling me how she went early that day to pick up her great-granddaughter just so she'd be there when I arrived. "For our meeting."

I look out into the darkness where shadowy branches wave stiffly in the howling wind and feel ashamed, guilty, thinking *this is written into our history, this caste system of black and white, and I've unwittingly obeyed its rules.* But of course, it's more than that.

Later that night as I huddle beneath the blankets, I wonder if Ora had been someone of my own class, my own race, would I have behaved differently: gone by, if only to say I couldn't stay? Made a more conscientious effort? Called sooner? Behind rudeness, there's always hierarchy . . . it's just a matter of stripping the behavior down to its roots. And I know that in white culture Ora is expendable; she's not worth interrupting a family crisis for. No matter which way I cut it, my own rudeness indicts me, aligns me with my dominant culture, which says that Ora doesn't count, isn't a part of me, is just a woman who sits in the backseat of our car. For years I've told myself that I'm different from other southerners, liberated from my past, but what if I'm not? Can I ever talk to Ora about this, not just about the racism, but the "classism" of our lives, the way even the style and value of a chandelier separates us? I shake my head, knowing that this is the conflict I'll never lose, this sense of myself as caught between two worlds, unable to speak.

As I'm fretting about this, I hear a loud crash as if something has exploded just outside my window. I sit up, heart hammering, excited but waiting for disaster. And yet when I lift the curtains to peer out, I realize it's only an avalanche of snow falling from my roof, thundering to the ground. I sigh with relief and snuggle back in bed, staring at the silvery moon frozen in a winter sky. But oddly, the metaphor holds: being southern I've often felt this same lurch of disaster, the surge of love and guilt crashing through my psyche, startling me to attention, waking me to a quivering rage. In the midst of this anguish, my heart seizes up, opens and empties, my nerves buzz like high tension wires. Just as I see the slit in the universe, I'm already falling, bathed in a blistering light. Maybe, for me, that's all the South will ever be: an emotional jolt, an arc of feeling, a racehorse in my blood.

I've thought for a long time that I'd simply grow old and die trying to figure it out, but lately I've come to see that this ambivalence *is* my southern identity, an ambivalence that chastens and frightens me, that lacks the sweetness of reconciliation. It's what the place can do to you; but, like Ora, I know I have to keep pushing against myself, pushing at the enemy inside, opening the circle and asking, What can you do for the place?

FANNIE FLAGG

The Truth the Heart Knows

My contribution to this book will be short, not because I have nothing much to say. On the contrary, my problem is I have too much to say and could fill this book and many others about what being from Alabama has and does mean to me. Alabama is so much a part of me and who I am as a person. It has shaped the way I look at the world, the way I speak, how I think and feel, what I like and dislike, even what I eat and drink.

Let me begin by saying I am a woman in love with her hometown of Birmingham and the entire state from north to south. So much so that all of my books are dedicated to Alabama and to the sweet people of Alabama. To this day, when I am anywhere other than Alabama I am not at home. As a matter of fact, when I first had to leave to go to New York for work on *Candid Camera*, every time I came home for a visit I would always leave carrying a shopping bag full of frozen turnip greens, bar-b-que, black-eyed peas, and cornbread to help stave off homesickness as long as possible. To me the North was a harsh and alien place where Yankees snapped their consonants at me and ate vegetables that were not cooked. I might as well have been on the other side of the moon. When I went into a restaurant, or as it was called up there, "deli," something we had not yet heard of in the South, the waitress did not smile and say, "Hi, hon. What are you going to have today, Sweetie?" It was a fast and impersonal: "What do you want?" Well, I wanted fried chicken and biscuits—but I got pastrami on rye. I knew I was not in Alabama anymore. It was then that I first started to realize who I was and what I believed.

Would I have even been a writer if I had not been from Alabama? No. More important, would I have even felt the need to write at all if I had not been from Alabama? One of the greatest incentives to any artist—writer, painter, dancer, musician, whatever—is to feel misunderstood and mistreated. To feel the great frustration of not being heard, of being dismissed and misrepresented. These are things I felt by the mere fact of my being from Alabama. To this day, just to mention you are from Alabama draws a lot of comment—mostly negative. I always was and still am intensely defensive about my home state. Alabama is like my family: I may not like a lot of things that go on in the state. I may even criticize it, but woe to non-Alabamians who belittle Alabama to me, especially if they have never been there.

Alabamians are fiercely loyal to each other. I know about the strong bonds between Alabamians firsthand. While filming *Candid Camera* on the streets of New York, if by chance I would meet another Alabamian, black or white, we would fall into each other's arms like long-lost family, thrilled to see each other. Living in the North we found out that we had more in common with each other than we did with other New Yorkers. Our culture was the same, our manners, what we ate, and what made us laugh. We knew and accepted each other instantly. But history has a frightening way of being rewritten in books and in minds. For history to suggest, as it seems to want to do, that all blacks and whites in Alabama hated one another and were always enemies is not the truth, not the whole story. The bond between black and white Alabamians that did and still does exist is a puzzle the North will never work out and a mystery so deep that even we cannot explain it in words. Words can never explain what the heart feels and knows to be true. But I saw it happen; I felt it. There are things in my memory I can never forget, when color did not stop another human being from being kind and caring.

When I was a child a classmate of mine was hit by a car. He was lying in the street waiting for the ambulance to come when his mother—they lived close by—came running out of her house and stood in the street in a thin housedress. It was a freezing cold January day. A large group of people stood by helpless, not knowing what to do. All of a sudden, a black lady who had been waiting at the bus stop on the corner—in mid-1940s Alabama, she was probably a maid on her way home—walked through the white crowd to the young mother, who was shaking from fear and cold, and took off her own threadbare coat and wrapped it around her. Then the woman quietly walked back to the bus stop as the young mother got into the ambulance, coat and all, and drove off. I have often thought of that sweet woman, and of my own mother, who after I was an adult wrote to me about Albert, the young boy she had working for her whom she later adopted. It never occurred to her to mention that Albert was black, or to tell me the color of the nurse she was crazy about, who helped her through cataract surgery and remained her friend until her death. I think of my father, who worked so hard to integrate his union at a time when this was not easy. Were my parents color blind? No, I don't think it was possible for anyone to be color blind anywhere in the country at that time. But the point is, I never heard an unkind world or a racial slur from either one of them or certainly anyone we knew. Which brings me to the moment I think was the beginning of my need to write.

The main reason I wrote *Fried Green Tomatoes at the Whistle Stop Café* in the first place was to depict the love and kindness that *had* taken place between blacks and whites in the South. My book was based on fact. My great-aunt Bess Fortenberry ran a railroad café outside of Birmingham, Alabama, in the thirties and forties, and when she died there were as many black friends as white friends at her funeral. One of the greatest joys in my life has been being able to tell the other side of the Alabama story. And if history is to judge Alabama fairly, then the lady at the bus stop and my Aunt Bess must not be forgotten, and kindness between the races must be recorded and remembered as well.

M ARY W ARD B ROWN

Swing Low

A Memoir

The first version of this memoir was to preserve a few scenes, often talked about and laughed about on our farm, between my father and William Edwards, a black man on the place. The bond between William and my mother, however, took over and propelled it. For the sake of narrative, I fictionalized when necessary and called it a short story, but the characters and background were real. The essence, as I perceived it, was true.

Years later, I reworked what I'd written for my son and his family, who were never to know either of my parents. My mother died when I was a boarding student at Judson, my father shortly before my son, his only grandchild, was born. The farm, south of Marion and southwest of Selma, was divided between my two half brothers and me. Cattle replaced cotton in the area, and most of the black people moved away. Finally, the way of life in which I grew up was wiped out altogether by civil rights.

Now in 2000 both races are silent about the way things were at the time of this remembrance. Black people, programmed by circumstance into the roles they had to play, would probably rather not look back. White people, especially those of good intention who accepted the status quo without moral questioning, are inclined to feel a communal, if not personal, guilt.

In any case, I wrote this story/memoir before the silence set in. By now, relationships such as the ones memorialized here hardly seem authentic. Still, I didn't invent them. Nor could I ever forget them.

His name was William Edwards (pronounced Ed'ards by black people on the farm) and he cleaned up our house. Winter and summer he came to work in baggy serge pants and a sagging Sunday coat handed down from my father. With a bustling air of importance and a quick "hidy, hidy" to Joanna, the cook, he arrived like a country preacher entering his church.

He called my mother Miss, like all of the black people on the place, and she was his boss, though in a way they were workers together, since they had the same lord and master, my father. My mother called my father Mister Ward, which was customary in the rural tradition in which she was raised, but a large part of the deference seemed to be her own. In return he addressed her as sweetheart (pronounced sweedart), no matter where or when.

Though she was his boss, my mother worked longer and harder than William, since she had two jobs. She ran the store, a farm commissary that stocked everything from groceries to bolts of cloth and horse collars, and she tried to run our house. In the store she kept books for the whole plantation-style operation and, with the help of a black clerk, Bob Spencer, waited on trade from whatever hour of winter or summer daylight arrived until it ended and the "hands" came in for the night. On Sunday, together with William and Joanna, she tried to put our house in order, and that was the day William usually showed up half drunk or hung over.

Sunday after Sunday, she would get up early and make a tour of the house, putting cross marks with her finger on dusty surfaces, checking under beds, spotting cobwebs in corners. When William arrived, a little late and reeking, but in a great, optimistic hurry, they could soon be heard behind some open door.

"I told you last week," she would say, "not to let my house get like this again, and here it is as bad as ever." She would pause. "So I'll have to tell him. I'll just say, 'Mr. Ward, you'll have to send William back to the field, and let me have somebody I can depend on.'"

There would be a short, wounded silence, interrupted by a sniffle. Half drunk and hung over, he could always muster up a few rheumy tears.

"Miss," he would say, "I want to ast you something. Could you be that *hard* on your old po' nigger?"

It always seemed to work. Her voice would emerge in another defeat. "All right, get the dust rag and dust the *legs* of that table. Then take the polish and polish it, please."

Before either of them could get on with William's weekly second chance, however, another crisis usually arose. My father did not work on Sunday morning but read the newspaper, smoked a cigar, and went to Sunday school instead. In the small country church we attended, he was not only superintendent of the Sunday school but teacher of the adult class as well. He took his duties seriously when the time came, but not before. His lessons were prepared minutes in advance and began with the finding of the Sunday school book.

"William," he would call out around nine o'clock. "Where's my Sunday school book?"

"I don't know, sir, Mister Wa'd. I ain't seed it."

"Ain't seed it? Why the hell *ain't* you seed it? Don't you clean up?"

"Yes, sir, but . . ."

Beneath my father's blue-gray eyes, one of which was crossed, the search would begin, through stacks of newspapers and farm magazines, the drawers of tables. The book was wherever my father had left it the Sunday before, in the store, the car, sometimes the church itself. He never looked for the book himself. Household crises were not his concern. He only looked at the people who were supposed to look.

"Hurry up, dammit."

My father had no patience whatsoever. Having lost his own father at the age of eleven and, with little further schooling or support of any kind except the prayers of his mother, he'd started out at odd jobs in Chilton County, his home. Little by little, he'd worked his way to the rich Black Belt, where he'd managed to build the world in which we all now lived. His calculating intelligence and driving energy were never turned off except during sleep. His coat pockets bulged with letters, kept not for matters inside, but for columns of figures running up and down the backs and fronts of their envelopes. Hasty blocks of addition and subtraction identified magazines and newspapers that he'd read. Whether from habit or heredity, he was unable to relax and wait for anything, large or small, to happen. On Sunday mornings he sat in the living room, paring and scraping his nails, a small but unnerving sound, with a black-handled pocket knife from the store. Search for the book moved upstairs.

"William?" he would call out. "You got it?"

"No, sir. Not yit."

"Well hurry up, dammit," he'd call louder. "I won't even have time to read over the lesson!"

At this point William would think of something. My father had a boss too, the God of the Baptists, who turned away His face from drinking, dancing, card playing, and profanity. William would reappear, still without the book.

"Mister Wa'd, let me ast you somethin'," he'd say. "What good do it do you, cussin' and gwine to church all at the same time? Don't you know somebody up there writing down all them hells and damns you be sayin'?"

My father's religion was so simple it bordered on superstition. It was not a thing to which he gave much thought. In his teeming brain, it was synonymous with the literal Bible, an authority he had no time to read, much less question. William was right, he thought. He wanted as few black marks against him as possible on the Day of Judgment.

"Well, y'all run me crazy," he said one Sunday. "Jesus Christ would cuss."

My mother was the one who found the book, brought my father a tie, and soothed him on his way. Then, with William sobered up beside her, they started on the house.

William's fingers appeared to be blunt and clumsy but were surprisingly careful. He didn't drop or break objects when dusting. He could lift heavy furniture and heft it about a room, scrub and wax floors on his knees, wash windows to shining clarity. My mother didn't have him do these things on Sunday mornings, however. She only set things straight and primed him for the upcoming week.

One of his merits as a cleaner was his conversation as they worked side by side. An inveterate gossip, he told her things which, as farm mistress, she needed to know.

"You know that little yellow gal fell out in the field yistiddy?" He would flick the rungs of a chair with a brown feather duster. "She didn't have no spell, like they say. She in a family way."

They usually wound up in warm rapport about the time my father got back from church and from visiting with neighbors in the churchyard. Occasionally, before coming home, he had to open up the store for someone, which temporarily sabotaged his Sunday good humor.

"You do such good work when you try," my mother would say to William as they finished up, watering potted ferns on stands in front of the living room windows.

"Well, you learnt me," he'd say. "Wadn't for you, I'd be ignorant as the rest of the folks on this place."

He would hang up his feather duster and put away the dust mop, dust rag, and red furniture polish. Then he'd go to the kitchen and sit down heavily on a straight chair, to wait for Sunday dinner.

Joanna would be frying chicken, frying corn, candying sweet potatoes, or boiling rice, cooking one or two meats and three or four vegetables, hot bread, and dessert, as she did every noon.

"She ought to run you off the place," she'd tell him.

"I know it." He'd shake his head. "She got a tender heart, though, thank God."

"I wish somebody would send me to the field," Joanna would say, sweating over the black wood-burning iron stove, winter and summer.

"Go by yourself, then," he would tell her. "Don't wait for me. Them rows git five miles long fo sundown. No, God. Let me clean up long as I live."

After Sunday dinner, my parents usually rested on the sleeping porch until three or four o'clock in the afternoon, when they rode around the whole place, grown now to several thousand acres. During the ride, my father often gave my mother a pointed opening.

"William was drunk again, I see."

"No, he was all right. He drinks a little of that cheap wine on Saturday night, but they all do that."

So the Sundays passed into years and William was never sent back to the field, but during my last years of high school his days in our household seemed to be numbered.

My mother had begun to feel the years of hard work and long hours. After a full week in the store, she was worn out by Sunday morning. Also, though no one suspected, she had cancer. Her weekly set-to's with William became more climactic, but she steadfastly refused to have him replaced.

Then came the episode of my father's bottle. Strict Baptist that he was, in his heart my father disapproved of drinking. But the years of struggle and unrelenting responsibility were taking their toll on him as well. His operation now included, besides the crops, a cotton gin, sawmill, planer mill, gristmill, blacksmith shop, beef cattle, and dairy. More than two hundred black people lived and worked on the place. He had a succession of overseers but was driven to oversee everyone and everything himself. On an especially hard day, he began to make quick trips to the house for a few swigs of whiskey straight from the bottle. It was soon obvious that someone else had the same idea.

"I thought there was more in this bottle," he began to say to my mother. Since his trips to the house had no regularity and his drinks were hasty, unmeasured, and quickly forgotten in the press of the day, he first suspected himself. But being by nature deadly accurate (he knew almost to the penny how much money he owed and how much was owed him, how many bales of cotton were made on each plot of land, how many feet of lumber ran through his mill in a week), he was not fooled for long.

"Joanna wouldn't touch it," he reasoned out loud one Saturday night. Joanna had once been in jail for a day and night and was fanatically law abiding. "So it's got to be William. I've been drinking behind that son-of-a-gun all this time!"

"Don't say anything about it, though," he told my mother. "I just want to catch him!"

But first thing the next morning, my mother was up confronting William.

"There's no use to deny it," she said. "You're just going from bad to worse. What on earth is to become of you?"

This was beyond tricks or cajolery, he knew. "All right, Miss." He held up both hands as if to ward off the rest. "You don't have to say no more."

The whiskey level didn't recede again, but something else always seemed to be missing. Pecans from the back porch, sausage from the smokehouse. A scuttle of coal was mysteriously emptied. We'd never used so much Lifebuoy soap.

"That old rogue," my father said.

My mother never failed to defend him. "But he leaves in broad daylight," she would say. "Empty-handed."

Meanwhile, William grew thin and quiet. His good, hardworking wife had died, and he was courting a young woman on another place. It was news he neglected to tell my mother, who heard it from Joanna instead. His young gal was making a fool of him, Joanna said. She didn't love him because he was too old, and, besides, there was nothing to her. All she was, was gimme, gimme. He'd already given her everything he had, including quilts pieced by his dead wife.

As if to bring the whole thing to a head, one of my brothers came home for a short visit. Ours was a mixed-up family. My mother was a young widow with a small son at the time she married my father, divorced and with a son the same age as her own. It was a case of my child, your child, and our child, with seventeen years between. Neither of my half brothers had ever lived or worked, except briefly, on the farm, however. The ins and outs of the situation had separated us, though not in kinship, early on. It was now my mother's son, living in Chicago and working his way through law school at night, who came home for a few days and missed ten dollars from a wallet left in his room.

My father might not have known but for Joanna, who considered herself under suspicion and meant to establish her innocence where it mattered most.

"God knows I ain't seed it," she said to my father, after the noon meal next day.

"Seed what?" asked my father, and the cat was out of the bag.

The morality of stealing in our house was ambiguous. To miss flour, sugar, lard, and small necessities was overlooked and even expected, but money was not to be touched. Small change and pennies were supposed to lie around indefinitely in ashtrays or on the tops of dressers. "He wouldn't take a penny" was the ground rule for honesty.

My father was not one to avoid embarrassing or awkward situations. His aim was not to please but to keep the farm going and solve its problems. He brought this one up at the first opportunity, which was the next meal.

"All right," he announced, as soon as he'd served his plate. "This thing with William has gone too far."

"I'll see him first thing in the morning," my mother said.

"No, I'll see him myself," my father overruled.

Always first to get up in the morning, my mother was downstairs before daylight to meet William. She had a fire going in the break-fast-room fireplace when he got there, and she called him in at once. Still in her long woolen bathrobe, her very looks must have told him what was coming.

"Have you still got the money?" she asked.

He shook his head, then eased over to the fireplace and held out one hand to the warmth of the blaze. My mother poked the coals and said nothing. Darkness blacked out the windows and a lone Delco light bulb, suspended on a cord from the ceiling, lit the room like a wan Last Judgment.

"You might as well go on back home then, I guess." She put the poker back in its wrought-iron stand and turned to face him.

He started to leave without a word, but she stopped him at the door. "Why didn't you ask me for the money?"

"You wouldn't of let me had it," he said.

"Mr. Ward is really mad this time," she said. "I don't know what he'll decide to do."

"Well, that's all right, Miss," he told her. "I don't belong to Mr. Wa'd like the rest of these niggers. I belongs to you."

He took his hat from a crisscross folding hat rack in the kitchen where it always hung. Joanna was making up biscuits. Smoked bacon was frying, coffee perking. Joanna didn't speak or even look at him. He'd put her back in the shadow of a jail, she thought, and she wanted no part of him.

It was a cold morning, my mother said later, and his skin had a whitish cast as if the frost had bit it. She thought his coat was too thin for the weather. She stood by the fire for a minute, then went to get dressed and open up the store, to see the hands off to work as usual.

If my mother had ever used artifice, even in appearance, she'd given it up by now. In girlhood she'd been considered pretty, and her good looks endured in straight features, clear olive complexion, and expressive dark eyes. But she'd become stout. She wore her hair short and straight because it was no trouble, used no cosmetics except face powder, owned no clothes except the plainest of work dresses and one or two, hastily bought on rare trips to town, for Sundays and funerals. Except for the cameo she wore now and then, the few pieces of jewelry she owned were in the lockbox of a bank. She didn't know how to be deceptive.

"The money's back," she told my father at the dinner table next day, in what was meant to be an offhand manner.

"What do you mean, *back?*" he asked.

She took a heavy envelope from her sweater pocket and handed it over. My father glanced at the dollar bills, the quarters and half dollars weighing down the envelope, and gave it back to her.

"Looks like your egg money to me," he said.

My mother said nothing.

"We can't have stealing in the house, sweedart," he said. "You can't abet a thing like that. I'm surprised at you."

My mother's face flushed all the way down to her neck. "It won't happen again," she said.

Years later, old, lonely, unhappy in a disastrous third marriage, my father liked to talk about my mother when he had a secret chance. "She was too good for her own good," he would say. Then, looking off into space, he would add with a sigh, "Still, she was no reed shaken with the wind."

My mother was right about William. Things stopped disappearing after that. His gal had quit him for some other fool, Joanna reported, and it was no longer "hidy, hidy" when he came to work. He was in and out like a shadow, polite but distant, his face a mask.

"What's eating on *him?*" my father wanted to know.

"He's just sad," my mother said. "He'll be all right."

"Sad?" My father shook his head. Only Negroes and irresponsible people had time to be sad, he probably thought at the time. As for himself, he was too busy.

When William recovered, he was changed for the better. My mother no longer smelled whiskey on his breath on Sunday mornings. There were no more dust balls under beds or cobwebs in corners. With his busy feather duster, dust rag trailing from a sagging hip pocket, he was someone to depend on at last. My mother began going to church with my father.

Like most people absorbed in work that they love, my mother had few physical complaints. She'd always been strong and healthy, so people leaned on her, both black and white. Her health seemed all of a piece with her character, which we took for granted. When she began to have symptoms, no one knew, because she didn't tell us.

It was not until she began to be wakeful at night that the fact was forced upon my father.

"What's wrong?" he would ask, hearing her up.

"Nothing," she would say. "I'm just taking an aspirin."

It was some time before he thought to ask, "Aspirin for what?"

Her trouble came from standing and walking all day, she said. Always at hand was what she called her "doctor box," equipped from years of doctoring people on the place. My father couldn't afford to call the country doctor, who was also a friend, for the minor complaints of so many people, so my mother had become of necessity, a kind of plantation nurse. Someone was always on our back porch, it seemed, soaking a hand or foot in a strong solution of carbolic acid and near-scalding water. She kept gauze and adhesive tape, rubbing alcohol, iodine, ear drops, toothache drops, stomach medicine, Epsom salts, diuretics, and a variety of pain killers. Now she doctored herself, and it was not until she began to lose weight noticeably that she told the doctor her symptoms.

From the first examinations, we heard the chilling phrase "too late," but always with a could-be or might-be. The hysterectomy was quick and decisive.

The black women cried out loud when they heard it. "Jesus, have mercy," they sobbed.

Their laments would float up from the little unpainted two-room houses on summer nights when we lay in our beds with open windows. First a high, clear, lone soprano would throw out a tentative line that seemed to hang in the air until a listening voice caught it, began to play with it, and a gathering chorus set the beat. Then the night would ache with music, half spiritual, half blues, saying that life is hard, almost too hard to bear. A ten-cent harmonica from the store would solo, a male then female voice would take over, until finally, abruptly, the soulful pathos would be cut short by a burst of laughter, loose, earthy, and totally free, which spread from yard to yard like rain after heat. Afterward, we would sleep.

My mother, helped by my brother, made a trip to the Mayo Clinic. She went through a series of X-ray treatments but had accepted her fate early on.

For a while she dressed and went to the store as usual. Where she'd once stood and walked, she now sat and watched. A cot was set up in the back out of sight, so she could rest when the pain pills took over. Confined at last to the house, with William to help, she went through possessions, cleaning out and throwing away or putting up for safekeeping. As long as she was able, she had the farm account books brought to her and posted them sitting in a pillow-cushioned chair or propped up in bed.

But it was now her turn to lean on someone, and she leaned most on William, who was always there. Joanna went home after the noon meal, then came back to put a supper of leftovers on the table and wash up the dishes.

William finished his own work by noon but began staying on of his own accord, sitting in the kitchen, usually head in hands, waiting for my mother's little hand-bell to tinkle. A practical nurse was brought in to take care of her and later a trained nurse, but William stayed on as well.

"You better go on home and try to get something done," my father would tell him, since everyone sharecropped on the side.

"Miss might want something," he would say, and go on sitting, waiting for some small errand such as a trip to the store, bringing a tablespoon, squeezing a lemon. In cool weather he kept the fires going, not too hot and not too cool, fussing over grates and coal-burning heaters like a living thermostat.

He took it upon himself to answer the back door, since black women came up every day to see my mother. Most came out of concern, but some were simply idle and curious, and William weeded them out at a glance.

"She sleep," he would say, opening the back door and seeing the wrong face. "Ain't no need to wait."

My father couldn't get over it. "William has turned out to be the best old scoundrel I ever saw," he would say, as before a real phenomenon.

My mother must have been lonely. My father was in and out during the day but never for long. He was without his good right hand and had to compensate as best he could. I was away at school, not far, but away. My mother wouldn't hear to my coming home. She was determined that I have the education she had missed. My brother was hundreds of miles away.

We were called home for the last week of her life, which was spent in a deepening coma. Once, at the beginning of the end, she unexpectedly came to and was lucid. My father, my brother, and I were hurried into the room. William and Joanna stood outside in the hall.

"I must have been asleep," my mother said in a vague, apologetic voice. "Is it night or day?"

"It's day, sweedart," my father said, leaning over the bed. "Ten o'clock in the morning."

She looked curiously from one face to the other, and we all moved closer, hoping to be recognized, even spoken to.

But an unmistakable sob from the hall interrupted. Someone hurried to shut the door, but my mother had heard.

"Was that William?" she asked, and called out weakly, "William?"

We moved aside to let him come, weeping without restraint, while all that was left of her seemed to focus on his grief.

"Poor William," she said. "Don't cry. . . ."

But it was too much for her. She shut her eyes, frowned, and turned her head. My brother led William from the room.

The funeral was held at home as she would have liked. The

house was thoroughly clean and in order. Friends had filled it with flowers. The short service, led by our country preacher, was attended by so many people they had to stand outside, all over the front yard and into the road. The newspaper obituary referred to my mother as a "beloved woman."

There was no music during the service. But at its close, a group of black singers, self-selected as the best on the place, stood outside under the carport and sang "Swing Low, Sweet Chariot" as they brought the casket out.

Joanna, William, and Bob were to ride with the family to the cemetery. A farm truck was to bring any of the rest who wanted to come. But when it was time to leave, William couldn't be found, so we had to go on without him.

It was not until we got home that we found him alone in the backyard, in a chair under the trees.

"She gone," he announced, when we went up to ask him what happened, and why he hadn't gone with us. "I ain't got nobody now."

My father went up and patted him awkwardly on the shoulder. "You got us," he said.

William looked at my father as if to say *You?* Then his eyes filled with large tears that began to roll down his cheeks and onto his clean, white, starched Sunday shirt.

"Nobody," he repeated. "Not in this world."

The Humanistic Black Heritage
of Alabama

There is something about growing up black in Alabama that has historically encouraged one to strive for excellence. I have researched the lives of a number of black men and women of distinction. My interest was, and always has been, wide-ranging. I have always considered "professionals" in a broad sense. I would include professional entertainers, for example: Erskine Hawkins, a native of Birmingham, who composed "Tuxedo Junction"; Big Mama Thornton, born Willie Mae Thornton in Montgomery; and Lionel Hampton, born in Birmingham. Also, professional athletes: Jesse Owens, a native of Danville; Willie Mays, born in Westfield; Hank Aaron, whose birthplace was Mobile; and, most important, Joe Louis, the "Brown Bomber," who was born in Lexington. My interest includes political figures, such as the first black mayors of several major northern cities: Kenneth Gibson of Newark, New Jersey, who was born in Enterprise, and Coleman Young of Detroit, who was born in Tuscaloosa. It includes military figures, like Brig. Gen. Oliver W. Dillard, the first African American to achieve this rank in the army, who was born in Margaret. It encompasses people who were in the forefront of the civil rights movement: the Reverend Ralph David Abernathy, born in Linden; the Reverend Fred Shuttlesworth, a native of Montgomery; Coretta Scott King, born in Marion; and, of course, Rosa Parks, who sparked the Montgomery bus boycott, which in turn ignited the direct-action civil rights movement. Mrs. Parks was born in Pine Level. I would like to study the lives of others with a view toward establishing a kind of "ecology." Much broader than Horace Bond's "ecology of academic excellence," it would be an "ecology of human excellence."

I realize some might think that "human" is too general a category—too much of an automatic "given"—to have much meaning. But to blacks like myself, who were born before World War II, the word *human* has a very important meaning. It was not for me, nor for the other people whose names I have just listed, a quality or a state of being that could be taken for granted at all. For the major part of our history here in America, we black people have not been accorded by our fellow inhabitants of this continent full membership in the human race.

When the Fourteenth Amendment, declaring all persons born in the United States to be citizens, was ratified, the former slaves were elevated to the status of human beings. Nevertheless, the legal, economic, and psychological mechanisms that had been developed to rationalize the coexistence of peoples who were the same in terms of biology only could not be immediately nullified. The majority culture was threatened by the change and resisted. Indeed, many white Americans are still grappling with this problem.

In the national mind—and especially in the mind of the South, where the former slaves who had suddenly become human beings actually lived—the radical change in the status of blacks mandated by law did not actually occur. Blacks were not elevated from slavery to full human beinghood. Rather, their status was raised slightly to a limbo-like state best described by the term *subhuman.* This term was fairly popular in racist circles before the civil rights movement and, in some quarters, enjoys favor still.

Without belaboring the point further, I will simply state that the people whom Horace Mann Bond studied, and the majority of "famous blacks from Alabama"—not to mention all the black Alabamians born before World War II who did not become lettered or famous but who tried to live good lives and to make life better for their children—all these people had a barrier to get past that no white Alabamian ever had to consider: they had to define their own humanity. For them, humanity was not a given, and it was not willingly accorded them by the majority culture. Humanity, in the philosophical sense, was something that they had to create for themselves.

On the most basic level, it is this historic ability to define our own humanity, and thereby to create a heritage of which we can be proud, that to me is the most significant aspect of being a black Alabamian. In a way, the very majority culture that denied full humanity to blacks for so long also presented us with one of the means to define it ourselves. I am thinking, of course, about the church.

Although the Judeo-Christian ethic, as defined by Americans, managed to accommodate slavery, it could not adjust to the presence of slaves who were also "heathens." Christianity was brought to us, and we not only accepted it but adopted it fully—especially its precepts about suffering here on earth in order to ensure a better life in the hereafter and about turning the other cheek. In fact, by taking such Christian teachings so thoroughly to heart, we outdid a lot of the white folks who had taught them to us. As a people, we were not innately "better" than whites. That we believed so completely in the concept of Christian humility reflected the reality of our legal existence. That we so patiently waited for our "Promised Land" was primarily a function of having nowhere to go but up. Still, that deep religiosity had a way of pervading our lives and of giving root to a humanitarianism of which I feel blacks should be especially proud.

Blacks, as a people, did not have to define their humanity by demeaning anyone else as subhuman. They did not need a negative foil to establish their own identity.

At least that was how I was brought up. The humanitarian philosophy with which I was imbued as a child encouraged the idea of helping others, not bringing them down. And I have an idea that other black Alabamians were raised on a similar philosophy. Renowned educator Marva Collins became famous because she believed that "unteachable children" could be taught. Big Mama Thornton spent a good portion of her career as a blues singer giving free concerts in prisons. Lionel Hampton has used part of his fortune to build low-cost housing for poor people. Joe Louis, during the World War II years, risked his heavyweight title twice and in both instances donated his winning purses to charity. Of course, none of these people—indeed, no one at all—can define his or her own humanity alone. Everyone needs the support of the surrounding environment.

In addition to citing the church as a crucial element of community support for family life, Andrew Billingsley has cited a good school and an intellectual atmosphere in the community. Horace Mann Bond's criteria for his "ecology of academic excellence" were (1) a history of family literacy; (2) a strong-willed father; (3) a loving mother with strong aspirations for her children; and (4) a good school. Are not these the same elements necessary for academic excellence in people of any race? And what is it about the Alabama environment that has historically provided the necessary combination of these elements to produce a marked proportion of black achievers?

When you broaden the standards of excellence, as I have, to include nonacademics, attempts to explain what is so unique about Alabama are even more difficult. My list of famous Alabamians includes people who have had very little formal education, people who did not have strong-willed fathers, people who were not particularly religious. Being born in Alabama, however, gave them some kind of incentive, some combination of the various support elements, some elusive "ecology of human excellence" that encouraged them to succeed. Some day I would like to track down that elusive key, or combination of elements. For the time being, however, I can only write knowledgeably about myself and about the elements of my growing up in Alabama that encouraged my striving for excellence.

Like Bond and Billingsley, I think first of the family. What my family and other black families in Demopolis imbued in their children was a firm belief that the social and legal distinctions between whites and blacks were not divinely ordained. I was taught that whites were privileged people who, in many instances, enjoyed unfair privileges. But I was never taught to perceive even the most racist of whites as other than misguided. These teachings on the part of my parents derived partly from church teachings. They also evolved from association with whites: Black women genuinely loved the white children they cared for. Some white women were honestly concerned about the black women who worked for them.

One of the white women for whom my mother worked gave me the opportunity to read books from the Demopolis Public Library. When I was growing up, black people could not patronize that library. When my mother told this white woman that I was a voracious reader, she volunteered to check books out of the library for me. I read *King Arthur, Ivanhoe, Treasure Island,* and other classics, among them H. G. Wells's *20,000 Leagues Under the Sea.* If not for this woman, the reading materials available to me would have been limited. But that would not have served as an excuse for not reading.

Albert Murray, who lives in New York, wrote a book called *South to a Very Old Place.* Published in 1971, it is essentially a chronicle of his return visit to his home place—Mobile, Alabama—by way of New Haven, Connecticut; Greensboro, North Carolina; Atlanta, Georgia; and Tuskegee, Alabama. Remembering what he was taught as a child growing up in Mobile, Murray wrote the following:

Absolutely the last thing in the world you could ever imagine yourself doing . . . was coming back complaining, "Look what they did to me," . . . because the only one you could possibly blame anything on, even if you did run afoul of white viciousness, was yourself. Absolutely the only thing you could possibly come back saying even then was: "I'm the one. That's all right about them. It's me." Because I already knew exactly what to expect and I still didn't do what I was supposed to do when the time came . . . that time. But that was that time, watch me the next time.

Like Murray, I was taught that if you go out into the world, you better know how to behave in that world. No excuses for messing up. And my parents were not just talking about the world of Demopolis. They were keenly interested in the world outside Demopolis, and particularly in the achievements of other black Americans in that larger world. They read *Ebony* and *Jet* and the *Pittsburgh Courier,* which purported to be the key "to understanding the progress of the race." Among the grownups, blacks who made it were a common topic of discussion. Demopolis was light-years away from the great cities of Europe, and the lives of my parents were equally as alien to the lives of cosmopolitan black entertainers like Josephine Baker and Bricktop. But it was a peculiar fact of existence for the average, aware black resident of Demopolis to be on intimate terms with the stories of those American blacks who had managed to achieve fame. My parents talked about Josephine Baker and Bricktop and Jackie Robinson and Ralph Bunche with as much familiarity as they talked about Cousin Eliza or Aunt Cindy.

What this kind of talk established in the mind of a small boy was not only a sense of horizons far beyond those of Demopolis, but also the idea that stars were people who were not essentially different from Cousin Eliza and Aunt Cindy.

I also attended an excellent school. It was segregated, of course. My classmates and my teachers were all black. My school did not have up-to-date textbooks or much equipment for extracurricular activities like music and sports. But it had superb teachers. Back then, when so many other professions were closed to blacks, teaching was a highly respected, even exalted, profession. In fact, when some other professions began to open up to blacks, older folks just couldn't relate to their children who pursued those different fields.

My teachers enjoyed the community support they received. They also earned it. For them, teaching was a true vocation, and it did not stop when school hours were over. When they traveled, they shared their experiences with us, brought back books for us. They did independent research on subjects they believed were important to us— black history, for example. It was not on the official Demopolis public school curriculum, but it was taught in my school. Not only did we learn about the lives of famous blacks in history, but most of the time their portraits stared down at us from the walls of halls and classrooms. They were removed on the occasions when the superintendent of schools came to visit with guests. The teachers in my school also got together and sponsored oratorical contests and talent shows. They were not paid to do this. They devoted additional time because, for them, teaching was not just a job.

Although I do not see myself as an apologist for segregation, I cannot help feeling that I actually benefited from a school environment in which both my intellectual and human development was of such genuine concern. In 1979 I visited one of my former elementary school teachers. She had taught me in the second or third grade and had just recently retired. She had a collection of scrapbooks full of pictures of her students over the years, and in one of them—one of the earlier ones—there was a picture of me. Hers was a loving and complete record of her years in the teaching profession. I don't think most teachers nowadays do that.

Once I left Alabama, an entirely different set of elements began to affect my personal "ecology," but the foundation of my Alabama upbringing prepared me to deal with them. It was the role models provided by my teachers and the preparation my parents gave me that encouraged me to become a teacher. It was, in part, my frustration with the "ecology of failure" that I encountered in my early career as an educator—teaching children in a special education class in Harlem—that led me to keep a journal of my experiences that was later published as my first book, *Diary of a Harlem Schoolteacher.*

My desire to provide my students with a window to the larger world such as that given me by my parents and teachers inspired my first forays into writing nonfiction for young people.

Many of my early books addressed political and social issues; for example, *Resistance: Profiles in Nonviolence; Revolutionaries: Agents of Change; The War and the Protest: Vietnam;* and *Profiles in Black Power.* In them, I endeavored to provide information on a level that adolescents could understand. I have also written books about the Vietnamese boat people and Cuban refugees, a multibook series of *Count Your Way* books introducing elementary school students to various world cultures—Africa, the Arab world, Brazil, Canada, China, France, Germany, Greece, India, Ireland, Israel, Italy, Japan, Korea, Mexico—by illustrating the numbers one through ten in the languages of those respective areas/countries with information unique to those cultures because I wish to instill a sense of inclusiveness in young minds.

Remembering the efforts of my teachers to provide historical role models for me, I have also concentrated on writing biographies of successful blacks who have earned a place in history. My hope is that young people will be inspired by their example.

When I say young people, I mean white as well as minority youth. In my many years of teaching—on the elementary, secondary, and college level—I have learned that there are white students who are eager to understand. Adults, too, want such information, and I have not confined my writings to the juvenile audience. Over time, I have accumulated a body of work—mostly biographies of blacks—for the adult audience as well.

In much of my work, I engage in "conversations with myself": I want to know more about something, and in the process of learning I try to convey what I have learned to a larger audience. My Alabama upbringing gave me the confidence to spread my own sense of humanity. And to believe in it.

ANDREW GLAZE

Growing Up a Poet in Alabama

Growing up as a poet in Alabama is—or at least used to be—not only a contradiction in terms, but also a pretty risky business, accomplished if possible, in secret. Because by traditional Alabama and southern standards, poets were parasites, communists, oddities, creeps, lepers, blasphemers, and Antichrists, unless they were little eighty-year-old ladies in dimity dresses with flowery hats, in which case they were tolerated as harmless.

Keep in mind you are a squid growing up in shark country. I had the word for all this from my father, who knew what he was talking about after a closet life of being a socialist, agnostic, occasional poet, and believer in sexual freedom and racial equality in the Deep South. Daddy trained me from the beginning to keep my mouth shut about all the things I believed, particularly those most impor-tant to me. So I learned to bow my head while others prayed, assuring myself, "If it makes them feel better, why not?" I shrugged when they cursed President Roosevelt, giggled (inwardly) when they gave ridiculous lectures in the name of sex education, although they knew less about it than I.

As a result of all this, I never suspected I was a poet. In a life surrounded by people doing *real* things, the very thought, if it had occurred to me, would have seemed both exotic and ridiculous.

In every direction, people were doing *real* things. For instance, on the slope of Red Mountain in Birmingham, a wagon driver would be fiercely lashing his poor mules, trying to make them struggle a load of coal up the curve in a nearly vertical driveway at 2811 Niazuma Avenue.

At Acipco, a workman was repairing a pipe mold and dusting it just before a giant bucket arrived along the rail line and poured it full of molten iron.

Mme Jeanne Youngblood was chain smoking halfway up Highland Avenue to the summit from Jones Valley on Altamont Road, teaching French verbs to a bored high school girl, while an Italian lady in a tiny delicatessen at fifteenth Avenue just off Twenty-first Street was dipping vanilla cones in chocolate.

Sheriff Holt MacDowell and his deputies were chasing bootleggers in the wild northwest of Jefferson County, dumping confiscated homebrew into the Warrior River. Daddy's friend Bob Williams, even while locked up in the insane asylum at Tuscaloosa, was making homebrew in gallon-sized pee cans hung up the chimney.

It was depression time, and people were moving out of houses where they couldn't pay the rent and moving in with relatives on farms. Farmers were converting the back axles of their broken-down trucks into primitive wagons powered by mules. They called them "Hoover Carts," in honor of Herbert you-know-who.

A confused and disoriented Mexican was wandering about the Five Points area selling hot tamales out of a wooden box with a hinged top. He thought he was in San Diego.

Mr. George Ward, chairman of Alabama Power, was holding a dinner party in his round house atop Shades Mountain, which was an exact replica of the Temple of the Vestal Virgins in ancient Rome. He called it Vestavia, and as soon as he was gone to that Roman Empire in the sky, some idiot developer would tear it down and build a tasteless bungalow on the spot. But just now, he was having a party, and his servants were clanking about in what he thought was authentic Roman armor, serving imported English gin.

Along the crest of the mountain to the southwest, his less-well-off neighbors were gathered to drink near-beer in the Linger-Longer Lodge.

All these things were "real"—considered indisputably so by the world that lay all about the unconscious poet that I was. Only one clue did I have to my nature. I felt in some way un-included in the life all about me. If my attention had been called to it, I'd have assumed it was somehow my fault. Daddy made sure of that.

I never had a serious glimpse of my real world until I was about fourteen years old. A group of Daddy's friends met to discuss literary matters. They met irregularly, a Birmingham writer of novels and travel books, James Saxon Childers; a *Saturday Evening Post* fiction writer, Octavus Roy Cohen; and three amateur lovers of "Literature," Daddy, Judge Charles Feidelsen, and a lawyer whose first name has gotten mislaid in the sands of time, a Mr. Rosenthal.

Cohen wrote stories about "colored" life in Birmingham, the sort of life that was chronicled in Charleston by Dubose Hayward, the creator of *Porgy and Bess.* Cohen's hero was a comic black of the Amos and Andy ilk named Florian Slappey, a fictional inhabitant of the amorphous area about Eighteenth Street and First Avenue downtown in Birmingham, then a black ghetto. Various comic mystery adventures came to Florian, and Daddy's group did its best to keep Cohen supplied with ideas. Needless to say, it was a never-never land of black life with little relation to what really went on.

This particular night one of these visitors happened to bring a book for Daddy to read. It was the poems of Emily Dickinson, and I picked it up and read a few of the pieces. It was the first instance in my experience of that phenomenon the English poet A. E. Housman called the only way to recognize a poem—having the hairs on the back of your neck stand up as you recite it to yourself while shaving.

I was too young to shave, but Emily made my neck hairs stand up. I wasn't sophisticated enough to know what had happened, but *something* definitely had. In an almost unidentifiable way, the direction of my life had taken some sort of bend, or perhaps *curlicue* would be a better word. I wouldn't read Robert Frost for a while yet, but I'd know instantly what Frost meant when he said, "I took the road less traveled by, / and that has made the difference." This was not the harmless piffle of Longfellow and Whittier; it was, in its own way, desperate stuff. Something in me felt oddly stirred up, in a way with which I was unfamiliar.

Daddy had certainly encouraged me. I was about four when I dictated a poem to him about Sloss Furnace, now dead but in those days a perfect fountain of steam, molten slag, whistles, mysterious lights, and noises. My poem was entitled "Watch the Choo Choo Pour Fire" and all that remains of it is the first line. "The fire was pouring on the lean"—a respectable iambic tetrameter. There was more to the poem, but along with a lot of other things, it was lost in the catastrophe of Daddy's death.

Daddy was always at the center of my childhood. I dearly loved my mother, but Daddy was a mysterious dark cavern of frightening excitement and surprise. I ask myself now, why? Why? And how does he hold such a prominent place in an essay about growing up a poet in Alabama?

Like most of Birmingham's inhabitants at that time, Daddy was not a native but drawn, like tens of thousands of other people, from elsewhere by the magical growth of the steel and iron industry in Jones Valley. He was born Andrew Louis Glaze Jr. at Elkton, Tennessee, son of a country doctor who in his early twenties served as a surgeon in the Confederate army. On horseback, barely twenty-five, Grandpa rode all over the South with Forrest's cavalry. And when the peace came, he took a formal medical degree at Nashville.

Daddy took a medical degree in Nashville and married a girl he met there, who came originally from the same county. Many years later, Mama, ninety-three, on her deathbed asked my sister, "Sis, who was I married to?" and when Sis told her, a look of pure horror appeared on her face as she said, "You mean I married one of those awful Glazes from Elkton?"

The Glazes were acknowledged to be bright, energetic, and creative, but dangerously unstable. Granny, a schoolteacher, was brilliant but manipulative. And Grandpa was stubborn. Which explains how she was known to stand on the edge of the well and threaten to jump in if she didn't get her way.

Daddy began to practice general medicine at Athens, Alabama, then became a medical officer in World War I, served through the Meuse-Argonne offensive, and was discharged a major. With his bonus money he studied dermatology at the old Skin and Cancer Hospital in New York, under the famous Dr. Pack, and set up an office in Birmingham, at First Avenue and Twentieth Street, in the Empire Building.

I, the future poet, was born April 21, 1920. Somewhere there is a picture of me lying on the bed in the family's first apartment, across from the old Presbyterian Church at the foot of the Twenty-first Street hill where it meets Highland Avenue—looking like a baby. We moved shortly. But then we were always moving. I remember four houses between Glenview Road to the northeast and Sixteenth Avenue S. and Twentieth Street to the southwest. All on the north slope of Red Mountain. Maybe it's why I have a predilection to this day for living on a northerly slope.

The comparative Eden of childhood came to an end one day when my mother took me firmly by the hand and led me off to school. Miss Stillwell's was a private kindergarten and first grade on the south side of Highland Avenue amid tremendous oak trees. It was a bit east of Twenty-first Street and not far from the Synagogue. I *hated* it.

Under Miss Stillwell's back steps
(White painted one by twos)
the paint flakes off. Through which he's been looking out

for some time now. Play, they call this? Kicking balls?
It's "dumb." But is as good a cage as any
to wall out those brawling boobies at their whacks.
The treachery! Mother leading him up this doomed path
through plug-ugly dark root trees,
putting his hand in the teacher's abstracted
(abstract) chalky paw.
She's bid him sit and learn. He will not.
Never could and won't.
Under these steps he'll sit, fingering gravel.
Someone's changed the rules.
Decide—now decide—(it's decided).
A lifetime of *pee* on the world.

Then the depression came. It turned Fifteenth Avenue into a
wasteland. All the friends I was just getting to know moved away,
and we ourselves soon departed also. We left behind us the miniature golf course we'd made out of cotton seed, and the tree-house
we'd built. I was beginning to learn about Daddy's temper. Once I
shot my air rifle carelessly, and he destroyed it, then replaced it the
next day. Typical.

Daddy had begun his anxious crusade to turn me into a genius. I
was sent for art lessons, piano lessons, singing lessons, public speaking lessons, French lessons, boxing lessons, golf lessons, typing
lessons, arithmetic and geometry lessons. First to Miss Hannah
Elliott for art. She lived on the Twenty-first Street hill in a ram-
shackle old house. Everybody said Miss Hannah used to be a "hel-
lion" when she was in Paris in her twenties. Which means she probably wore her skirts up to the ankle and said "damn" a couple of
times. But she quickly determined that I wasn't patient enough to
be an artist. And I wandered about and got into such things as her
father's old sword from the Philippine insurrection. "Still covered
with blood," as she said to me sternly.

We moved to the house on 2811 Niazuma Avenue. The tremendous two-and-a-half-acre lot was neighbored by Northingtons on

one side and Nelsons on the other. Across the street lived lawyer Jim Simpson and his son Joe. Daddy paid $11,000 for a house that cost $50,000 to build. The front lawn required Alpine equipment to mow it. Getting up the driveway demanded a powerful car. There was a garage big enough to hold Mama's big Buick coupe and Daddy's big Buick sedan. In the living room was Mama's baby grand piano, on which she played and I practiced my piano lessons, which I took with Hugh Thomas at the Birmingham Conservatory. My Glaze fingers were too clumsy to do much with a piano, no matter how much I loved music.

Daddy's ambitious program to turn his son into a genius was risky. Would it turn me into a prodigy or a harassed, neurotic child? At any rate, it certainly shattered my self-confidence, at first. What a constant struggle to keep up with what Daddy wanted of me. And he was so inconsistent. He announced he was opposed to corporal punishment but then slapped me because I was afraid to pick up a crawfish on one of his fishing trips. In his eyes, I was shaming him in front of his friends.

My public speaking lessons were probably the most useful. I discovered a love of theater and began to try out for children's plays at the Little Theater.

In our new house, my brother Bobby was born. All of us adored him. Daddy let him alone. "This one," he said, "is going to love me." So Bobby never lacked for self-confidence. He was far smarter than I, particularly in the area of the sciences, which fascinated but defeated me.

I carried my books and lunch down the mountain into the smog to Lakeview School. I did very well academically, except for the eternal P in handwriting. But I was afraid to fight. Daddy took me down to the Boy's Club and had the gym instructor inspect my boxing stance. What I lacked was not technique.

"I don't want to fight," I told Daddy. "What for? I'm not mad at anybody."

"Because if you don't, they'll always pick on you," he said.

Finally, with a sigh, I decided to provoke a fight with the smallest of the boys in my class, Charles Nice. So, one day, with a scared sense of adventure, I took a poke at Charlie as he walked by. And we had a fight. I was disconcerted to find that once involved, it wasn't so bad. That was the last time I ever had to fight. As though I'd passed some sort of test, the boys in the class actually started a club and elected me president (it never had but one meeting). I decided boys were crazy.

Miss Mamie Brown, my eighth-grade teacher, was the first to notice that I had a talent for writing. But she didn't know anything about poetry, and I didn't know anything about poetry, and the library teacher gave us nineteenth-century poems about death and failure like the "Ancient Mariner," some of whose opening lines I thought (and think) were ugly and unpronounceable. "By thy long grey beard and glittering eye, wherefore *stops't thou me?*"

I lived on broadcasts of baseball games. When the Barons were out of town, these were presided over by Eugene "Bull" Connor, in the future to be a highly incendiary racist demagogue. All he had was a telegraph ticker to signal the game. "A Whi 1b rf" meaning "Abe White, single to right field." By the time Connor got through with it, it would be a highly dramatized version of the base hit. "LOOK AT THAT!" he'd say. "One swing of the bat, there she goes, higher and higher, higher, yowee, look at it—over the fence, it's a HOME RUN." Connor got his nickname from a humorous editorial columnist who used to write daily in the *Birmingham Post* during the late twenties and thirties using the acronym "Dr. B.U.L. Connor."

And I read monthly pulp magazines such as *Secret Agent X—The Man of a Thousand Faces* and *Amazing Stories* and *Astounding Stories,* as well as the magazines about World War I flying combat, *Wings* and *Flying Aces.* And of course I read everything I could find about adventurous, romanticized war, by H. Ryder Haggard, Kipling, even things like *The Young Carthaginian* by G. A. Henty, that Victorian popular writer of historical war fiction for boys.

But I loved Eddie Rickenbacker's *Fighting the Flying Circus* and the nostalgia of World War I flying combat high above all the grim slaughter.

Every month when the pulps came out, I'd go with Mama to Five Points, and while she went into the Piggly Wiggly or the A & P (Daddy's office was across Twentieth Street in the Medical Arts Building), I'd curl up in the backseat and disappear from this often disappointing world. It was in *Amazing Stories* that I first came across the name of L. Ron Hubbard, who would in future times found a religion (Scientology). To me he was just one more goofy space writer.

Years later I would meet several of them through Breadloaf Writers Conference. Those names had always a certain aura of gilt-edged glamour about them. As though they came from another world. (Believe me, they did.)

What was I going to do for a living when I grew up? I didn't like to think about it. I didn't want to be a doctor. But I knew I wasn't going to be a salesman or a preacher.

If I was incautious enough to tell Daddy any problem, his injunction was always to tackle whatever it was head on. I mentioned that our closest park had no decent place to play baseball. Daddy insisted I write to the paper about it. They published my letter and to my infinite embarrassment, Bull Connor, now a city commissioner, sent out a crew to build us a baseball field on one edge of the nearby Roebuck Golf Course (now Boswell). My friends immediately lost interest in playing baseball.

As soon as I was comfortable at Ramsay High School, age fifteen, I was sent away to a school in Tennessee so strange I couldn't have imagined it. Webb School in 1935 was like a return to the nineteenth century. For the lower high school grades, the school used an old teaching technique called the "trapping system," invented many decades earlier, so that one teacher could handle a class of 200 or 300 students. The teacher would ask a series of questions in rapid-fire order. If the first student couldn't answer, the question passed to the next. If five, ten, or fifteen failed to answer, the one who did answer rose up physically and went past all those who couldn't answer and took a seat near the "head" of the class. If you succeeded in staying at the head of the class all day, the next day you "went foot" and started back up again. Your grade at the end of each month was based on how many "rounds" of the class you made that month.

I thought it was exciting, great fun, a sort of game, and it explained what old books meant when they talked about being "head" of a class. Old-fashioned it may have been, but it gave me a thorough grounding in Latin, which has been useful all my life as a writer and history freak. Daddy strongly disliked the school's peculiar "honor system," which required that if you saw somebody else do anything against the rules, and they didn't report it, you were supposed to report *them* at assembly the next day. Luckily, I never even had to report myself. The punishment? To study in study hall instead of outdoors.

Mr. Follin, my senior English teacher, genuinely loved English literature and was the first teacher who ever noticed that I had a considerable gift. And he had us memorize some good poetry. For instance, the prologue to Chaucer's *Canterbury Tales,* speeches from *Hamlet.* I still recite those wonderfully musical Chaucer lines to myself when I lose faith in the power of poetry.

He was a truly imaginative teacher, though not a handsome man (we knew him as "the goon" after a character in the Popeye cartoon). Naturally his son, in my class, was "Goonlet." Mr. Follin had us dig a grave in the lawn by the school office to perform the graveyard scene from *Hamlet* (I was Hamlet). And he was much struck by several themes I wrote about an imaginary land. He had me read them to the class.

In college I heard about a whole string of poets I'd never known about. Walt Whitman, from teachers who despised Walt Whitman—also Edwin Arlington Robinson, A. E. Housman, Robinson Jeffers, Hart Crane, Marianne Moore. I wrote my senior thesis on W. B. Yeats. To start my last year, I applied to a writing class taught by a name that meant nothing to me: Theodore Morrison. I knew nothing about him except that there was no other course in creative writing. Only much later did I find out that he was Robert Frost's best friend and founder of the Breadloaf Writers Conference.

Filled with apprehension, I submitted poems and short stories for his approval, as required.

One day, he called me in for an interview, stared at me a while, and lit his pipe, said he assumed from my accent that I was a southerner. After a considerable preamble, he looked at the poems on his lap. "I'm not quite sure what to tell you," he said. "You're far beyond my help. I don't quite know what I can do for you. You're a first-class talent. But I'd love to have you in my class." How unexpected, how dizzying, even frightening! It would take me months to sort out my feelings, to separate the pride, the fear, the overwhelming sense of responsibility from the joy of having something of my own, nothing to do with Daddy. When you've never had acceptance, it's hard to take.

My talent, which I had always cherished and enjoyed, had always been like something outside of me. I didn't think of myself as a poet. I was a person who wrote poems among a multiplicity of other doings and responsibilities.

And all that year, I kept expecting Morrison to change his mind, to tell me he'd been mistaken. At the end of the academic year I made a small mimeographed edition of my poems and slipped them under the doors of all the English faculty in Leverett House. They were totally ignored.

In later years I was to get the same reaction from practically every literary magazine in America. Stupid young man! If I was as good as Morrison thought and as I felt, why didn't I get encouragement?

It's the hardest thing in the world for any creative person to have an original way of looking at things. Most people in the arts feel uncomfortable with work that breaks old shibboleths and tries to insist on a new way of looking at things. If I'd written timid but recognizable and acceptable poems, I'd have been better off. But I didn't know how to write such things. The poems I read in literary magazines seemed to me sterile, imitative, and dead. Nor, being very shy,

could I court the people you need to court to succeed when literary
reputations are being doled out.

    World War II interrupted all that. I joined the Army Air Force.
Waiting to be called, I pumped gas from a filling station in Mountain Brook. Between customers, I'd struggle through Joyce's *Ulysses.*
My ancient copy still has oil stains on it. One day, an old pickup
truck parked nearby and the even older man who drove it called out
a little army of tiny dogs who performed dances. Many years later, it
came back to me for my poem "Dog Dancing."

Dog Dancing

Big Fred Carey hobbled over to me last night
in a dream, giving his heart-sworn thunderous grin,
reminding how he'd once paid twenty a week
as I pumped gas from a Pure Oil Station in Mountain
    Brook—
and how one time an old man parked his busted pickup
next, on the grass, some strange, lank kind of a fellow,
whose beard was dirty, whose eye was witty,
whose truck was square in the back
closed off with a delicate netting of wire.

When he'd gotten a sack of day-old buns and rolls
from the bakeshop down the street,
he opened the veiled doors behind and called out a company

of trim little dogs like grasshopper children,
fox terriers and kindred mongrels on spindly legs.
He watched them shake themselves,
then cranked his old Victrola.
Hearing its stately scratches, the dogs began to dance.
What a strange sight, to see those dozen dogs
gravely turning about in slow pirouettes, hopping,
spinning in schottisches, somersaulting over their heads.
The old man stood there, watching,

slowly nodding, bidding them persevere
with squashed bits of stale bakery trash.
They silently waited with anxious fortitude
and gnawed crumbs in the wings like refugees.

On a tiny lady dog he strapped a pink skirt.
She treadled beneath the ruffles.
While the needle squeaked a bag-pipe wail,
she did a slow and mystic spin
with paws upraised and eyes in a heavenly transit,
turning and hopping, mincing her toes below.
When she'd done her turn, she took the old man's tambourine
between her teeth and grandly made the ring
of those who watched, and took their nickels and dimes.

I saw the thought fester in Big Fred's eyes,
that this old man, who should be safe somewhere,
sucking his pipe, reading the weather—
he and his dogs were out on the whim of the world.
"One morning he'll wake up dead," he said, whisking his
    hands.
"I mean, all right for him, he won't know better,
but what about the dogs?"
What was there I could say that he would believe?
And what did I know about the demands of art?

My four years of World War II weren't very exciting. There were
far more of us keeping the planes flying, the radios working, the
runways paved, the parts counted, and the papers signed than there
were coming in contact with an enemy. A buzz bomb once went
over my head. I watched bombers come home to Norfolk spouting
flares, which meant they had wounded aboard. I found my excellent
French more useful than aiming a rifle. I studied a little bit of Rus-
sian, learned a bit of Welsh history while living in a seaside mansion
near an air base on the island of Anglesey.

Sometime during those years, Daddy wrote me a letter that bewildered me. "Everybody else seems to have seen it, forgive me for not recognizing that you are not only a poet, but an absolutely first-rate poet."

I memorized his letter. To me it meant, "After all this time, you're free. It's okay to be you." So I decided to go back home after the war, study medicine, and, when he retired, take over his practice.

What a dreadful mistake that would have been! But it wasn't to be. Daddy killed himself.

Not till the war was over did I hear the full story.

It was the old uncontrollable temper. He had an affair with a girl who worked in his office. She tried to break it off, take the car he'd given her, and leave with another man. He shot her and then himself.

My Father Invented the Submarine

It's the last report we shall have,
in a moment or two you will rise,
you will lift the fiberglass hatch
above the steel cone,
stretch vertically the long iron grille
built with your impregnable
bars of honor and grit,
—hesitate—

Make ironical bows to the harbor, to the birds,
—to us—and climb in,
and down, and lower the hatch
above you like a lock.

There you will shut out
the daily obscenity,
the wastage of mean thought,
the slither underfoot of superficial manners,

the daily lies of refreshment and love,
the sneaking ambitious flat-worm hearted sky.
Be off—to adventure, surely,
Nervously twisting the dials
about you, sinking
in the emerald foreshore like a rock.

Where have you gone, Daddy?
Down there?
Cruising, sliding somewhere beneath the sunless sea
and riding along hallooing corridors
glowing like a phosphorescent bead,
inside of me?

I think I see you, I hear you—
slowly floating deeper, deeper, grating upon
the center of myself, on my soul's sea floor,
aground upon the reefs of your wrecked science.
Are you alone—at one?
God knows Daddy, I wish, I hope so—at one.
Or are you falling
into one of the old mad un-accepting rages
to find the same thing happening over again
that has happened and happened
since the original catastrophe began?

Are you aground there
in the most unacceptable place of all places,
trapped—caged like a beast—
forever—

bound in the hateful burning place of flesh,
locked, blocked, chained and barred,
for as long as I am to be myself,
In the un-surrendering humanness of my heart?

In the chaos, everything changed. Mama sold our house. All my books and beloved record collection disappeared.

Invited by Theodore Morrison, I went as a fellow to Breadloaf Writers Conference, which became a second home for me. I did six months of graduate work at Stanford. But I didn't want to teach. I was in love with words, with the English language, with southern speech. So I threw up graduate work and came home to Alabama.

I needed to get to know my city, my state. So I made the deliberate decision to get a job in Birmingham.

I'd starve, maybe, but that wasn't dishonorable. Through editor Jimmy Mills, I got a job as a reporter on the old *Birmingham Post*, later the *Post-Herald*. I met a girl, was married, we bought a house. My daughter, Betsy, was born.

At the same time, Birmingham was plunging deeper and deeper into the cauldron of racial animosity, hatred, confusion, contradiction which was Birmingham in the 1950s.

To me as a poet and writer, it was a splendid, scary, unforgettable, exalted, terrifying learning experience. I witnessed something surprising, every day, about the contradictory, amazing city I sprang from. I was growing up at my own speed, doing it in a conscious way.

A few people in the literary world began to recognize me as a growing poet. *Poetry Magazine* of Chicago gave me its Eunice Tietjens award. John Ciardi published me in the *Saturday Review*.

I was a junior reporter when Robert Frost came through for his annual reading at Birmingham-Southern; he asked if someone could contact me and invite me to spend a day with him. The good professor who called me was obviously baffled. Who in the world was Andrew Glaze? Why in the world would Robert Frost want to see him? Frost was notoriously impatient with younger poets, but he was kind to me, I've always suspected, because I never asked him to read my manuscripts. And he knew I'd never write a news feature about him. It was treacherous to my responsibilities as a reporter, but anyway it made for a nice day.

My boss, Duard LeGrand, the city editor at the *Post-Herald,* was one of the best people I've ever known. When my days as a courthouse reporter brushed up again the race issue and I had to give controversial testimony, he snatched me out of what he feared might be a dangerous situation and gave the courthouse beat to another reporter. But that couple of years was fun.

My poem called *I Am the Jefferson County Courthouse* (for which there's no room in this essay) tells of that experience. Now the time had arrived for a serious change in the direction in my life. My wife and I decided we must move to New York. She wanted to study acting seriously. I wanted to see my plays staged. In Birmingham they won prizes but couldn't be produced because of unpopular subject matter. We both hoped to make a living doing what we liked most. And our daughter, Betsy, wanted to take advanced ballet classes.

So the die was cast. We sold our house. Dorothy took Betsy and went ahead to the big city to find a place to live. When I could afford it, I would follow. It was a wrench.

My last Sunday in Birmingham before leaving, I visited the sidewalk art show that was held in the Lane Park woods near where these days there's a zoo and botanical gardens.

Sidewalk Art Show

Life, with frantic indifference, had broken through,
and valiant, riding a trailer of household Gods and Devils,
he proposes to head off north, towards home,
though what he takes as home neither expects nor welcomes him,
does not take the trouble, even, to bother to care.

He has in mind to make a sort of perverse ceremonial,
and climbs Red Mountain one more time,
it's a dazzling April Sunday,
Lane Park is full of what the papers call "Our Sidewalk Art
    Show."

For sidewalks there are sandy paths—and for art,
squadrons of monster loblolly pine soaring straight at heaven
like galleon masts, with flapping between them, hung on
    strings,
hundreds of timid copies of poster art.
As though Redon, Van Gogh, Renoir,
had gotten strained through the skewed eye of the *Ladies
    Home Journal.*
and sit there staring contemptuously at one another
—primitive Baptist Christs, chipmunky flowers,
funky watermills and happy country cabins—
He longs for the rough edged pictures
he'd not the gift to make, of Governor Wallace
skinning the eastern bankers, of Happy Hal Burns
riding his perky guitar-stallion yodelling cowboy tangos,
up the fiery Red Mountain sky on the trail of life! life! life!

But he'd got to do whatever there was to do,
—With this—. With all these awful artists
squeezed out like paste on a toothbrush crying me! me! me!
Like awful him, yelling I'm hungry, feed me fame! fame!
—or anyway, fifty cents—.
Is that all he wants from the far away wilderness
of a foreign city which lords it over his dreams?

He stands there in the rain squall of his own comic despera-
    tion—
remembering, as he must every day,
how daddy went on the prowl one night
with a .45 resting beside him on the seat,
to slaughter the girl who dared humiliate him.

And remembering it once more, he shivers.
"Uncle Andy" someone speaks his name, and he raises his eyes
to see gentle nephew John,

standing beside him, puzzled by the face full of wild waves.
"You okay?" John whispers,
and leads him over in the peaceable tree-dark
to where he is selling, out of a wooden booth,
Staghorn Orchid, Spider Plant, Bilbergia, Tradescantia,
a trackless wilderness unrestrained, of tangled leaves and
    stems.
Simply touching the cool, dry, self-contained
matter of fact-ness about them, calms him.
It's the same quiet with-ness
which once rocked and soothed daddy's tumbling wits,
when he rooted up and around
these wooded valleys digging hands deep into the humus
for hidden flowers to set in the earth,
like little wild gifts to himself and his loved backyard trees.
But why is it never enough, in what we call our world—
to give the gift of yourself to a quiet thing?

The memory never fails, if it knows what it's doing. It may be wrong or confused, but in a life of art, it is always right. Whatever my life became afterward, I'd managed it without doing violence to myself either as a poet or as a southerner. And though I was leaving the South, physically, I was and always would be a southerner and an Alabama writer. And the poet in me would always live in Birmingham.

H E L E N   N O R R I S

Stalking an Early Life

It gives me pleasure to report that my first memory, a most vivid
one, is of standing on the observation platform of a train backing
into a station. I am holding my mother's hand. Surrounding us in
the station are many people shouting and waving their arms. They
do not seem to be angry, but they are certainly noisy. I look up at my
mother and ask her, "What is it?" She says, "The war is over." At
that moment my grandfather leaps onto the train, which has come
to a stop, and picks me up in his arms. End of memory. Set apart
from all else. It is, as I came years later to realize, a memory of the
end of World War I. My mother and I were on our way from Montgomery, my home, to Miami, where my grandparents lived, where I
had been born, and where my eldest brother would in three weeks
be born. I was too young at the time to know any of this.

I like to recall that my first memory was one of joyful celebration for the end of a war, indeed of the war popularly hailed to be "the war to end all wars."

There is another memory that challenges the primacy of that memory of peace. I am being chased by a gander in the backyard of my home. I am screaming in terror as I half turn to find him gaining on me. I glimpse a man bending and heading him off. I assume the man was my father. Later in my life, I was told that the gander gave chase each time I entered the yard and that no one ever understood why he did. It is tempting to regard as my first memory one of being chased by a man. But I reject the total terror of myself as prey in favor of joyous celebration for the end of all war.

Somewhere along the way is a memory of losing my mother in Woolworth's and howling like a banshee till I got her back. Nothing else until the age of six, when I was driven by my grandfather, in his open touring car, along with my grandmother, mother, and brother, all dressed in linen car coats, to visit relatives in New England. I was aware that my relatives all lived in what now I would describe as style. I remember the occasion when, decked in my best lavender dress, I disgraced myself at the formal dinner of one great-aunt by emitting a pronounced and loud whistle at the table. I had simply wanted to show that I could do it. Life is a series of painful lessons as to what you can't do. It's never what you can do. It's simply that you do it and discover that you can't. By the time you've got it nailed down, they nail you down.

I grew up on a 500-acre farm just east of Montgomery, where I'm told I was taken when I was eight months old. The location is now officially and geographically the center of the city, but in those days it was certainly a rural scene. No electricity, no telephone, no radio (it had not been invented), and a newspaper delivered two days late by the postman. We never worried about the weather, since we never knew what it would be until it was. You might wake in the night and think, wow, what a blow! and then go back to sleep. When the mailman brought *The Advertiser,* my father would look first for the weather prediction in the lower left-hand corner to see if the weatherman had got it right; 90 percent of the time he hadn't.

Our neighbors relied on the *Farmers' Almanac* as being more reliable than the weatherman's guess. But my father was a man of science and would have none of that. One day the headlines reported that west Montgomery had blown away—that was three days before. So we all jumped into the family car and drove at full speed to see if it was so, and it was, more or less. Something left for seed.

It was really a nice thing to have no telephone. If my father had a word to say to a neighbor down the road, we all hopped into that family car and went along for the ride, and invariably the lady of the house would make us get out and stay. We weren't hard to persuade. It was why we had come. They had just made a pitcher of lemonade and a batch of cookies or were just about to cut a watermelon on the picnic table. So we stayed and ate and laughed and talked, and when it was bedtime went home. I never laughed or talked. I was painfully shy. I was like a little sponge that soaked it all up.

The farm we owned had fields of alfalfa, lespedeza, oats, corn, sorghum, and johnsongrass for the hay. It had forty acres of a deep and magical woods, where I could get lost whenever I chose and where in the spring we picked armfuls of white lilies and purple violets. Everything I've ever written has in some sense come out of those woods. On the half acre where I now live I never cut or prune a tree that wants to live, to the universal disapproval of neighbors and blood kin. I tell them that I'm a one-woman protest against the deforestation of the earth, but it's mostly that I'm trying to recover that lost woods.

In early spring, there were fields of wild dewberries and blackberries, which we loved to pick, then red and yellow plums, muscadines, and persimmons in the fall. Deep in the woods was a wide place in a stream where a sloe tree dropped its blush-tipped fruit to float in the water. I tell you all this because it was extremely important to me. We had, of course, peaches, pears, apples, and figs, but they were cultivated. There is something about picking wild things to eat that makes you know that you are living in a world that likes you.

The farm we owned seemed to accumulate in no time at all a

dairy full of milk cows, 7,000 laying hens, 2,000 turkeys, two large hatcheries, an assortment of mules, beef cattle, sheep, goats, pigs, pigeons, guineas, geese, ducks, one burro, two peacocks, and an absolutely incredible amount of manure. To this day I rebel against buying the stuff for my plants, because it was once so much and so free. Manure was not needed for fertilizer then, since the farm was in the Black Belt and the soil was black and rich as Croesus. The Atlantic had once covered it, my father said. My brothers had collections of the sharks' teeth they found. One portion of the farm became our "sleepy lagoon," where manure was dumped.

I believe my first self-generated awareness of beauty in the world around me occurred when as a first-grader I was walking with my father in the winter a mile down our gravel road to the Vaughan Road, where the school bus would pick me up. I saw in the road a cow pile densely covered with frost and gleaming like diamonds in the early sun. My father was struck by my exclamations of delight and referred to it as long as he lived. He called it my discovery of "beauty in the commonplace." Whatever.

Fortunately, I was not expected to do anything about all those creatures that produced the manure. There were people around to take care of all that, though I found the creatures of interest.

Turkeys, for example, are interesting to observe. They vie with sheep for being the dumbest things God ever made. But at one time they were profitable, though always difficult to raise. My father practiced diversified farming. When the price of one thing goes down, another will go up. That's the theory, of course. Unfortunately, I came along in the Great Depression, but turkeys were up. My father liked to say that turkeys put me through college.

You haven't lived till you've passed a large pen of turkeys with colds in the head, all sneezing like crazy and shaking their running beaks. This is an undesirable development, since in their misery they don't eat and gain weight, and weight on a turkey is the name of the game. In case it's of interest, the treatment goes like this: Persons on the payroll are sent into the pen to grab the suffering things, choke them till they open their beaks to get air, at which time a vitamin A pill is stuffed down the gullet. Not a lot different from getting medicine down a suffering child. In turkey-colds season the dining room mantel was always lined with vitamin A bottles beneath the Donatello of the infant Jesus trailing swaddling clothes. It had been a wedding gift for my parents. My father was fond of that Donatello. I could tell that he liked to say the name "Donatello."

I was a useless child. I believe I experienced vague compulsions to make the world a better place, but they were unfocused. I cannot recall a useful act that I ever performed. Perhaps churning for butter, but that was given me to build my character. Soured milk was poured into a crock of a churn that was always on the back porch just inside the door. I was seated before it, handed the plunger, and told to plunge. I plunged forever. I was taught the traditional butter song: "Come, butter, come. Come, butter, come. Johnny's at the garden gate, waiting for his butter cake. . . ." I was never told who in tarnation Johnny was or what a butter cake was. And whoever promised that song would speed up the process had lied in his throat. I thought of all the fun things I'd rather be doing. I saw myself as an old woman bent over that churn.

But then, when hope has failed, miracle of miracles! the butter comes. There is little more rewarding than reaching the end of labor with that glorious golden mess. You scoop it out and wash it seven times in water. You smash out all the water, and you can go out and play. For lunch, there is nothing better in this world than a glass of fresh buttermilk with a sprinkle of salt and all those flecks of butter that you couldn't corral. As one enters the pearly gates, the buttermilk angel approaches with a brimming glass. And those who don't like it can go elsewhere.

Butter and cream. We grew up literally awash in whipping cream. Each morning my father walked out to the dairy to see that the milking was going right and returned with a quart of cream, which we consumed in a single day. My parents' coffee was half cream. A cup of tea was the same. And when we children made a brew from sassafras roots we'd dug up in the woods, you guessed it—the pan was half cream. On Sundays my father brought us two quarts of cream. My mother put one in the ice cream freezer. No one had thought of saying no-no to cream. My father said that its A and D vitamins rendered its consumption a necessary thing. I long for those days when we were directed to consume two quarts of cream in a single day. Surely in heaven there will be thick cream—which means, I suppose, that cows will be there. But no manure. My faith forbids it.

Memories don't arrange themselves in the order they are received. The brain is a shuffled deck of dog-eared cards. No, it's more like a stew pot with everything dumped in, or more like a Frenchman's *pot au feu* on the back of the stove, where things are added as they come and simmered together till it's time to dish up.

It's time to dish up my battle with leprosy, which blighted several years of my early life. It came about in this way: Cecil B. deMille made two films called *The Ten Commandments*. The second was made for the talking screen and did big things for the wrath of God. I had begun to take transgression in stride, and I thought deMille was showing off for God.

But that first silent film—now, that was a killer. It shot straight from the shoulder. And it certainly broadened my conception of sin. I had seen transgression as something settled with a hairbrush. Now I saw that God was in on the deal.

Each commandment had an episode all to itself, headed by "Thou Shalt Not . . ." and a different cast. Well, of course the cast was different. The preceding characters had been mowed down for what they'd done. They didn't have a clue they were headed for trouble. It was sort of like whistling at my great-aunt's table. They didn't know they shouldn't do it till they did, and then they knew. I recall the awful earthquake when the earth cracked open and the hordes of guilty people fell down through the crack. I don't recall what they'd done.

The part that stayed with me was the Seventh Commandment. The details of it were seared into my very soul. I hadn't the foggiest notion what adultery was. All I knew was that God said don't do it; if you did, you got leprosy. I hadn't the foggiest notion what that was either, but the way that man carried on when he got it, I knew it wasn't for me.

The story went this way: A woman from the Far East smuggled herself into this country in a bale of cotton. I've been uneasy with a bale of cotton ever since. She wasn't a pretty lady. She looked more like a wicked stepmother to me. But when she clawed her way out of the bale in the warehouse at this end, the warehouse owner was around, and in spite of her mean looks they somehow got involved. We weren't shown how. In no time at all he had leprosy. He knew by looking at his forearms. In all the early films people knew they had leprosy by pushing up their sleeves and viewing their forearms, first the left, then the right. And if God healed them with a miracle, they knew it with the same double-forearms test. Although the screen was silent, I could tell by his gestures that the man blamed the bale-of-cotton woman for his forearms and was furious with her. We never got a look at hers. Immediately he died. He felt himself going, going, gone and grabbed a hold of an arras (you know what they are; they're all over Shakespeare). In falling he pulled it loose from its pole and the arras fell over him and covered him. He was dead!

My mother explained adultery in a hazy way. Frankly, I never got it. But, boy, did she give me an earful of leprosy! She said that you could bypass adultery and get it. The germs were on things in public places. Like doorknobs, she said. After that, doorknobs were anathema to me. I became convinced that downtown Montgomery was a hotbed of the germs. Especially, I thought, they probably infested the big new post office, where people came and went all day. If my father sent me in to mail a letter while he circled the block, I had to stand and wait till somebody opened the door, and then I slipped in. It was like that everywhere. I had to be careful I wasn't smushed in the slam of a door.

I remained free of leprosy. Eventually, mercifully, the epidemic subsided, and I could get on with growing up. Since then, we've learned that leprosy isn't all that easy to catch. But deMille and my mother were convinced it was. And I'm reasonably sure the *Britannica* was too. We always consulted it for any disease and were treated by it, except when our bare feet stepped on a rusty nail. We were given tetanus shots, which my father and *Britannica* and Louis Pasteur agreed was the thing to do.

When I think of my childhood it is always summer and always morning. Winter was something I'd as soon forget. It was full of schoolwork and rain and cold. Our house had been built in the previous century, entirely of heart pine, impervious to termites, so it never fell down. It was where there had lived the overseer of the plantation devoted to cotton until the boll weevil made a mockery of that. It was nothing like Tara in *Gone with the Wind*. It was made with a long porch at the rear, open on one side to the elements and on the other to dining room, storage room, and kitchen. It was obviously a design from the days of slavery. Heat from the fireplaces rose to the twelve-foot ceilings and there it remained. Sometimes I caught a whiff of it on the way up. We closed in the back porch, lowered the ceilings, and double floored. It was a morsel of help. In my opinion, central heating is the greatest thing the world has to give. I put it right up there with oxygen.

I have a distant memory of a commissary behind the house in my earliest years. I suppose it was for the workers on that cotton plantation. It wasn't there for long before it disappeared, but I recall the long empty shelves and the long countertops on either side of the room and the smell, as I entered, of smoke and salt. It's a strange thing how odors will pursue you down the years. And then they will creep into the things you write.

School was an annoyance you wouldn't believe—coming, going, and in between. My brothers and I rode the worst school bus the county could offer: number 17. It broke down on an average of three times a week.

My mother was a firm believer in ankle support. My own hightops that laced up the shin were purchased at the old Montgomery

Fair downtown. They were Buster Browns. I'm not clear why they stocked them, since I was the only girl child I ever knew to wear them.

One of my vivid memories is of winter school mornings as, still groggy from sleep, I munched my oatmeal at the dining room table. My mother stood behind me combing my long hair and braiding it into pigtails. I screamed at intervals from pain. She tied the ends with black ribbons. Except for birthday parties, they were always black ribbons, as if I were in perpetual mourning. I'm sure they were to match the ink in Dick's well, for as soon as I reached class, Dick Hudson, who sat behind me, dipped my braids in his inkwell, and untied my ribbons. No one would have known me without ink-dipped pigtails and dangling ribbons to match. Boys of my day were uncivilized beings and should have been caged. Dick went on to publish *The Advertiser,* but he never, in my eyes, outlived that daily dunking of my braids. School desks were all outfitted with inkwells, since we wrote with quill-type pens. Fountain pens had just come on the market, were expensive, and beyond the reach of most. Each child was sent to school in the fall with a bottle of Waterman's blue-black ink with which he filled his inkwell. And that, I submit, was the major error of the education system of my day. You wouldn't believe what a child with a full inkwell can dream.

I'm back with the oatmeal: As soon as my mother had finished the braids, the school bus honked its lungs out from the top of the hill to tell me it was coming and I'd better be out there and ready to board. At this point my mother promptly dropped to the floor, crawled under the table, and laced up my high-tops while the school bus was arriving to cough and snarl a little and threaten to leave. Sometimes it did and I had to chase it. I guess it was a good thing I had ankle support.

But I dream of the summers when high-tops were out. The first act upon being released from school was to shed one's shoes and spend a week toughening one's bare feet for walking on gravel, rough stubble, and the like. A neighbor boy my age would demonstrate for us a walk on ground glass. Then we roamed all day, walked literally for miles, to swim in muddy ditches, catch crawfish in ponds. I had a brother so quick with his hands that he could catch any fish, no need for a hook.

We always somehow made it home for meals. My memory of meals is not of the food, for my mother was proud of the fact that Wellesley had offered no courses in home economics, but of my father reciting snatches of Shakespeare and Byron and Marcus Aurelius and William James and extolling the virtues of Dante's *Divine Comedy* and of Greek as a language more capable of subtleties than ours. My mother taught all her children as soon as they could speak the first part of the *Canterbury Tales* in pure Chaucerian. Not one of us ever forgot a word. Sometimes at meals we'd recite a chorus of it. At family reunions we would all recite it—and still do today. All this reciting made a profound impression on me.

I believe I was most impressed with my father when later he told me that in farming calculations he used trigonometry, which I had found the most senseless affliction anyone could endure. But in those early years I was largely aware that he had studied premed, had majored in bacteriology, and knew all about germs. We grew up a thoroughly germ-conscious family. No one ever drank after anyone else, or even after himself. When the maid arrived each morning, she was greeted with a groaning drainboard of glasses to wash. And when neighbors, who drank from family dippers (oh, the horror of it!), offered us water out of their dipper, we retreated as if we'd been presented with cyanide. Pasteur and Darwin were household gods.

My father had wanted to become a doctor till fate intervened. But all the workers who lived on the place would come to him whenever health was a problem, and he would prescribe. They called him "the little doctor." He was secretly pleased. Whenever they got into trouble (usually Saturday nights), they would come to his bedroom window at any hour and call to him for help. One morning he reported that Will, a middle-aged black man, had waked him at 2:30 to say that he'd been involved in a wreck and the law was after him. He had concluded his plea for help with the

words: "I'm just a little boy lost in the tall grass." I was so overcome
with the beauty of his words that I begged my father to help. He
had already agreed to do it. Those words were the first I'd ever discovered on my own to be poetry. If poetry is a way of coming
straight to the point in a roundabout way (as I think it is) those
words will do it.

One of our main pursuits of the summer was the catching of
crickets for pocket money. Teague Hardware in town had a going
rate: one cent for two crickets. The fishermen bought them for bait-
ing their hooks. The hardware folks bought only the live because
the fishermen bought only the live because the fish ate only the live.
I think of fish as being pretty dumb, but it seems they distinguish a
dead cricket from a drowning one. So we were at pains to keep ours
alive, popping them into our mayonnaise jars, a little water but not
too much, holes punched in the lids to give them air. In haying time
there was ample harvest. Under hot summer sun we followed the
dumprake and swooped up the crickets as they came swarming out
of the johnsongrass hay. Ours was a furious bonding with churning
earth.

There was something grand about being one of an army of
predators. We roasted in sun like pigs on a spit, smelling the hay,
feeling those crickets raked out of their homes bathing and tickling
our faces and arms, between our toes; and then, when we had our
jars full of them, trekking back to the house, with crickets crawling
out of our hair and shirts, our bare feet now inured to the stubble.
The crickets we wore got loose in the house and ate some holes in
our winter clothes. One of them always crawled into the hearth and
sang all winter.

When we were afraid our harvest would die, we were taken to
the store. The cricket man gravely counted them out, sliding them
into a galvanized tub. He gave us no quarter; if he found a corpse he
would lay it aside, then give it back in the empty jar. We watched
him to see that we got fair price. After all, he was buying our summertime.

My mother had her eye on a Wilton rug for the living room. It was forty-eight dollars, an enormous sum for that day. We might be willing, she said, to pool our cricket money and buy her that rug. We went into action. It took us the rest of the summer, but we got her that rug. So I guess I was really of use after all.

On summer evenings it was too hot to stay inside and read, so we rocked on the front porch and maybe harmonized a "round" or two. If my grandfather was visiting he taught us children all his Amherst College songs. But mostly we heard tales recited by our elders, memories or fiction, and told our own. We talked the daylight out of things and pressed them flat against the night. Words spoken in darkness are heard in a special way. I tried to capture this quality in a poem:

> The words are clear and always near,
> Closer than the air you breathe . . . .
> The teller fingers them like beads.
> No prayer was ever rounder said.

When I wasn't into crickets or roaming the woods, I spent my summer days reading, dreaming, and writing. I wrote my first poem when I was eight. It felt so good I was hooked. A first novel at nine, a second at twelve, and, in between, numerous plays, operettas, and musicals, which I somehow talked brothers and neighbor children into performing for captive parents. (I gave myself the best roles; that goes without saying.) We raided their kitchen pantries and made candy, which we sold to them at intermissions. We were merciless with them.

About the time I was twelve a family moved within walking distance, meaning one and a half miles if you cut through the field. They had seven children, all of whom were writing novels. Even the father had one in progress, but we didn't include him when we crossed the Vaughan Road and way back in the field found a deep, dry ditch, which we thought had never been discovered before. An utterly virgin, primeval ditch. Several times a week we met and climbed into the bottom of that ditch and read aloud to one another our latest chapters. We never wrote stories; they come to an end. But novels go on forever, and we wanted that. Samuel Johnson has said that nothing concentrates the mind like a hanging. I submit that if you happen to lack a hanging a novel will do. We were into making novels before we knew the facts of life.

Well, we thought it great fun. And what else could we do, with no telephone, no radio, no TV, no drugs (except for a random aspirin), and only a family car which the father drove? And besides, we were colliding with the Great Depression. Fun had to be cheap. Pencils were cheap.

Through all the lean years we had our Jersey cows that have a winning way of turning green grass into yellow cream. And we had our words that don't cost a thing.

My parents, it must be told, were obsessed with words. They delighted in meanings, pronunciations, derivations. In the early days, we children were appointed guardians of the *Century Dictionary,* alerting them if the youngest got into a volume of that sacred set printed in England on onionskin paper and hence vulnerable to a child's depredations. Later on, when *Merriam-Webster Unabridged* supplanted the *Century,* we gave my father for Christmas a freewheeling stand that he kept beside his Morris chair. Whenever in conversation a word ruffled his composure he would reach for *Webster* and rein it in. My mother would pause and ask with her little word-smile: "What is it, Daddy?" And he would smile his special, happy, quizzical word-smile that would invite our challenge. In the course of time this procedure was guaranteed to send my three sisters-in-law up the wall. I have tried to tell them that this was never done in a critical spirit but in the spirit of a game. My parents hated Monopoly, checkers, and cards. But they liked to watch you deal yourself a hand of words and then they watched you play it. It was more like slapjack than anything else. I was used to the game and never uttered a syllable I hadn't looked up first. It was also in the spirit of a thirst for knowledge, for my parents were actually eager to stand corrected if they'd had it wrong. Words were that important. They mattered a lot.

The bosom of my family was always heaving with words. My mother was keen, as Tennyson said of Hallam, "to track suggestion to her inmost cell." After we secured a telephone, I have known her to put every librarian in the city on the trail of a word or phrase that was giving her fits. She put them on the rack over "agenbite of inwyt." That was a toughie. One of them at last came up with origin and meaning. My mother relaxed.

I loved words myself and liked to push them around, but something happened when I was nine that might have turned me off them forever.

I must explain that in my mother's psyche there lay something deeply competitive in nature, which her life, as she lived it, failed to satisfy. She absolutely could not let a contest go unentered if it had to do with words. She never entered one herself. I became her surrogate. I am working up to telling you about the major contest of my existence, which, as I ponder it, contained in microcosm my future life.

The children's shoe department of Montgomery Fair was replacing its Buster Browns. It advertised in the paper a total of seven prizes for the most words derived from the letters comprising the new line: Robin Hood Shoes. It set my mother on fire. She even made my brother enter. He was two and a half years younger and not much good with words. He'd had a terrible time in the first grade with "Big Billy Goat Gruff." My father got so sick of Billy Goat Gruff that he threatened to leave home more than once that year. But Mama made my brother enter and did most of his words.

I had to do mine myself. She had a system that worked if you put in the time. I sat on the guest room bed with all five volumes of the *Century* nudging my budding hips, and I went through them all, prone, supine, shoulder stands, leafing through the onionskin pages of words, current, obsolete, and on the make. Talk about Hercules and his twelve paltry labors; they were nothing to mine.

I sat cross-legged on the bed, my chest caved in like the letter

C—not one of the few in Robin Hood Shoes—gnawing the ends of my pigtails with their taste of ink. The bed was the kind that had suspension springs. (Innersprings were on the horizon.) I sank to the middle and the books slid down upon me in an avalanche of words. I could hear the carefree voices of my siblings in the yard. I should have been with them tumbling in the clover, even churning for butter. I felt consumptive.

The only thing that kept me going was a glimpse of the grand prize, which I'd had at the store. It was a $7.50 yellow scooter, state-of-the-art with rubber tires and bumpers. You could have a choice of that or a pair of Robin Hoods of equal value. I had my eye on the scooter. I already had shoes. Once when I was visiting in Miami, some little boy had let me use his scooter for a quarter of a city block. I fell in love with the thing. Imagine kicking off with one foot, getting up speed, then lifting that foot to the floorboard and riding free, free, with nothing to power you but your own past steam. It was heaven to me. My mother, it seemed, had her eye on the shoes.

At last I came up with an absolutely incredible 700 words. My brother had 400, but my mother did most of his. The manager of the shoe department went into shock. No one else had come close. No one else had the *Century*. No one else had my mother.

Of course I won the grand prize. My brother won shoes. He had no choice. When I chose the scooter my mother looked pained. She said it would never work on a gravel road. But if I'd chosen shoes, I knew they'd be high-tops, and good Lord! I hadn't gone through what I'd gone through for another pair of those. So I got the yellow scooter, but my mother was right. It didn't work on gravel. Yet I kept it all my life until a few years ago. It symbolized something. A dream I had worked for that didn't work for me, still a beautiful dream.

And when I got married my mother brought it out and said, "Well, here's your scooter," and I took it along. I'll bet I'm the only bride whose mother sent her off with a scooter in tow.

In all the places I lived I never had a place I could ride that scooter. So at long last I kissed it goodbye, and I gave it away. It was still a virgin. I was very sad.

But life is fraught with irony if nothing else. And here I am living in a cul de sac with plenty of sidewalk and too old to care. If they hooted when I scooted I wouldn't give a hoot. I see myself scratching off, sailing down Sagewood on my rubber-tired scooter and on into Woodmere, down the Boulevard, hanging a left at Blount Cultural Park, gliding down the asphalt, whirling around the lake where the snooty swans preen. They'd remind me of the gander. I'd park my old trusty and go in to hear Bill Shakespeare mess around with words. He knew a lot of words. But I bet you, I bet you a dollar to a doughnut, he couldn't pull 700 out of Robin Hood Shoes.

Growing up, I would sometimes regret living away from the center of things, with no electricity, no telephones. Now I see how lucky I was to be freed from "progress," which promises to free but ultimately entangles. It soaks up time and mind and spirit. It blunts the sense of a beautiful earth. I was born without a sense of direction (directionally challenged, I've just heard it called). In place of that sense, which I certainly could have used through the years (I've been lost many times, in many countries, but I've always been found), I was granted a keen awareness of the hereness of things. I might not know where, geographically, I was, but I always felt around me the land, its living presence, its every contour, as if my body were laid upon it. I mean literally laid upon it. I was aware of the pebbles, the roots, the weeds, the wild hedge, the smell of soil, the bumps and hollows, the shape of trees as in a body they rode the earth. I delighted in them. They are what I am. And it's better to know.

W AY N E   G R E E N H A W

Learning to Swim

During the summer when I was eight, a white-haired black man showed up in the field behind the red-brick schoolhouse and promised the world. His name was Jed, and his eyes burn into my memory unto this day. They were coal-black eyes in a sea of red-veined liquid white, bulging from pain-pocked scaly-looking dark skin, like the skin of a lizard. When he was a baby, he said, he had fallen into a pot of boiling lye soap, and the burn had seared his face for life.

He had only one leg, and he walked with the help of a hand-tooled crutch fashioned from a sycamore limb. When he talked his words flowed like the creek at the edge of the old Civil War foundry on the hill behind the school. It was our private playground, where we could hide and become Confederate soldiers or cowboys or whatever our imaginations desired. Back there, where no one else went, we sat with him and listened to his version of history.

"I don't reckon there's been anything that ever happened that I didn't know about," he told us as he leaned against the trunk of a huge oak and reached down and scratched the end of his stump where it had been amputated just above the right knee.

"Once upon a time I could out-run a rabbit and retch over and snatch him up, just pretty as you please. I'd have him in my pocket quicker'n you could snap your finger." His big black head raised up against the sunlight, sweat glistening beneath his eyes, and he nod-ded slightly with self-assurance. "It was like that, back then," he added. As though "better than now" was understood.

Later, when we were walking home through the park, my best friend, Lester, said, "That old man's some more full of shit, ain't he?"

I shrugged. The old man's poetry was already settling on me, cov-ering me with a world from which I would never escape, although I had no idea at the time what was truly happening in my psyche. I listened to his every word, watched closely his every gesture, heard the hurt in his gravel voice, felt the agony of his uneasy movements.

The next day, when we met at the same place, he commenced to tell about growing up in the time when Jesus Christ roamed the world with his disciples, talking the tales of being brothers to all men, sharing and touching, never looking down on another human being. "That's what Christianity and the Bible's all about," he said, "doing unto others," and I found myself nodding.

When I told his words to Mama, she said, "He sounds like a smart old man," but there was a hint of giggle in her voice.

And when I told the stories to Granddaddy, who was the smartest man I'd ever known, he smiled knowingly. His eyes twin-kled and he said, "I reckon old Jed's been around quite a bit."

For days Jed told us he was going to teach us how to swim. He had us sit on the hillside overlooking the pond where the concrete dam backed up the water and made it still and deep. "I want y'all to sit here and study that water and know in your minds that it's something you can conquer without the least bit of trouble. Just look at it: see how flat it is, how still, how peaceful, then, when you get in, you will know that you can take care of yourself."

After we sat and gazed at the surface, he said, "Now, tell me what you see."

Lester said all he saw was water that didn't do anything and was about the most boring thing he'd ever looked at. I said I didn't see anything either, but I was trying. With his big watery eyes bulging, Jed asked, "Do you see underneath?"

I shook my head.

"You don't see the fishes? The little bitty minnows? The big fat bass hiding over yonder under a big flat rock?"

I squinted.

An hour later, when the sun came in at a bright slant, its reflection danced like thousands of diamonds glittering on the water's surface. "See there, how it's changing? How it's becoming something other than what it is?" His words dug into my mind. That night I went to sleep studying the vision of what he'd said.

Two mornings later, Jed announced, "This is the time. Take off your clothes."

Lester and I looked at each other and all around.

"Nobody's here but us," Jed said. He started unbuttoning his shirt that smelled of yesterday's sweat.

Naked and self-conscious, we followed as he hobbled out onto the dam. When he saw that we were covering ourselves with cupped hands, Jed laughed and said, "What y'all think you doing? You ain't got nothing to be so proud of. Look at me." He was hung like a stud-horse. "Now, I got me something to hide, but ain't no need to hide it." Chuckling, he suddenly jumped into the water.

We watched, amazed, as his head broke through the surface, and he slung water from his head. "Now, what I want you to do is jump in here with me, kick your feet, and paddle your hands. Remember, you got twice as many feet as me, so you ain't gonna float away, you gonna come right up."

We leaned forward, looking down at the water, mysterious questions coming to mind: how deep? what lurked beneath the surface? will something suck us under? I inched toward the edge. "Jump!" Jed said, and I refused, looking toward Lester's shivering body covered with goose bumps as he too stared down at the dark water.

Nervous fright consumed us both as we gazed into the pond and wondered. Then Jed clapped his hands and said, "Jump!" and I reached out toward him with hands outstretched, turning loose of some fright that had held me back.

I gulped as I went down, feeling a quick panic. I kicked against the water and slapped my hands. I came up coughing and spitting, afraid momentarily, until I kicked and slapped myself straight into Jed's arms. He turned away, and I grabbed around his neck, holding tightly to him. "That's it," he said. "Ol' Jed don't have no extra arms to hold you with." Moments later, Lester splashed into the water. Somehow, miraculously, within minutes we were swimming among the hundreds of tiny minnows and the old bass. We climbed out of the water and strutted like two veteran bank walkers, naked and proud, across the dam to the deepest part and dove in head first. We kicked and paddled, laughed and shouted, and for the rest of the summer the water became our second home. The next year, after Jed had vanished, going off somewhere for further adventures, we suspected, we were ranked among the best swimmers at Camp Winnetaska.

Limon

When I first wrote about the summer with Jed I was sitting next to a tree on the patio of a hacienda where I lived during the summer of 1958 in San Miguel de Allende, Guanajuato, Mexico. What I wrote were awkward words trying to relive a place and emotions of my childhood—a time that, I believed, meant more than the words and the actions.

Because I was the youngest and most inexperienced in the creative writing program at the Instituto Allende, I tried hard to be the most sophisticated—a struggle which, of course, reversed the desired effect. For weeks, West Coast and midwestern teachers attempted to squeeze the southernness out of my writing. I remember well being criticized for using words like "yell" and "holler" and "y'all" and being warned against the use of regional slang. I took their warnings to heart and did my best to sound the way they sounded—flat and objective—which they called "professional." They urged me to read F. Scott Fitzgerald's short stories about growing up, and I did, and I tried to write like him but failed miserably.

Returning to Alabama in the fall, I entered freshman English composition taught by a young British professor fresh from his first job teaching at a British prep school for boys. He urged us to "write like you talk," which horrified me after my long summer at the Instituto, where I had been trying not to write with a southern accent. "You are unique," he told us in his own particular accent. "You are different. That makes you stand out in a crowd." And he spoke of writers like William Faulkner and Flannery O'Connor and Truman Capote, all of whom used their southernness effectively.

I read stories by these writers and fell in love with the poetry, the words, the cadence of the sentences, and the lush world they described. Some of Faulkner's narrative, I discovered, sounded exactly like Granddaddy talking, telling stories. I did as the professor asked and delved into my background and wrote it the way I would have told it. I composed a five-page story about me and my brother and a mysterious train that Daddy had told us would take bad boys to Birmingham. If my brother or I misbehaved, Daddy warned that the train would stop at the crossing just south of the Cahaba River and would pick us up and take us to the reformatory he had pointed out: a dark place surrounded by a twenty-foot-high wire fence behind which gray, frightened faces tried to hide from passersby.

As the teacher counted down his "prize-winning stories" he did not call my name until the end. I had won "the grand prize," awarded an A. He lauded me with grandiose adjectives and, after class, asked if he might forward my paper to Hudson Strode, the renowned teacher of creative writing. Until that moment, I thought the closest I would ever come to the great Strode was carrying his groceries to his car at the supermarket where I had worked weekends during high school. I had read his book *Now in Mexico*, which had vividly described San Miguel and made its world come alive for me even before I traveled there. Once, several years earlier, my father had happened upon Strode in the downtown post office and had brashly told him, "My son is going to be a writer," and I turned away, embarrassed as only a fifteen-year-old can be embarrassed by his proud father.

A week later, my English professor asked if I could accompany him to Strode's office. I stammered a quick reply. And that afternoon we entered the hallowed office nestled in the dogwood-and-azalea-splotched woods behind the Strode house on Cherokee Road on the outskirts of Tuscaloosa. Sitting at a bleached desk sent to him by Sigrid Undset, after the great Norwegian writer had been his houseguest, he looked the picture of sophistication. With gray hair brushed back from his high forehead, a neat little trimmed mustache, and a blue silk ascot that fit perfectly with his cashmere jacket, Strode studied me.

Under his sharp eyes, I felt ill at ease as I intertwined fingers in my lap. In a clear baritone that he used brilliantly in his famed class on Shakespeare's tragedies, making Hamlet's voice boom through Morgan Hall, he said, "Your story is remarkable. I find traces of genuine talent. You have the ability to make good choices. However, you need training, discipline, knowledge. Do you write regularly?" I answered that I wrote every day, a habit I established early and continued. Again, his eyes wandered the geography of my face.

I learned later that he always judged people on first appearance. He asked when I was born. I told him: February 17th. "Ah!" he exclaimed dramatically. "The stars tell us everything. You're a noble Aquarius. You have a heart larger than your brain." His words stayed with me. I was not sure whether he was praising me or saying I was dumb as a post. Whichever, I knew he was correct in his assessment.

Standing, he clasped my shoulder and welcomed me into the

world of creative writing. Then we were invited into the Japanese garden between the house and his office for tea. Mrs. Strode, a handsome lady whom I soon knew simply as Therese, served hot English tea and elegant little lettuce or cucumber crustless sandwiches. Settling into a wrought-iron chair in her impeccable straight-back fashion, she stared at me and instantly remembered, "You're the nice young man who always packed our grocery sacks at Jitney Jungle." Before I could answer, she said, "None of the boys are half as nice now. We much preferred your service." And Strode stated, "And he has the most remarkable father," recalling the night at the post office and what Daddy had said. I cringed again.

Inside the Strode house I perused the thigh-high built-in bookcases. A long section was filled with books that had been published by Strode students or former students. There were literally dozens in a row, book jacket to book jacket, including *Buttermilk Road* by Thomas Turner and *Redbone Woman* by Carlysle Tillery. I reached down and carefully removed a book I had heard about but had never read. It was a novel called *Rachel's Children* by Harriet Hassell. "She's my mother's cousin," I said. Strode was amazed and had me map the genealogy, how Miss Hassell had actually been my grandmother's first cousin. "She was my first success," Strode said and recounted the story about how this shy young farm girl from north of Tuscaloosa came to him and begged him to help her write a novel about her family. He did, taking her manuscript chapter by chapter, reading it, making notations, asking questions, always careful to allow her to do the work and make the choices. "I believed in her," he said, as though stating a universal truth. It was his way, forever staring into you with those strong eyes. He told me to take the book and read it. "It's about your family," he said. "But guard it with your life. It's my only copy."

From that moment on, I was a member of the Strode team. He seldom had more than twelve students in his writing class. If you were chosen, he made you feel as though you had already accomplished a writing feat; you were among the chosen few. At his table, you were sitting with the great.

Strode was a cheerleader for his writers. Not that he didn't criticize. He did. And often his words cut to the bone, an incision that hurt so badly the writer would carry the wound back to his typewriter and spend hours correcting and rewriting, polishing and perfecting, then bringing the work back for another reading, another close examination, followed by still more reworking. He moved us all to strive for perfection.

The teacher held class in a rectangular room on the fourth floor of the library. At the far end of a long conference table was the professor's padded captain's chair. From this throne he conducted class. At least one student-writer sat at the end near the door—for speedy retreats, we surmised—and read a story or a chapter every Wednesday night. Class members sat and listened intently, jotting notes. Strode fixed the reader in his relentless stare and waited.

He listened with even more intensity. He scribbled notes. When the reader finished the last word, silence exploded through the room. The reader waited. Strode was always the first to speak.

What we all waited to hear break the silence was a clear throaty "Awww" that he awarded to only the very best, such as the end of a particularly poignant chapter read by a Japanese woman who as a child had lived through the bombing of Nagasaki or after a short story by a young man writing about the agonizingly slow death of a child. When he said "Awww," it was like he was clearing his throat after a long swallow of a perfect drink.

Sometimes it was excruciating, listening to the painfully inept sophomoric outpourings of a young writer's heartfelt prose, and often he would close his eyes and clasp his fingers before his face as though in prayer. When the last tear-and-sweat-soaked word was nervously uttered, Strode's face would rise to the occasion like a master actor. He spoke out forcefully but never hurtfully. If a story was good but missed the point in the telling, he cut through to the core of the problem and dissected it cleanly.

"See through the character's eyes. Feel through his or her heart. Step into the character's shoes. Know *why* a character says the words that come from his mouth. Know *why* he walks a certain way or reacts to a situation." He made the young writer think. He gave him promise for having been chosen to sit at his table. "You have the talent. Now you must learn to do with it," he stated. "Reach out. Stretch your talent. Do not be afraid to display your talent."

Always aware of the dramatic essence of any scene, Strode presented himself as a dandy. In fall and winter, he wore a felt fedora, cocked just so. In the spring and summer, he wore either a Panama or a flat-top straw hat. Colorful bow ties matched the sport coat of the day. In winter, he covered his shoulders with a Burberry trench coat, wearing it like a cape, never fastening more than the top button and never putting his arms into the sleeves, always ready for its use as a stage prop.

If a student-writer's work did not meet his expectations, Strode would not urge the student to continue. He once told a particularly bright young woman that she might never write a great or even salable novel, "but you will succeed at whatever you choose to do." She later became a high-paid executive with a company in California. He enjoyed his students' successes, whether literary or otherwise. However, if he saw promise in a story, he would delve into it, asking questions, listening to answers, allowing the student to find his or her own way, not unlike the way old Jed had shown Lester and me the water and how it changed in front of our eyes.

Toward the end of my second year in his class I read a short story about a middle-aged professional golfer who was going blind. When I finished, I waited. I could hear my heart pounding. I did not receive the favored "Awww," but he held his strong chin cradled in his hand and nodded. "You have something here," he said. "It's powerful, but not because you have created a memorable character." I wanted to scream, "Well, why then?!" Strode was so ambiguous in his comments that I left the room in a quandary. I actually stormed downstairs, threw my story into the trash, and didn't stop until I was downtown at a beer joint called The Chukker, where I proceeded to drown my sorrows. I was later joined by several classmates who said they thought he was wrong. "No," I said. "He's right. The story's too damn stilted, forced, plotted." The others tried to cheer me up, but I would not have it.

Before the next class, Strode invited me to tea at his home. In the kitchen, Therese mixed a martini and slipped it into my demitasse cup. As I sipped it in the Japanese garden, Strode told me, "You wrote about golf with deep feeling. You have a passion for the sport." Then others arrived and he let it drop.

All of his students other than his obvious pets—of which he had at least one every year—had a sweet-sour relationship with the man. He was pompous and self-centered, and he always heaped praise on his chosen. He had favorite sayings, which we all repeated over and over again: "Simplicity is greatness." "Stickability! If you succeed, you have to display stickability." "If you don't have that much talent, stickability will get you through." "Be natural. Find your voice and let it flow." "Work! Don't think! Too much thinking destroys creativity." "Your characters must act or react. If they're too introspective, you will lose your reader." And on and on.

"I cannot teach novel writing or any other kind of writing," he confessed more than once. "But I can spot talent and encourage that talent to grow. If a person has talent, it will grow if you nurture it. Do not allow your talent to stagnate. Use it! Work with it!"

Early in his career as a professor one of his students brought to class a packet of letters from his girlfriend. The girl, who was then sixteen, had written what Strode thought were "original" letters showing "a keenness and a sharpness; they were pungent, slightly racy, and humorous."

"I have always been able to spot talent. The girl had talent to an extraordinary degree." The girl was Zelda Sayre. Several months after he read her letters, Strode arrived at Montgomery's Union Station, where he met Miss Sayre, who was, he recalled, "touched with glamour. I never thought her beautiful, but with her gold hair, green eyes, fine complexion, she had something about her that was arresting and even exciting." Four years later she married F. Scott Fitzgerald. She became a celebrity, known as the ultimate southern belle and 1920s flapper. She wrote numerous fine short stories and a novel entitled *Save Me the Waltz*.

In the fifties, Strode's most successful student, Borden Deal, a Mississippi farm boy who grew up near Pontotoc and who came to the University of Alabama after a stint in the navy during World War II, moved back to Tuscaloosa with his family. While still a student under Strode he wrote and published several short stories, one of which was selected for Best American Short Stories. "Antenaus," the tale of a farm boy who moves to a big city, where he cultivates a garden on the rooftop of his apartment house, was anthologized numerous times. Deal also started a novel in Strode's class. After he married Babs Hodges from Scottsboro that novel became *Walk through the Valley*, a saga of the rural South that was highly acclaimed and sold through several printings.

When the Deals came back to Tuscaloosa, his second novel, *Dunbar's Cove*, a lengthy story about a north Alabama family being displaced during the Great Depression by the Tennessee Valley Authority, was due out soon. And Babs Deal's first novel, *Acres of Afternoon*, about growing up in a small north Alabama town, was also soon to be published. Both of these books received fabulous critical attention and sold very well. *Dunbar's Cove*, written on a Guggenheim grant, was picked up by several book clubs, condensed by *Reader's Digest*, hit the bestseller list, sold to the movies, and was published in many languages.

It was not long before I was welcomed to become part of a small group who sat on the Deal front porch on Eleventh Street and drank coffee during the afternoons and beer or bourbon at night and talked and talked about everything under the sun. After classes I babysat with the three Deal children while Borden and Babs played golf, went out to dinner or to the movies. They were writing people and talking people.

The campus at Tuscaloosa was generally a quiet place. The block on Eleventh Street where they lived was quiet and shaded by great oaks. But the Deal house had an atmospheric rhythm. The early mornings were filled with the chirp of children preparing for school, invariably one bickering with another, the loud shout, "Shut up!" followed by abrupt silence.

By the time I arrived after first classes, there was the click-clack of Borden's IBM Selectric in his downstairs office. Babs, more subtle, worked upstairs in silence. I poured coffee and waited for their break. When one broke, the other followed shortly. The conversation was never simple. It was never understated. Almost never did they talk about their work. There was always an edge of turbulence in their voices, words spoken loudly, sharply. I imagined it was because they both worked in their own silent solitude. When they quit, they had to speak in fast, frantic tones.

In the evenings, we tossed I-Ching, which I once asked the same question twice about a current girlfriend, and the Oracle answered, "The young prince who asks twice is a fool," and I marveled over the ancient Chinese fortune-telling device. And once we asked about President John F. Kennedy's political career. We loved JFK. And the Oracle said, "The young prince will never cross the bridge," which we thought meant he would not win reelection. Borden marked the question and the answer and noted the date, and a year later, on that fateful day in November when Kennedy was shot and killed, Borden went back to the I-Ching and read it, and we all shivered in stunned disbelief

It was an exciting place with exciting people who wrote for a living, and I fell in love with the lifestyle as well as the people.

Now and then the Strodes would visit the Deals, and now and then we would travel out to Cherokee Road for tea or dinner. Borden credited Strode with his success as a writer. "Hudson Strode was a legend in our time," he wrote later.

Every person in the class, I do believe, stood more or less in awe of him. Indeed, he ruled our universe. We devoted more thought, speculation, legend-making, worship, and fear to this god of our creative writing world than to any other person, subject, or theme of our lives.

Like most gods, Hudson Strode left something to be desired. A small, plump, often self-important man, he was the first real snob I had ever known—the names of kings and princesses and Shakespearean actors fell naturally from his lips.

He played outrageous favorites. Every year there was in the class a chosen white-haired boy whom he groomed with tender care for literary stardom. For these favorites, he was known to prescribe diets, attitudes, sleeping and working hours, and to arrange love lives, submissions to and meetings with New York editors, adequate housing, foundation grants, and teaching fellowships.

I was never Hudson Strode's teacher's pet. Indeed, there seemed to exist an unspoken strain of antagonism between us. Yet I respected his criticism, his story sense, and he, I think, respected my talent.

When I read this years later, I knew that I had felt similarly. Perhaps that was one of the reasons Borden and I became such friends.

When Borden spoke about "the night of discovery," which he later wrote about in *Writers Yearbook,* he told me, "Some day you will have your own night of discovery," and I believed him. I followed his advice: work, work, work, stubbornly rewriting piece after piece. Suddenly, after years of work, a light will shine brighter with a certain clarity. There will be an awareness about what you are and how to apply your trade, knowing that you must find the rock first before you begin chiseling. Like a word sculptor, you chink away at the rock, removing a little piece here, a tiny triangle there, a sliver. Then you will know the time to back away and examine the product of your labor and realize that you have a finished piece of work.

It first happened for me in 1966 while working as a reporter for *The Alabama Journal* in Montgomery. I was twenty-six years old. Early in the morning before the sun came up, I sat at my typewriter in a minuscule apartment on Boultier Street in Cloverdale. I worked at my fiction before going downtown to the *Journal* to face the real world. Suddenly one morning, as the sun peeked over the horizon, it came to me. It was not a false dawn. It was real light. Strode's words flashed in my memory. Not the words from class but ones he spoke later: "You write about golf with real feeling. You have a passion for the sport." I would write about golf, something I knew about. My brother was a terrific golfer. I'd heard him talk about it in a passionate way. Years earlier I had caddied for him in tournaments. I had met Arnold Palmer and some of the other big names of the game. I would write about a professional golfer, a young man who desired to play the game but who had character flaws that kept him from being great. He was good, but he had many obstacles to overcome.

Thus I began my first real literary adventure. And months later, when I looked down at my finished product, I again thought about Strode. Every year he brought New York editors and publishers to Tuscaloosa to speak to the class. Even then he believed in networking, getting to know people, looking into their faces, hearing their words, learning what the people in publishing were looking for. In the year after my class, he brought down Tay Hohoff, who had recently edited the Pulitzer Prize–winning novel *To Kill a Mockingbird* for J. B. Lippincott. She had been the editor who worked with Alabama novelist Harper Lee, someone Strode always wished had been in his writing class. She had actually taken his class in Shakespeare, so he tried to claim her in that regard. I had heard from students that Ms. Hohoff had invited them to submit manuscripts. I had not met Ms. Hohoff, but she didn't know that. I wrote a letter saying I had been in Strode's class. I told her I had finished a novel. Did she still wish to read it?

Within several weeks I received a short letter saying she would read my work. I sent it. And the weeks and months that followed seemed an eternity. Finally she wrote that she liked the book but wanted others to read it. Again, I waited. Finally she wrote that the editorial board would meet next Monday.

All day Monday I watched my phone at the *Journal*. Every time it rang I jerked it to my ear. By night I still had no final word. My editor, Ray Jenkins, knowing I was anxious, invited me for a drink. Halfway through a martini, Ray said, "Here, use my credit card, call the lady." I did. After hearing my inquiry, Tay Hohoff chuckled. "We love your book. We want to publish it. Of course, we'll need some rewriting. You will receive my letter in a few days." One year later my first novel, *The Golfer*, was published. I was at Borden

Deal's house in Sarasota, Florida, when I first saw a photo of the jacket in *Publisher's Weekly*. I sat and stared at the page. Tears seeped from my eyes as my fingers began to shake. Borden and Babs laughed. It was a good, deep, heartfelt laugh that knew the joy I was feeling.

Since then, writing has not always been as easy as swimming. In fact, it never is. But I no longer hesitate on the dam before jumping into the water. I know that Hudson Strode and Borden Deal and old Jed were my teachers. As Jed instructed more than fifty years ago, I know that each time I approach a new piece of writing I must first know the territory into which I am about to enter: I must look beneath the surface and see its depth and find something new and vital in its being. I know that I have to strip away the layers of clothing until I am naked to the subject. I know that once again I will use the techniques I learned in the past, and each time I need to add to these or modify the old ones to make the writing shine with a new quality. After thirteen books and more than a hundred pieces of short fiction and nonfiction, I look back at the process and know that it all began that summer when I was a boy, discovering a new world while learning to swim.

N A N C I   K I N C A I D

The Other Sun of God

We had an old brown Chevy, the kind that was all curve and bumper and made you think of a solid-built woman wearing chrome jewelry. In the summers my parents, two younger brothers, and I climbed in the womb of this wide-hipped, slow-going car in hopes of eventually being delivered someplace far more interesting than home. Our favorite trip (practically our only trip) was to Alabama to visit our grandparents, who lived thirty miles from each other—one pair on a farm in Macon County and the other in a college town in neighboring Lee County. While they all lived in Alabama, they also lived in totally separate worlds, which explains I think, at least in part, why my parents did.

I was lucky on these trips to get the coveted spot in the car, most conducive to pleasant, relaxed travel—the rearview window shelf on to which I folded myself just perfectly. The vantage point was ideal.

The view may have come to me secondhand and backward, but it was all mine when it came. My parents looked straight ahead into their dark future together (although at the time we didn't yet know it would be dark). My brothers could only look to the right or left, and I am sad to say that at the time they were the types to be satisfied with that. But I could lie still and wait for the two views to merge into a whole. I might have been unsure of where we were going exactly, but I was absolutely certain of where we had been.

At the time, our family lived down in Tallahassee, Florida, fondly and accurately referred to as the Sunshine State, vacation mecca for Yankees everywhere who were moving there in droves and, according to some people, messing everything up. Mostly they were messing up Miami and St. Petersburg and Jacksonville—the big cities with beaches. But we suspected that in time, if we weren't careful, Tallahassee could be next.

Already a Yankee family had moved on our street. The McClouskies. They were from *Up North*—that vast, anonymous, cold place where none of us had been and none of us ever wanted to go. We thought the people up there talked too loud and put too much nose into their words, giving them sort of a honking quality when they said things. We thought they had more than a lot of gall making fun of the way we talked, but people mostly overlooked it because nobody expected Yankees to have decent manners. We also knew they thought they were better than us—smarter or something—because sometimes they came right out and said so, which was totally rude—and just proved our point perfectly. We'd seen Yankees on TV all bundled up in their coats and scarves scurrying around, doing we did not know what. We had read about their children in our schoolbooks, dragging their sleds around and losing their mittens and tromping to school in their galoshes. We felt sort of sorry for them. And now here were some of them right in our midst. It was every bit as exciting to me as if outer space aliens had landed on our street.

The McClouskies had six children (like our family eventually would) and their daddy was the chef at Howard Johnson's, which meant they could swim in the motel swimming pool free anytime they felt like it, while we had to pay money to swim in the sardine-packed city pool, where everybody peed in the water and everybody knew it. They could also walk up to their daddy's restaurant and eat french fries and double-scoop ice-cream cones free anytime they wanted to. This seemed strange to me—getting special treatment like that. Up until then I had never met people who got things for free. Especially not a free lunch—which I had heard a saying about. *There is no such thing as a free lunch.* And now look—Yankees eating free lunches. It was enough to make you pause and wonder.

We, on the other hand, were the kind of people who always paid for what we got. And if we couldn't pay for it, we didn't get it. And if we knew we couldn't have it, then we pretended we didn't even want it. Didn't like it or need it and wouldn't take it on a bet. It was a pretty decent plan I thought. Maybe even genius. But getting stuff for free definitely seemed like a better plan. The only thing we ever got for free was use of books that technically did not belong to us, since my daddy was in charge of all the school textbooks for the state of Florida. But I don't think anybody ever envied us over a bunch of math and social studies books. If you are going to get something for nothing, french fries seem better.

Besides being Yankees, the McClouskies were the first Catholics I ever knew personally. I understood from my Baptist neighbors that the Catholics did not stand a ghost of a chance at heaven since they went about everything religious in the wrong way. Wrong, wrong, wrong. And, as my neighbors explained, *God's love and forgiveness would only stretch so far.* Although, the best I could tell, the Catholics were not the least bit worried about it.

For one thing, they had the Virgin Mary on their side. She was all over the place, hanging on their car mirror, sitting on their coffee table, on their bookshelf that did not have any books, on chains around their necks, in pictures on the walls of every bedroom—even the boys' room. They were all crazy out of their minds over Mary. Myself, I thought Mary looked like a pretty woman who was so sad she didn't know what to do. I had seen that look that was on her face on the faces of a bunch of colored women—and some white women, too. I thought maybe it had something to do with getting pregnant before you were ready, you know, having a baby but no man who truly loved you—no real husband at least—to help you out. Mary had that same worn out look so many women in the South had. That disappointed look that made you turn your head away when you saw it. So I didn't quite know what to make of the Virgin Mary—except to sympathize.

It seemed radical and exciting—nearly everything the Yankee-Catholic family did—but especially acting like Mary was even more of a big deal than Jesus. It seemed such a dangerous thing to me— to ever act like a woman was just as important, maybe even more important, than a man. I didn't know a single soul in the world who ever thought that way.

I made friends with the McClouskies's daughter, Ann Marie, even though she and her brothers didn't go to the regular school with the rest of us, which seemed tragic and I was sure would ruin their lives in the long run. While the rest of us waited for the school bus in our shorts and flip-flops, Ann Marie's daddy drove them to some mysterious school we had never heard of before called Blessed Sacrament, which did not even sound like a school. It sounded like something for foreigners—like *chop suey* or *synagogue* or lasagna. They waved to us in their hot, out-of-style uniforms, which made me think of movies about orphans or something, those saddle oxfords and sad white button-down shirts. We heard the nuns were cruel and slapped your palm with a ruler every time you made a mistake. And they made you pray even if it wasn't Sunday, and once in a while made you get in a dark closet and confess all your sins to an old man who might forgive you or might not. My mother had warned me never to get in a dark closet with some old man I didn't know—not even if he was nice and went to our church, and not even if he claimed to be somehow kin to me. And especially not if he was wearing a dress.

Ann Marie told me *sin* was the main subject you studied at Catholic school. Already she was an expert. She knew sins I had never even heard of yet. *Impure thoughts* was a particular favorite of mine. As far as I knew, Baptists and Methodists were allowed to have impure thoughts. But Catholics had to apologize for every nasty idea that flashed through their minds. I felt sorry for Ann Marie because of this. It made me think Ann Marie's parents were mean since they were causing her to miss out on Lillian C. Ruediger Elementary School—where everything that really mattered in life happened as far as I could tell. At least to white children. It was like you had to go to Lillian C. Ruediger if you were white and wanted to grow up to be normal—even though I guess it might have already been too late for Ann Marie and them.

Also, Ann Marie's parents drank beer right out in the open and did not care if people saw them. Not even children. I had never seen anything so brazen and glamorous in my life—except for Elizabeth Taylor, who besides drinking to excess in public also stole other people's husbands and showed up with them in movie magazines. But she got away with this because she was so beautiful. This was something all southerners completely understood and forgave—the privilege of beauty. Besides, Elizabeth Taylor was not somebody I knew in person—like Mrs. McClouskie. Mrs. McClouskie drank beer out in the yard in front of us, right out of the bottle, sitting in a folding chair while Mr. McClouskie cooked some kind of strange-smelling meat I could not recognize on his barbecue grill. This made me totally nervous. I didn't see what the fun of drinking was if you took all the sneakiness out of it. I liked the Baptist way much better, where you said one thing and did another. It made more sense to me. The way Ann Marie's parents did it did not give the feeling that they were getting away with anything—so what was the point?

I tried to warn Ann Marie that for some people hell lurked at the bottom of a beer bottle, which I had heard Oral Roberts say on TV when he was laying on hands and healing people—drunks, I guess—who fell to the floor at his feet. But Ann Marie would not believe me. She insisted that God didn't have anything against drinking. She said, "He was the one who showed Jesus how to turn the water into wine, wasn't he? Besides," she said, "all the priests drink and so does the Pope."

I didn't see how this could be true. How could you let a bunch of single men wearing what amounted to long, hot dresses with big gold jewelry around their necks drink like a school of fish—while they ran a whole religion? I didn't see how they could get any women to take them seriously. And then suddenly it made sense to me why they had Mary plastered all over everything. It was like a Catholic trick, to make women think the religion had something to do with them.

All I knew was that all around me in the South were women who had devoted their lives to trying to get men to stop drinking. It was like a southern pastime that went hand and hand with women trying to get their men saved and baptized and born again so they had half a chance at heaven. And here was Ann Marie insisting that the Pope himself liked to take a drink. I had to take her word for it since I didn't know much about the Pope. He seemed to me like an imitation king in all those elaborate outfits. And the Vatican looked like a castle too, with gold decorations all over the place—which my mother said were way too showy and therefore not in good taste. My mother said Mexico was full of Catholics so poor they didn't have shoes on their feet or food to eat and that the Pope ought to be ashamed of himself hoarding and displaying all that gold while his people were suffering so bad. She said she bet it made Jesus turn over in his grave. And my mother was known to be an authority in this area—what would break Jesus' heart and what would make it glad. So to tell the truth, it was sort of hard for me to grasp a fancy religion like that, which got just as mad at you for thinking about something as it did for actually doing it.

My mother also mentioned to me that the Catholics ran their religion in a foreign language—Latin—so none of the regular people ever had the foggiest idea what the priests were even talking about. She said she couldn't help but wonder if maybe they did that on purpose too—you know—to keep the people from knowing what exactly it was that they were so busy believing—so then they wouldn't be likely to ask many questions.

"You know what Latin is, don't you?" my mother said.

"What?" I asked.

"A *dead* language."

Just hearing this gave me the shivers. Up until I met the Catholics I had always thought the Baptists were the strangest people alive.

We liked Ann Marie and her brothers. We liked for them to spend the night at our house and for us to spend the night at theirs. Their family was not like us and didn't do anything the way we did it, which made me both feel deep sympathy for them and be completely crazy about them at the same time.

So it was not that Florida was a boring place. It wasn't. It was just that to us Alabama was even more interesting. Both places were hot as fire and full of snakes. You couldn't hardly take a step either place without stepping on some kind of serpent. It made people mostly keep their heads down, for one thing. I know I did. In my case, I think growing up in Alabama and Florida completely shaped my entire future, since I have been on the lookout for snakes pretty much nonstop all my adult life. For the longest time I thought everybody was.

My daddy used to say going to Alabama was just like *going back in time*—which I choose to think he meant in a good way. Southerners usually like the way things used to be more than they like the way things are fixing to be. I know my daddy did. He was the kind of man who did not trust in the future. He had no faith in it at all. To him all the future did was open up possibilities that things might get even worse than they already were. Since he was raised out in the country with mostly all colored people, it gave him a dark view of things—since without ever meaning to he had started to see the world the way they saw it. And so some modern sorts of ideas had cropped up in his mind even though he had never really wanted to be a modern man. He had seen things that made him think the world needed to change—but he was also afraid of what would happen if it did. Any modern ideas Daddy had our Alabama relatives could attribute to our living in Florida, which, as they said, *was not the real South.* It was too full of foreigners and retirees and escaped convicts and such. It seemed like living in Florida just automatically made us more modern than the average southerner—never mind the average Alabamian—which both tortured and pleased my daddy—and me too.

Anyway the trip up to Alabama was a major undertaking. We packed the car like it was a stagecoach and we were taking out in search of gold or at least a new life—when really it was the old life we were in search of. The remnants of my parents' childhoods were available to us—and to them—in Alabama. Even if we lived in Florida, we understood that Alabama was our real home. It was where our people mostly were. It was where our history was.

Back then it was a long, long trip to Alabama, partly because my father never drove any faster than thirty-five miles an hour and also he liked to stop often for boiled peanuts or salted peanuts, which he dropped in his RC Cola and taught us to do, too. Our favorite thing was to come upon a cane grinding, with the mule going around and around in a circle and that sugarcane juice pouring into a vat that you could dip a glass into. We gulped down all that liquid sweetness until we felt sweet ourselves, all over, much sweeter than we had been before drinking that potion. It worked like a miracle medicine that maybe you didn't really need—but you wanted it because it gave you the feeling of being *cured of something.* Your spirit, at least. Then we would each take a few stalks of sugarcane with us in the car and chew the flavor out of each bite and spit the pulp out the window.

We also stopped frequently for good barbecue, fried pigskins, Grape Nehi, and anywhere along the way that looked to have good homegrown tomatoes, sweet corn, butter beans, watermelon, or fresh peaches. This was because we did not have our own garden—since we were so modern. But our grandparents had big gardens that took up much of their land and time and provided them both good food and a good topic of endless conversation. As far as I could tell, a person with no garden in Alabama was at a total loss when it came to conversation.

In Alabama, back then, gardens were like their own kind of religion. Most everybody believed in them because it was where you could learn faith and patience, not to mention the rewards of hard work. And if things went right, God would richly reward you with all the tomatoes and squash you could ever eat and enough ripe watermelons to make it through the summer. I used to think it would be pretty hard to starve in Alabama unless you really put your mind to it. It seemed like the earth itself was warm and loving—even if sometimes some of the people weren't. Gardens even inspired people to share their bounty with the less fortunate. Even poor people could usually have a garden of some description if they wanted to—a patch of collard greens in the sand, pole beans climbing up the side of the house, corn in a line like soldiers saluting the sun. I guess a garden might make poor people feel a little less poor, at least when the harvest came in. It seemed that gardens were a practical way to put some blessings in your life. The most basic of human rights—a little piece of land to grow something on. Some seeds to sow. A bounty to reap. I think it was one of the main things that made Alabama people believe in God. That and pure fear.

These were the days of two-lane roads, back when nobody thought about or cared about a direct route—because there was no direct route. In fact, in all the South I don't even think we had the concept of *direct* anything. There was no hurry going on anywhere in Alabama, which was nice. Whereas the hurry was just beginning to settle into Florida, since we had all those Yankees zooming down there in their fast cars with all their fast talk, taking their loud vacations, snapping their elaborate camera equipment in our startled faces. But as far as I could tell since Sherman and them came through in the Civil War with their torches blazing, I didn't think a single Yankee ever lingered in Alabama long enough to bother anybody or try to mess anything up. I certainly never heard of Yankees looking around Alabama and deciding to stay just because they wanted to. Although some—like my own grandparents—got sent down to Alabama to do a job and ended up staying forever, maybe because they just got too old to leave. So the Alabama of my childhood was more or less still in its original state—except that the colored people who could were moving away looking for a better version of the American dream than the nightmare some of them were experiencing in Alabama. Otherwise not much had changed there since my parents had been born. It was like history was just standing still. Or maybe, after so long, squatting.

When traveling through Alabama—those *Heart of Dixie* tags on the secondhand, finned cars that floated and sputtered down the roads like big pastel motorboats, sometimes packed with every last member of a family plus a few distant cousins hanging out the windows—we occasionally had to stop just to get out from behind a homemade, one-family, unintentional traveling sideshow. Or there might be an old man alone at the wheel chewing his toothpick, his elbow stuck out the window, who did not seem to understand that my father's swerving behind him was indicative of a desire to pass. The farmer would simply lift a finger in a friendly wave. His pace made my father appear to be a genuine speed demon, a false image that thrilled us and made us feel that we alone, our singular family, had an important destination, while those around us were simply in the usual *no hurry* to go the usual *nowhere*. Sometimes we would become so frustrated trailing a twenty-mile-an-hour produce truck or a ten-mile-an-hour tractor we had no choice but to pull off on the side of the road and eat something.

Occasionally we stopped at those white-painted cement picnic tables that sat on the side of the road among the weeds, next to a large trash bin—and if God was smiling on us, under a shade tree, too—and ate the olive loaf sandwiches we'd brought from home and drank the grape Kool-Aid Mother had in the thermos that was warm and watery now since all the ice had long ago melted. Even warm it could leave you with a fine purple mustache and purple tongue like the gums of those blue-tick hounds people love so much.

For some reason these uncommonly substantial cement picnic tables, built so that they could never be stolen and could in fact withstand all manner of abuse and even deliberate attack, and which were doused regularly with institutional white paint, always made me think of convicts. I don't know if it was because I occasionally saw convicts painting the tables while a guard sat nearby in his truck with his shotgun across his lap. Or if it was the institutional white, which I associated with public places—both prisons and schools— where people, mostly male, were inclined to destroy things.

One thing we learned on our Alabama travels was that if you ever had car trouble you better hope some poor people came along, because that was who was most likely to stop and help you out. My mother said, "Poor people know how it is to have trouble," as if that alone proved they were both wiser and kinder than well-off folks. In fact, we had proved this to ourselves on several flat-tire occasions when our rescuers coasted to a stop in such rattletrap contraptions that it hardly seemed possible they could be out traveling the roads, never mind trying to save us from our automotive dilemma. But they were and they did. And ever after we always watched to see who was helping whom with roadside car trouble. We saw that it was not usually the Cadillacs that stopped but the torn-up cars and trucks that looked like they'd been running on empty all of their lives. It was an interesting thing to know, too. Ourselves, we didn't always stop every single time we saw people with car trouble—but we did almost always pick up hitchhikers if they were wearing army uniforms.

We also learned something about the Alabama state troopers and the police, which was interesting to note. It was my mother who pointed this out, after which it practically became a game to me—looking to see if her theory held. The theory was that law officers were partial to stopping colored people, poor white people, and women traveling alone—in that particular order. You were not likely to see a white businessman in his necktie pulled over on the side of the road getting a ticket. Not unless he was so drunk he had veered off the road and into a ditch—in which case he would likely get a friendly warning. But it became clear to us when we were too young to make sense of it that part of the job of law enforcement of that era was to punish poor people for being poor. And to bother women because there was nothing women could do about it. Either that or else white men in neckties were most likely to travel the speed limit and obey all laws, which was why they got all the breaks. My mother was always noticing stuff like this and pointing it out to us. And our daddy was always wishing she wouldn't. Of course, in this case, he himself was a white man in a necktie. It was he whom the world in general—and Alabama in particular—was set up to accommodate. Although I don't think he ever fully appreciated this fact.

Sometimes my family was forced to pull over at isolated rest stops just so that my brothers and I could—theoretically—cool off. This meant our tempers and our boiling brains—not our bodies. We had all been born into the world preheated and fully expected to simmer our way through this relentless fire drill we called *life*. We checked the trash can for possums or snakes or maybe drowned puppies tied up in a knotted croaker sack. We hit or kicked each other as a means of getting even for some injury to body, mind, or spirit that had occurred in the car. *He touched my leg! She put her nasty foot on me!* Afterward, when we had exhausted our deep-rooted longing for some higher justice that completely eluded our parents—either satisfied or spanked—we would lie on top of the hot picnic table, legs crossed at the knee, eyes squinted, and sacrifice ourselves to the hot fireball sun, a god of sorts in our sweaty lives, which—although it had mostly the characteristics of hell—lurked, we believed, in the general vicinity of heaven. This was the other sun of God. Everybody believed in it. You didn't have to join a church to prove you believed either. All you had to do was look up and you could know for sure. The sun did not have any chosen people either. It pretty much chose everybody.

This roadside ritual tended to occur after some moderate brawl in the car that had caused our father to have to lean back over the seat and swat us, which caused our mother to shriek for fear the distraction would cause him to steer right into a tree and kill us all. It was like we stopped, submitted ourselves to the bald sun for purification—to get ourselves and each other forgiven enough to reunite peacefully in the car like the loving family we aspired to be. We were all sun-browned, but my mother and one brother got so dark people thought they were foreigners. I always liked the feeling of forgiveness on my skin—the way it burned itself in. That way you knew for sure it was working. Like if God touched you with His hot finger.

While the outbreak of a family fuss could inspire a stop, we were far less inclined to stop for bathroom reasons, which according to our father would prevent our making good time. We more or less accepted this sort of logic. And we only made bathroom stops for my mother and me—if we carried on convincingly. Otherwise, we traveled with an empty RC bottle in case nature happened to call one of my brothers. They never raised any objections (that I remember) to this efficient method of saving time. For all I know, they preferred it to the outhouse options that often awaited us out behind gas stations or roadside vegetable stands. We had all heard the stories about outhouses and shade-seeking snakes and consequently had developed an appropriate fear of both.

This was back when life was totally unairconditioned. Neither our home nor our grandparents' homes had air-conditioning, although there were the enslaved oscillating fans churning the heavy

air with their gears complaining and box fans perched in the windows like cats. But cars were another story. There, speed determined
the movement of air. We drove along with all windows down and an
occasional foot or two hung out the back windows and we sweated
like crazy. We wore sweat necklaces and our palms and bare feet left
wet prints wherever we set them down. Our clothes were soaked
through. Our hair was wet and plastered to our faces, except where
it curled around our ears. You could not get away from the fierce
eyeball of the sun anymore than you could escape God Almighty
watching every move you made. You knew that to try was hopeless.
Nonetheless, it was necessary for us to stop often on the blistering
back roads of rural Alabama to avoid totally roasting like pink-
skinned sausages in our Chevy oven on wheels.

Also, from my reclining posture in the rearview window I could
look into the cars that followed us—rode our bumper as was the
Alabama custom—and see if the people looked nice or mean, rich
or poor, interesting or boring. Most everybody in Alabama looks
Baptist. If you live there you know what I mean. Whether people
are rabid Baptists or relapsed Baptist, there is a look that goes with
it. I was then and still am both interested in and afraid of Baptists.
My own father was a Baptist, although over time my mother had
managed to talk him out of it. Now he went to the Methodist
church like the rest of us. I have always been grateful to her for that.
My father's Baptist upbringing had taught him to believe every
word of the Bible, even though he had never actually read much of
it himself. Even now he preferred to read *U.S. News and World
Report* and *Changing Times*. But I think, like me, he was half scared
not to believe every word of the Bible for fear he would be struck by
lightning or contract leprosy. I didn't hold his blind believing
against him because I was trying pretty hard to do the same thing.
Just in case.

My mother, on the other hand, was a Sunday school teacher
who had read the Bible cover to cover but had found any number
of mistakes in it and was not afraid to point them out. This caused

my father to shudder. And I think that if our preacher had known how many questions our mother had in her heart he would have fired her from the Sunday school. She might have had to stand trial in front of the whole congregation and confess her doubts publicly, after which she would be punished through eternity and end up burning in hell with the rest of *those of little faith* who did not have sense enough to fake it. Mother used to say to us, "God would not give us a perfectly good mind and then dare us to ever use it, would He?"

Yes, I thought. Best I could tell He did it all the time, didn't He?

As a child I interpreted the phrase *Bible Belt* literally as some huge whip God had and was not afraid to use against nonbelievers —or, as in my case, sort of a failed, lackluster believer—to beat his love into us if he had to, if we insisted on being stubborn and sinful. He would do it the same way earthbound fathers tried to beat some sense into their children with their snakelike weather belts. (Ever since Eve got in trouble for wanting to partake of the tree of knowledge I've always associated snakes with God's angry side.)

Already, just by looking around Alabama, I knew for a fact that a person's life could be so full of pain and misery and hatefulness that there was no real explanation other than that God was punishing them for something, the way he did Eve. I had a sneaky feeling that people got punished all the time for things they did by accident, you know, like getting born someplace they shouldn't have. Maybe getting born to a worn-out mother and no daddy at all. Or a mother who wasn't but thirteen and a daddy who already had a wife and family and grandkids older than she was. Or a mother who never said yes to the man that forced himself upon her and now never will say yes to the child who is also forcing himself upon her. Making God mad would be the least of a person's intentions at the time of their birth. But they were born already sorry. I saw people like that all the time. People with such hard lives that it was clear to me—if not to them—that no matter what the Bible said, God simply didn't love them. If he did and if he was really all-powerful then I thought he would prove His love some way. The only reason these folks believed that God loved them was just because they wanted to. As far as I could tell there was not an ounce of evidence anywhere you looked. Unless maybe they had a little plot of garden providing them a decent yield.

It was like religion had all these rules and for some reason—in Alabama—God had left the Baptists in charge of interpreting and policing his commandments. This bothered me because my mother had told me, "The Jews are God's chosen people. Not the Baptists." I took great comfort in this, although I wasn't sure I really believed it. I did believe you had to count your blessings to keep from losing them. And so I counted mine. One of them was the fact that our father never actually used his *Bible Belt* on any of us—he just swatted us with his huge open palm and for the most part got excellent results. He had no need for a back-up plan. But, nonetheless, I knew most of my friends had the kinds of fathers who said to them regularly, "Don't you make me take off my belt." Consequently, God the Father, was not always a very comforting image. Almost everybody I knew was afraid of God in one way or another.

Secretly I felt God was not doing a very good job running the world—particularly in Alabama. And, like I said, I especially did not see how any poor people or colored people ("black" people had not come along yet) could love God hardly at all, and yet it seemed they were the ones who loved Him most.

This seemed to make perfect sense to my mother. Many of God's ways baffled me, but she had explanations for them, which she made up herself and seemed to me better than what the Bible said. For years I used to wish God would step down and turn the world over to my mother. I thought she could do a much more loving job of things.

Two religious questions haunted me—actually I was thoroughly haunted by religion, but these two things haunted me in particular—Why was I born white instead of colored? (At the time I hardly knew there were any other possibilities—like Jewish or Cuban or

Italian or Cherokee Indian. That came much later.) What came instantly—practically the day I was born into the black-and-white world of the South—was the sense that I had been born on the wrong side of something and that that fact made me lucky. I could see clearly that to be on the right side of the thing would cause you to suffer and have a miserable life. I knew very, very early that being born lucky could be the worst kind of curse in the long run. That life was going to be full of tricks like that.

And second, why was I born average instead of poor? How did God decide who the poor people would be? And why didn't he choose me? I felt like He'd done me a huge favor and now I owed Him something in return—but what? Should I memorize a hundred psalms and maybe win a blue ribbon at Training Union? Should I walk the aisle for Jesus every Sunday of my life? Should I get down on my knees and confess my unworthiness? I knew that in the world I lived in being born these two things—white and middle class—were two strokes of incredible good fortune. Blessings were what I thought they were. Everywhere I looked I saw people struggling and suffering because they lacked one or both of these blessings. It made people who suffered seem more interesting and braver to me than people who didn't suffer. Even so, at the time, I myself didn't want to be interesting badly enough to voluntarily suffer for it. Besides, I really hated making people mad. Even stupid or mean people. I wanted every single person on earth to like me. So already I was split into the real girl who lived in my head—and the pretend girl who lived in the world as I found it.

This is the crazy kind of stuff you thought about when you went to Alabama. I don't know why. I wasn't the only one it happened to. We all got mesmerized looking at the Alabama landscape, the cotton fields, the kudzu, the red clay, the pines, the little semi-towns that you could not tell if they were just getting started or just giving up, the big houses with the tree-lined drives, and the little shacks clustered together under one huge old shade tree. The folks that hung out at the gas station stores, the old men on benches, the boys on bikes, the barefoot girls eating Popsicles on their walk home. In Alabama you used to be able to look at a person and know his or her life story practically in a flash. This was partly why the people were always so friendly to strangers—because just looking at you they felt like *they'd been knowing you.* It wasn't a particular talent of any kind. Everybody pretty much knew how to do it. For one thing there were very limited possibilities on what a person's life story could be—and mostly it showed on their faces. Like you could just look at somebody and know if he had been to prison or not—or if he was likely to go any time soon. You could tell if a person was good Sunday school material or a member of one of those families that got the Thanksgiving basket delivered to their door. You knew by looking if a boy's daddy drank too much and beat the fool out of him, because then he was always the one on the lookout for somebody he could beat the fool out of. You could tell if a colored person sang the gospel or sang the blues. You could tell if a polite person was sincere or not, which in the long run didn't really matter much. You knew when a woman had man trouble or a man had money trouble. You knew the first day of school, just glancing around, who would get picked on and made fun of—and you knew why. And you could look at the teacher and know right off whether or not she was going to do anything about it.

You also knew this—that everybody had secrets—and some of them were not much and others were pretty bad. You also knew that nobody was going to ever tell you the absolute truth about anything that ever happened in this life—and you came to count on this and appreciate it. Instead people told things like they wished they were or thought they ought to be. It takes a little imagination to be a good Alabamian. You have got to think of ways to word things so that they sound better than they are and yet don't actually make you out to be a liar.

In Alabama a good story is always better respected than the actual truth. This has always worked out pretty well for me. The truth gets so far-fetched sometimes that it is downright impossible to take it seriously. So stories lurk all around, most of them with some shred of fact in them and then embellished by the hungry-hearted people telling them. You can use the stories like salve if you want to. Some of them are known to have healing properties. You can collect them so you have something to show for yourself—same as if you collected guns or arrowheads or quilts your grandmother made. You can hide things under them and make things out of them. You can dress people in them or strip folks naked with them. You can feed the hungry-spirited with stories of love, the cowardly with stories of courage, and the wicked with the beautiful sorts of lies they are most likely to become ensnared in—like flies in a delicate web. They are the staple of the Alabama culture-stories. This is the thing I love the most of all.

I would think about all this when I was baking like a cupcake in the rearview window of the car. I would just look at all those Alabama faces looking back at me—and it just automatically made me know things. Sometimes I waved at the people in the cars behind us. Mostly they waved back.

In Alabama I still love to rent a car and take the long way almost everywhere I go. Last year I went through Elba for the first time and saw an impressive fleet of buzzards lift a writhing snake into the air just seconds before my car was about to hit them. I took it as a sign from God because—it seems like in Alabama—everything is. God still works primarily in mysterious ways there. I sincerely appreciated His removing a snake from my path. Even after all these years I still think the only good snake is a dead snake.

I know a place outside Tuscaloosa where I used to go maybe once a week, just to drive past a little homemade red tarpaper church with two funny steeples like huge ears. Sometimes people inside were singing their heads off, but usually the place was deserted. Once my daughter and I came upon a loose cow out there that had been hit by a car and had a bone jutting bloody white from her leg, which she was still trying to stand on. We went to the nearest house to get help and they sent us down the road to an old black man, who, when we told him the trouble, fetched a handheld hammer and got in the backseat of our car. He spoke the old kind of black that I remembered from my childhood but had almost forgotten how to understand. When we got back to the suffering cow, he got out and pounded her in the head with the hammer until she fell to the ground, more or less dead. Afterward he was dripping with sweat. He told us he would come back later and dig her a grave when it wasn't so hot. Then he directed us to a torn-up country store and we all got cold drinks before taking him back home. Alabama might be the only place that can still make me think of a hammer as an instrument of mercy. Violence as an act of love.

I still go by what used to be my grandfather's old farm at least a couple of times a year. It is twelve miles outside Tuskegee, and the people who own it now have built a nice catfish restaurant next to the house. It seems to do a good business. My family has eaten there on several occasions. They have great banana pudding. I think it might be *white only,* too—at least it has been whenever we were there—but we don't ask. We only wonder among ourselves where the black people are. They like catfish too, right?

They have modernized everything on the old farm, too, which for some reason, sort of breaks my heart. Not that I liked watching it fall apart and rot either. Sometimes you wish a thing could stay the way it was—no better, no worse—forever.

The old Milstead post office, where my grandmother was postmistress—and where together we read every postcard that passed through the place—is torn down and gone now, so is the cotton gin, and the train hasn't thrown off a mailbag in years. This was where my grandfather once shot a colored man who was running to get away from a posse. People say he shot the man off the caboose of the mail train as he was trying to climb on. There were some witnesses, I guess. Maybe this was the definitive moment when my grandmother stopped loving my grandfather forever—or maybe she never really loved him at all in the first place, which is what I have grown to suspect.

But we, his grandchildren, always loved our grandfather—even years and years later when we found out he was a murderer we forgave him—because he had the power to call any animal on the farm in a special language that the animal understood perfectly. The animals always came to him, too. They were never afraid. We thought it was an amazing gift to have. We didn't know a single college-educated person who could do it either. It seemed like college people mostly just read about what other people did and wrote papers on what was wrong with the way those other people did what they did—but the college people could not actually *do* anything themselves. So we were proud of our grandfather's unique talents. We didn't want him to feel bad just because he could hardly read a word.

We didn't know until we were grown the stories about him killing a person—or maybe two. The stories of the killing have come to us all broken and torn up so that no two versions ever match, and all we can do is choose one we can work with. So I choose the one about the posse and the train. I hate it. But I know I can't be allowed to ignore it either. Even if the story is not one hundred percent factual, I have come to understand the nature of stories enough to realize that the truth lurks at least somewhere in the vicinity of the story and that's about the best we can hope for. It is the rarest story that holds *the truth, the whole truth, and nothing but the truth* entirely inside its perimeter. Only fools believe that stories—or memories—can actually do that. It is the spirit of the truth—not the facts—that keep stories alive and well. It is the spirit of the truth—not the facts—that haunts us.

Once, years later, my dead grandfather appeared to me in a dream. He was dressed in all white, like Colonel Sanders, and he tried to cheer me up. Even in death he did not tell me the truth, although I got the strangest feeling he had managed to get himself forgiven and made his way to heaven in spite of everything. And I assumed the dead man was (or men were) up there with him. I pictured them playing checkers or something. I dreamed that they have worked things out and made eternal peace. All I really know is now Milstead, Alabama, is like an empty place where the heart of things used to be.

Not far from there, on your way to the Greyhound races, is the county hole where we used to swim with the snakes and bathe in the murky water with bar soap and wash our hair with dish detergent. Some kids jumped off the bridge and lived to tell about it. The way I remember it, my brothers and I were some of those who did. We worked up the courage. We did not let pure terror prevent our having a small moment of victory. That's the way I like to remember it. I know it was a high and rusty bridge with lumber trucks and farm trucks rattling over it, shaking the world below. Besides snakes in the water, there were stumps to worry about, and rocks, and we had heard the stories of mangled children, their bodies broken, their spirits broken, their mothers' hearts broken. But I like remembering that we jumped anyway. We did not overcome fear, we just momentarily joined ourselves to it, to see how it would feel. We let ourselves free-fall into the depths, and when our heads miraculously bobbed up like corks seconds later, suggesting that we were, in fact, going to be allowed to live—to continue our small lives so far off to rather shaky starts—no one was more surprised or grateful than the three of us.

Afterward we roasted hotdogs and marshmallows in the dark night with our mosquito-proof grandparents, who had built a fire out of sticks and scraps of paper. They wrapped towels around our trembling shoulders. They poured ketchup on our hotdogs and Kool-Aid in our cups, not fully realizing the impact of the event they had witnessed, not realizing that we—their own flesh-and-blood grandchildren—had transcended the ordinary perhaps for the first time ever. That we had dabbled with courage, taken a leap of faith—and come back from the depths of fear alive and inspired. Their failure to fully understand this didn't matter. The fire they'd built was hot and alive and just dangerous enough to please us. We leaned toward it, our faces glowing.

ROBERT INMAN

The Ghosts in
My Grandmother's Attic

There are ghosts in my grandmother's attic. They are quite durable and persistent ghosts. They have survived floods, wars, and assorted other human and natural tragedies. Maybe they have endured because the attic is a safe harbor, a place where ghosts feel at home, no matter what ill winds blow outside.

The attic is a magical room that peeks out at the world from under the eaves of a rambling white frame house in Elba, Alabama. It is the one place, above all others, that made me the particular kind of writer you call a storyteller.

There is a story everywhere, and there is a good story about how my grandmother's attic came to be. Like all good stories it is about people.

Elba is a river town, settled almost a hundred-fifty years ago in a valley along the banks of the Pea River in southeast Alabama. It got its name quite by accident. The settlement was first named Coffeeville, in honor of Gen. John Coffee, a hero of the Creek Indian War. The county in which it was located was also named for General Coffee, so the citizens of the community came to desire their own distinct name. Being of a democratic bent, they decided to draw a name out of a hat. One local fellow had been reading a biography of Napoleon and offered up the name of the island off the French coast where Napoleon was exiled. And that's what came out of the hat.

Those early riverbank settlers, as it turned out, had more imagination than good sense. Throughout the town's history the Pea River has periodically risen out of its banks and flooded the small valley and anything that is in it. Elbians have simply cleaned up the mud and rebuilt. Stubbornness is an abundant commodity in Elba.

My grandfather, Bob Cooper, was the mayor of Elba in the late 1920s and a successful lumberman. I suppose he figured that with all the rebuilding Elbians periodically had to do, lumber was a surefire thing. He prospered in business and was of the opinion that if you lived in a place you should give something back to it. What he gave was civic leadership.

But all of Bob Cooper's good deeds and intentions couldn't protect him from the river. In the spring of 1929 it rained unceasingly for several days while he was away on a business trip. The river flooded the town and washed his sawmill and lumberyard down the river. My grandmother, Nell Cooper, escaped out the backdoor of her one-story home in a rowboat with her four small children and fled to a two-story home nearby, where they stayed with other refugees, among whom was an extremely pregnant woman. Before the waters receded, she delivered a fine healthy boy who was aptly named Noah.

When Granddaddy Bob returned home, he rebuilt his sawmill and used some of his new lumber to build a second story on the family home so that if the river flooded again, his family would have their own refuge. Then he lobbied the folks in Washington to build a levee around Elba, which they did. During most of my lifetime the levee kept the Pea River at bay. The river would get swollen and angry and lap at the bottom of the levee, but that's as far as it got. The Great Flood of '29 was simply part of Elba's lore, a sort of odd badge of honor.

But the river has proved to be an inexorable and undeniable thing, despite man's best efforts. In March of 1990 Elba got a week-long deluge of rain. The river rose and kept rising. Finally it began to spill over the top of the levee, which broke under the pressure. The river entered the town and stayed there for several days until the levee broke at the other end of town and relieved the pressure. It was a disaster of major proportions. When I watched aerial footage of the town on the TV network news, I spotted the second story of my grandparents' home, sitting high and dry. Bob Cooper would have been proud.

By that time, of course, Bob and Nell Cooper were long departed. The river never flooded again during their lifetimes. And the attic—"Mama Cooper's upstairs," we called it—became the family dumping ground. It consisted of one large room and four closets tucked under the roofline at the corners. Each of the four children had a closet, and when I was a boy, rummaging about in the upstairs was my favorite activity.

It was there that I rediscovered the joy of reading. It happened in the summer of my twelfth year—an awkward time for a boy when you are too young to chase girls and too old to play in the dirt with the little kids. I was at loose ends as summer vacation began, and so my mother suggested I go to Mama Cooper's upstairs and find some books to read.

My mother and three uncles had always been great readers, and one of the closets contained several shelves full of the books they had read as children. The books had been there for perhaps thirty years, gathering dust and patiently waiting for me. I spent a great deal of that summer in the swing on Mama Cooper's front porch, traveling the globe with the characters in those books. I helped Nancy Drew and the Hardy Boys solve some unsolvable mysteries, flew in Tom Swift's airship, and went with the Bobbsey Twins to the seashore. Those books were a powerful stimulus to my young imagination—rich soil and warm rain, nurturing a seedling of a storyteller.

But the books were not all I discovered in Mama Cooper's attic. I found my family there, at least parts that I would otherwise have never known.

All of the boys—my father and three uncles—went off to serve in World War II. And when they came home from the war they brought their trunks and footlockers and duffel bags full of personal effects and stored them away in the attic closets. I had no respect whatsoever for their privacy. I went through everything, and in doing so shared their experience in a unique way. There were photographs—two pilot uncles standing beneath the wings of their planes, the one sailor on leave in London, my father the infantryman posing with his buddies in front of the Eiffel Tower. There were bits and pieces of war experience: an empty bullet casing, a map, a can of C-rations, Chinese currency, a document in French. And there were packets of letters, received from wives and girlfriends and mothers back home.

I discovered World War II there in the attic and came to appreciate how completely it altered the world. But I could also see how profoundly it changed the lives of these young men who went off to war and the lives of all those they left behind.

They were all great storytellers, but they rarely talked about the war itself. They had tucked it away in those corner closets. But now, I could read between the lines of their stories and know what unexpected twists and turns their lives had taken. When it was over, they came home and became merchants and doctors and game wardens and postmasters, raised good families, and pretty much lived quiet small-town lives. But they had seen strange places and heard strange tongues. They had known the horror and exhilaration, the loneliness and boredom of war. The world, and they—my flesh and blood—would never be the same again. And they took on a new fascination for a boy with an overactive imagination.

I occasionally let that imagination get the best of me. My Uncle

Bancroft was a fighter pilot during the war, flying missions out of England in support of Allied bombing raids and ground operations in Europe. On one mission his plane was crippled by anti-aircraft fire. He managed to make it back to the English Channel but had to bail out there and be rescued by a British ship. I could just see it in my mind's eye—billows of oily smoke pouring from the engine cowling, gallant Uncle Bancroft shoving back the cockpit hatch, crawling out on the wing, and diving into space while the plane plummeted to a watery grave.

In Uncle Bancroft's footlocker in the attic I found a small parachute. It was, I learned later, a parachute that had been attached to an aerial flare. But in my fertile mind it became the very parachute he had used to save his life in that terrifying moment over the channel. So I affixed the parachute with a piece of rope to my shoulders, crawled out an attic window onto the second-story roof, and leaped into space. As I plummeted toward the nandina bush below, I realized I had done a foolish thing. I escaped with a sprained ankle but always knew that if I were forced to parachute from a burning plane, I could handle it.

The family I found there in Mama Cooper's attic—Uncle Bancroft and all the others—taught me that there is a depth and texture to any life that is not readily visible. Each human heart, as Faulkner so wisely told us, has its secrets. Each soul has its demons and archangels with whom it wrestles. It is what makes us individually unique and thus infinitely fascinating.

Realizing this is essential for the fiction writer who wants to create true and honest characters. You allow them to wrestle with their own demons and archangels, make mistakes, experience joy and pain, thrash about in the underbrush, bump up against each other and make sparks. Sometimes my characters make me angry. Sometimes they embarrass me. Sometimes I rejoice with them. Just like family. They *are* family, and they are born in my grandmother's attic.

North Carolina novelist Reynolds Price says that in the South our families are our entertainment. For the writer of fiction, they are an irresistible wealth of material. In a large, extended southern family there is one of almost everything, from the steel magnolia to the black sheep. There certainly is in mine.

My grandmother, Mama Cooper, is a good example. She was a feisty, independent soul, left with four young children when my grandfather the mayor died in the early thirties. She raised and educated them all, using up the family treasury in the process, then supported herself in her later years as a piano teacher. She loved her extensive covey of grandchildren, but she brooked no foolishness from us. "Nasty stinking young'uns," she would say, "if you don't get out of my flower bed, I'm gonna pinch your heads off." We knew she wouldn't. Or would she?

Mama Cooper had a rather cavalier attitude toward time, and that is probably what allowed her to live a long and mostly happy life. Whatever age she was, she seemed to enjoy it and make peace with it.

Take for instance the great daylight saving time controversy back in the sixties. The Alabama legislature debated fiercely about whether to observe daylight saving time. The Farm Bureau opposed it. A spokesman said with a straight face, "It will confuse the farm animals." A lot of folks were confused about the concept of losing or gaining an hour. But Mama Cooper had a simple solution. During the months when daylight saving time was in effect, she slept an hour later every morning. During the summer, she rose at eight. During the winter, at seven. It worked for her, and she was able to concentrate her mental energies on the truly important things, such as whether to have sweet milk or buttermilk with her supper biscuits.

Mama Cooper's attitude about time extended to human basics. She believed that given time—and a little help—everything that was supposed to work out would work out. One of my indelible memories of boyhood was entering her kitchen door to the smell of prunes cooking in senna leaves. For the uneducated, senna is a powerful laxative. A prune by itself is artillery. A prune cooked in senna is an artillery brigade. If you were feeling "puny," as Mama Cooper put it, or even looked as if you felt puny, she would administer two prunes and a spoonful of juice. Then let time take over. You would stay close to home for several days. You had nothing *but* time.

Mama Cooper's kitchen was a marvelous place, and time was an important ingredient in everything that came out of it. Her recipes were ancient things, time-tested concoctions handed down through generations, everything made from "scratch." During the winter months, when prunes weren't cooking in senna, my favorite aroma at her house was of homemade rolls rising atop the gas space heater in her living room. They took their sweet time, but if you were patient, you were rewarded with a roll so light and fluffy that blackberry jelly fairly floated atop it. Fast food to her was warmed-up leftovers. She was suspicious of things that came out of cans.

One of Mama Cooper's specialties concerned blackberries. In the late summer she would buy gallons of berries and then spend days in the kitchen making jelly, nectar, and—just for cooking, of course (she was the teetotaling daughter of a Methodist minister)—a small amount of wine. Everything took time, especially the wine, which had to "work" for days on end. In her later years, Mama Cooper would occasionally get confused about which jar contained nonalcoholic nectar and which wine. One of the relatives would find her pleasantly tipsy, letting time take its own course.

Mama Cooper also had an accommodating attitude about the course of human events, large and small. I suppose you had to be that way to persevere through tragedies like a flood that ruined your piano and widowhood at a young age. Whatever came along, she seemed to make a place for it in her life. And that, too, is probably what enabled her to live so long. Take, for instance, the great Piggly Wiggly caper.

When I was a small boy, there were two gracious older homes across the street from Mama Cooper's white frame two-story on Buford Street in Elba. At the time, the community's housewives did their grocery shopping at two small mom-and-pop stores on the courthouse square several blocks away. The selection was limited and the walk downtown, especially on a blistering summer day, could be a chore.

Then, in the mid-fifties, came the Piggly Wiggly. The supermarket chain announced that it would build a gleaming modern store in Elba. Folks got excited about what they considered a hallmark of economic and cultural progress. That is, until Piggly Wiggly announced its location: right across Buford Street from Mama Cooper's house. The Piggly Wiggly folks bought those two gracious old homes, bulldozed them, and built the supermarket. Most folks in Elba viewed the matter with ambivalent alarm. Progress, yes. But demolishing two pieces of the town's history?

Mama Cooper had no qualms at all. Ever the pragmatist, she viewed the Piggly Wiggly as convenience, pure and simple. It was marvelous to be able to walk a hundred yards from your front door into the air-conditioned comfort of a well-stocked supermarket. There would be no hot treks to the courthouse square, and she could buy what she needed when she needed it, a decided advantage due to the capacity of the tiny, antique refrigerator in her kitchen. Other townsfolk, she said in so many words, should get a grip.

Piggly Wiggly, aware no doubt of the controversy surrounding the new Elba store, announced that the opening would be accompanied by a prize giveaway. Whenever you made a purchase, you would receive a prize card. If you could match the numbers on two cards, you would win anything from a small grocery item to a $1,000 grand prize.

On one warm June morning shortly after the store opened, Mama Cooper checked her pantry and discovered that she was out of peanut butter. So she put on her hat, picked up her purse, and marched smartly to the Piggly Wiggly, where she purchased one small jar of peanut butter. She got a prize card.

Late that same afternoon, Mama Cooper decided on her supper menu: a glass of buttermilk and a peanut butter and banana sandwich. But she found that she was out of bananas. So she armed herself again with hat and purse and returned to the Piggly Wiggly. She got another prize card. She compared it with the one she had received that morning, still in her purse, and calmly announced, "I've just won the grand prize."

You can imagine the commotion. Townsfolk were delighted and envious over what Elba in the mid-fifties considered a huge windfall. And the *way* she had won it evoked the kind of awe and wonder previously reserved for the Great Flood of '29.

Everybody asked Mama Cooper what she planned to do with the money. Members of her immediate family were especially interested. Every one of us had a great idea for helping her spend it. But to one and all, she was maddeningly noncommittal. In fact, she went to the grave years later without telling a single soul how she spent her winnings. The only purchase we noticed was when she turned up in church wearing a new red hat. There was no new roof on the house, no new car, no gift to charity that any of us knew anything about.

We did know one thing she *didn't* spend it on. My mother, after several months of family speculation, got up the nerve to ask, "Did you pay taxes on the money?"

"Of course not," Mama Cooper shot back. "What are they going to do to an old lady? Put me in jail?"

"Well, they might," said Mother.

But they never did. As far as any of us knew, the tax man never questioned Mama Cooper about her Piggly Wiggly largesse. If he had, I imagine he would have gotten the same kind of defiant reaction as did my mother. I'm sure Mama Cooper faithfully paid taxes on her limited income. But she probably considered the prize money a gift, a reward perhaps for good behavior—something between her and the Lord and Piggly Wiggly.

There is something essentially small-town about Mama Cooper's ability to reconcile herself with the passage of time and the parade of human events in a small place. There is a character in one of my novels who says, "You can't stay mad at somebody when you have to look 'em in the eye every day." That's of course not universally true. I know people in my hometown who have been mad at each other for years. But mad or not, they still somehow manage to get along because there is no alternative. In a small town, you sit next to your fellow sufferers in church and at the high school football games. You do business with each other. You are forced to rub elbows, consider each other warts and all, look each other in the eye, and, above all, accommodate. That's America in microcosm: somehow managing to accommodate, despite our great differences and diversity.

Mama Cooper lived proudly alone until she was ninety-two years old, and then called my mother one day to announce that it was time to go to the nursing home. The last visit I had with her, before her death at age ninety-four, she was bedridden and barely aware—or so I thought. I sat with her through a long afternoon and held her hand. Then suddenly she turned and looked at me with absolute clarity and said, "Bobby, I've give out, but I haven't give up."

I thought that I should write a book about someone like my grandmother, and so she became the inspiration for a character named Bright Birdsong. Bright's biography is different from my grandmother's, but there are similar traits of character. All her life, Bright has been surrounded by powerful and famous men, but she has managed to make her own mark and leave her own legacy. She is feisty and independent. In my story, she is nearing seventy. I suspect Bright will live to be ninety-four, and at the end, she will give out, but she will not give up.

I even made use of Mama Cooper's great Piggly Wiggly caper. I gave Bright Birdsong a grand prize at the Dixie Vittles supermarket across the street from her house—in this case, fifty thousand dollars, just to liven things up. And I peopled the story with lots of other folks who want to help her spend her money—or, like my family, want her to let *them* spend it.

The novel, *Old Dogs and Children,* is a story about how a singular woman makes choices and faces consequences. She takes charge of her life and gives account of herself in the same manner my grandmother did. If you asked me how I came to know Bright Birdsong, I would say that I found her in my grandmother's attic. She's one of the enduring ghosts of that magical place.

The windows of the attic look out onto the slightly larger world of that town where I grew up, to a small stage where you could observe human nature at close hand over time.

I came to realize that the town grew up out of the land and that its values were of the land: reverence for time and place, loyalty to family and friends, respect for the institutions of community—school and church, home and courthouse.

When I was in junior high school, I convinced the editor of the local weekly newspaper, *The Elba Clipper*, to give me a job. He put me to work back in the print shop, getting ink under my fingernails and in my blood, learning in a very physical way how a newspaper becomes a community gathering place, how people and events are turned into words for everybody to share.

On Saturday afternoons, my job was to clean up the place. It was hot, dirty work, and when I finished, I rewarded myself with an RC Cola and a Moon Pie. That is, except in the summer, when the RC was replaced with one of the finest beverages known to man, pure sugarcane juice. A fellow who lived out in the country near Elba had a cane patch and a cane press, complete with a mule that walked around and around at the end of a long pole, the other end of which was connected to the press. The farmer fed in stalks of cane from which the juice was squeezed. Most of it he used to make cane syrup. But he would save some to put in soda bottles with a cork stopper in the top, and he would ice it down and bring it to town for sale to the folks who had come to transact business of various sorts at the courthouse and the commercial establishments on the square. The cane juice was so incredibly sweet you could only drink one bottle. It was liquid heaven—the nectar of the land, the product of the sweat of a man's brow.

There is another, similar memory—waking up in the middle of a late August night in my room on the front of our house to hear the sound of metal wagon wheels on the street outside. Wagons full of cotton, picked during the long hot days and then taken to the gin during the cool of night. When I mentioned it to my mother the next morning, she called it the sound of meat and potatoes. Like the cane juice, it was the fruit of the land. And whatever the cotton farmer and his family and hired hands had produced during that southeast Alabama summer had to sustain them through the lean time of winter.

The realization of all that gave me an appreciation for how the roots of a small town and its surrounding area go deep, through soil and blood and generations. There is a sense of legacy, of history—the personal, intimate, and intriguing stories of people—that doesn't exist in places where uprootedness is the norm.

I observed all that about my small town, and I observed human nature up close. I saw good and evil, charity and greed, wisdom and ignorance, elegance and tackiness in my hometown—all out in the open for everybody to see, no matter how hard we tried to hide them. My town was and is an extended family, and thus an ever-widening source of fictional characters. And the town itself, as a concrete place, has been—like Mama Cooper—a model and inspiration for my fictional work.

The town that is the setting for my first novel, *Home Fires Burning*, bears physical resemblance to Elba in many ways. People who live in Elba read the book and try to figure out who the characters really are. And they tell me that I put the fire station in the wrong place. Well, I tell them that I put the fire station where I did because that's what suited the story. And I tell them that yes, they are all there. Because they are.

In many respects small towns are the last vestige of the way we were in America before we lost the last of our innocence. There are lingering things about small towns today that remind us of an America of fifty or more years ago, before the boys went off to war and saw Gay Paree.

In telling my stories, I suppose I am somewhat of a literary preservationist. There are many things about the place and manner in which I grew up that are worth preserving. So I have written books full of biplanes and automobiles with running boards, town council meetings and natural calamities, good and evil, elegance and tackiness. Because all of that is part of who I am. And the only thing I can share through my writing is myself, something out of the well of that sum of all things—people, places, things, writings, fears, joys, assorted notions—which is my experience.

A writer friend tells about his daughter being asked in her first-grade class what her father does for a living. She answered, "He stares out the window a lot."

Someone asked me once how you write a book. "Well," I said, "you stare out the window for awhile and think up something. Then you put it on paper. Then you stare out the window some more and think up something else, and put that on paper. You do that over and over until you're finished. And then you write 'THE END' and send it all off to your publisher."

I was being flip, but both my writer friend's child and I spoke the truth. Staring out the window is an essential part of the writing process, probably the most essential. When I stare out my window, I don't see what's outside. I look through a hole in the real world into my own imagination. And what I write has to be first imagined. Everything else is just typing.

I haven't been in my grandmother's attic in probably thirty years. And I don't want or need to make a physical visit, because it's not the same. I prefer it the way I remember it. In memory it is a lively place, full of intriguing ghosts who whisper in my ear and tell me things to write about.

ANDREW HUDGINS

Alabama Breakdown

A stag dance, wrote Captain W. L. Fagan describing an 1827 housewarming, . . . was necessary on the opening of every dance, "for the young men possessed such an excess of agility that a 'breakdown' was needed to render them sufficiently graceful to be partners to the ladies."

—Joyce Cauthen, *Alabama Heritage*

I

In my late twenties, when I was living in Montgomery, I was invited to read my poems at a brown-bag lunch at the Center for the Study of Southern Culture. The cheerful people who showed up on the University of Mississippi campus for lunch that day had not come to see me. They couldn't have. I'd published only a handful of poems in literary journals. I'd been invited because a professor from Ole Miss wanted to help a fellow southerner. I understood that. But not until I was actually sitting before this talkative gathering did it sink in that these people had come to the Center for the Study of Southern Culture to see SOUTHERN CULTURE, and for the next thirty minutes I'd be Exhibit A. Sitting there, smiling nervously at the people rooting in their grease-spotted brown bags, I raced through the characteristics I'd memorized ten years before in a southern lit class: a sense of the living presence of the past; love of landscape and the natural world; cruel humor; and a preoccupation with religion, family, violence, race, and the grotesque. I was bemused to discover that I and my writing possessed every item on my memorized list. Not most of them. All of them. I was astonished and perplexed. How had this happened? How had I become what I clearly was?

When my father received orders transferring him to Montgomery, we were living in military housing outside Paris. For the three years before we moved to Paris, we had lived in California. I thought of myself as a citizen of the world. I was thirteen.

"Alabama!" I said to myself over and over again.

The boys at school repeated it, too, mocking my fate. "Alabama!" they sang out when they passed me in the hall.

"Alabama!" We stretched the word out—*Aya la baym uh!* We hoked it up with caricatured southern accents—Scarlett O'Hara or Foghorn Leghorn, depending on our mood.

Our images of the state had been formed by photographs in newspapers and *Time* magazine. Bull Connor unleashing attack-trained Alsatians on peaceful marchers in Birmingham in 1963. George Wallace, also in 1963, standing on the steps of Foster Auditorium at the University of Alabama, his face swollen with rage and his right hand raised to say stop to the black students James Hood and Vivian Malone. And in 1965 both *Time* and *Stars and Stripes,* the military paper, were full of stories about the Selma-to-Montgomery march.

So this, dear God, was where I was going. I was no stranger to the South. I'd gone to first through fifth grades in North Carolina and spent many summers with relatives in my parents' rural hometown of Griffin, Georgia. But the Alabama I read about in the papers and saw on TV seemed as distant as the lower Orinoco River basin—harsh, strange, and brutal.

In world history one day, a bunch of boys, hunched over the sports section of *Stars and Stripes,* called to me, "Hudgins, come here. Look at this!" They held up a picture of Bear Bryant and three of his players holding a huge silver trophy. Alabama had defeated Nebraska 39–25 in the Orange Bowl and taken the national championship. Because I was looking for a reason to get enthusiastic about going to Alabama, I tried to share my friends' excitement. Wow! I was going to a state that was the national champion in something! Football would suffice.

My impressions of Alabama were almost exactly those held by the nation as a whole: virulent racism and good football. Those two qualities were embodied in George Corley Wallace and Paul "Bear" Bryant. In state, all you had to say was "George" or "Bear," and everybody from Birmingham, corporate lawyer to Lowndes County subsistence farmer, knew whom you were talking about.

As soon as we arrived in Montgomery in the fall of 1966, I was enrolled at Sidney Lanier High on Court Street, a three-story fortress of a building with crenellated parapets. It looks like a huge National Guard armory. I was afraid, physically afraid, every day I walked into that building. In California I'd been beaten up a couple of times by a Hispanic kid simply because I was white and walked home alone. I learned to dodge him. But Alabama was different. The rage and fear were pervasive.

One morning, juggling my schoolbooks, I got in the car driven by a boy down the street. As I pulled the door closed behind me and turned to say hi, he slugged me in the mouth and split my lip. He shook the steering wheel and screamed at me. The afternoon before, in a car full of joking boys coming home from school, I'd said something that he felt should not have been uttered in the presence of his mother, who was driving. I had no idea what I could have said and I was mortified to think I had besmirched the honor of a lady. He drove back to his house and stood triumphantly beside the car while I apologized to Miz Scaggs through bloody teeth that she seemed not to notice. I would have apologized if he had just asked me to, of course. He didn't need to hit me. In chivalry, doesn't the demand for satisfaction precede the blow? That was how it was done in Sir Walter Scott. But chivalry in Alabama had gone haywire, and violence had become not so much a means to an end as an end in itself, the only balm for our wounds, a necessary and outward expression of inner rage and self-loathing.

The year I began at Lanier, 1966, was the first year black students were allowed to attend the school. In my six classes, there was one African American.

Washington Baldwin sat on the far left side of my English class, third seat from the front. He was a large, good-natured boy with a big smile, a gold tooth, and a nervous desire to please the teacher. On Fridays he wore his ROTC uniform to class.

People said, "You know, they"—meaning black leaders, meaning the NAACP—"pick out the best nigra students and send them to Lanier so we'll think all of them can do good schoolwork and get on well with whites. But if these are the ones they picked out, God help the rest of them."

Though I have no idea if Washington Baldwin was chosen to represent his race at Lanier in that first year of integration, I do know he was watched. I watched him.

I watched him closely enough to see that he got C's and D's on his tests. I could hear him struggle to keep his subjects and verbs aligned when he spoke, and when he messed them up and Miz Tisdale corrected him, he responded with a self-conscious smile and a sideways jerk of his head, annoyed with himself. I wondered if I should try to talk to him though I had no personal connection, just a vague sympathy for what I assumed must be a hard row to hoe.

And wouldn't it be racist to seek him out for a friend because he was black, especially when, as a new kid in town, I didn't talk to anyone who didn't talk to me first? I felt bad about studying him, too, though I studied other people, the prominent ones—pretty girls, class officers, teachers, weirdos. And Washington's skin color made him prominent.

I also watched how Miz Tisdale dealt with Washington. He never volunteered to speak, and when she called on him to answer a question, which was rare, she smiled carefully, freezing her face into a simulacrum of encouragement. Since Washington was not a good student, she had to exert herself to keep her smile from pursing into a moue of contempt.

She was much more at ease when he fell asleep in class, which he often did because he worked nights at a grocery store and came to school directly from work. His head flopped backward, his mouth dropped open, and he snored.

"Washington!" Miz Tisdale called, smiling openly, amused.

When he didn't wake up, she called his name again, fractionally louder, "Washington!" and she conspiratorially arched a plucked and penciled eyebrow at the rest of us, inviting us to share her amusement. He was a deep sleeper. Sometimes she called his name four or five times before he jolted awake and found the whole class staring at him. He shook his head ruefully and grinned an embarrassed grin, silent but elaborately deferential. Miz Tisdale was almost joyous at these moments. Her face shone with pleasure as she informed him that we were now on page 102 of *Silas Marner*, and he could join us there if he so desired. She happily played the lady of the house who had found the butler napping in the pantry. She knew exactly how to mix surface respect with elegant and deniable contempt—because, for all she knew, the NAACP just might be monitoring how she treated Washington.

When she wasn't watching for Washington's head to loll, Miz Tisdale waxed poetic about the lazy magnolia charms of the South.

"We live," she said, "a slower and more gracious life here than they do in the North. We talk slowly, taking pleasure in our words. We take the time to get to know one another. We aren't like the Yankees, who rush, rush, rush. They talk fast and harshly and they don't care about people as people. They are only interested in what you can do for them."

Miz Tisdale was not gladdened when I said that the southerners in my Southern Baptist Church weren't slow at all. After the eleven o'clock service, they blasted out of the parking lot like Richard Petty so they could get home in time for kickoff. But Miz Tisdale, a Presbyterian, did not consider Southern Baptists to be southerners, except in the most technical sense. We were mountain folk who had moved to town for jobs. We were hillbillies with pretensions.

The following year, in American history, Miz Reebles celebrated southern life even more rapturously than Miz Tisdale did in English. Miz Reebles extolled the filial—no, the spiritual—ties that bound slave to master as strongly as it bound master to slave. All this business about slaves being whipped was grossly overstated. Why, a slave back then cost as much as a Cadillac Coupe de Ville did today, and people don't go beating on their Cadillac cars, do they?

I was dubious. In the parking lot of Biff Burger, where I'd worked that summer, I'd seen a boy whose girlfriend had dumped him punch and kick his Ford Galaxy until it was a misshapen lump of steel. After two hours, he sank to his knees on the asphalt, sobbing and retching. His hands were raw, bloody shreds. One knuckle shone out of the torn flesh like a white marble.

And just as you'd polish your Cadillac every Sunday, Miz Reebles said, masters took good care of their slaves. They had a big investment in them, and if recent history had taught us nothing else, it had taught us that Negroes, once they're free, didn't know how to govern themselves. And now they want to bring all their violence, crime, and illegitimacy over to our side of town, where it is not wanted.

But they're not stupid. Most of them knew they couldn't take care of themselves, and when the Yankee soldiers came to them and said, "Grandpa, you can go now. You don't have to stay here, working for your master," the old slaves told the Yankees, "Where would I go? No sir, it's fall and I got a crop to get in."

Recent research, Miz Reebles assured us, proved that the absolute best diet for someone doing stoop labor all day was cornbread, greens, and blackstrap molasses. And that was exactly what the masters fed their slaves. There's a powerful lot of vitamins in blackstrap molasses. Why, she herself took a tablespoon of it every day.

Oh, children, we were poor, poor, poor in the South. The Yankees had robbed us blind, robbed us of everything but our pride. Why, the Yankees had even forced poor helpless widow-women *at gunpoint* to dig up the family silver buried in the backyard and turn it over to rapists and murderers. But even worse than the wah-uh was the oppressive yoke of the Supreme Court, under which we labored today. *Brown* vs. *Board of Education, Topeka, Kansas,* was a simple travesty of justice. It was based, God knows, on psychology and sociology, not constitutional law. Psychology and sociology!

Some teachers went even further, deliberately twitting those twelve black-robed busybodies on the Supreme Court. In my senior analysis class, Miz Gorrie conducted daily Scripture readings. She passed the Bible around the room and when it got to you, you could read a passage out loud or pass it on. The first couple of times the Bible ended up in my hands, I, feeling coerced, blandly read the great clichés of the faith: "For God so loved the world that he gave his only begotten son"—a verse that about half the readers chose—or "And now abideth faith, hope, and charity, these three; but the greatest of these is charity." The next couple of times that it came around to me, I smirked and passed the Bible to the girl sitting in front of me, just to show that I could. But, later, convinced that no one actually listened, I began to read random, disjointed selections. No response. I read lurid, violent passages from the Old Testament. Miz Gorrie just smiled and nodded pleasantly at me. The other students stared ahead as blankly as though I'd just read John 3:16 again. So I began to read the verses of the passages backward. No one seemed to notice, and with typical southern cussedness I was both gratified to get away with my small blasphemy and appalled that nobody was appalled by it.

II

I was becoming southern, or rediscovering myself as a southerner—an understanding that crystallized for me one morning as I walked down Court Street to Lanier from my family's rented house on National Street, a long trudge in the cold. I was talking to myself out of boredom when I suddenly realized I was talking with a southern accent and that it felt good. The lengthening i's, the dropped g's, the fading postvocalic r's felt natural on my lips, felt right—and I experienced them for the first time as a sensual pleasure. Before, when I was living in California, I'd tightened my jaw and clipped my vowels, trying not to sound southern, because the other kids called me a hick, a hillbilly, a farmer—*farmer* being the preeminent term of contempt in Orange County in the early sixties. Rediscovering my southern voice in Montgomery locked in a sense of "This is who I am, a person who talks like this," and since I talked southern, southern is what I must be.

At the end of my senior year—in 1969, the height of the Wallace era—I was involved in one of the first episodes of interracial dating at Lanier. Maybe *the* first. When I called to ask Monica Goldman to the graduation dance, she agreed to be my date and then cheerfully informed me that she'd really wanted to go with Luther Simmons, a black student, but her parents had refused to let her. Though she made it clear I was her second choice, I felt I had to go to the dance with her: I'd asked and she'd agreed. I did not possess the cool presence of mind to inquire of Monica Goldman, "Why are you telling me this?"

We double-dated with some friends of hers, and at her door I presented her with the corsage I'd ordered two weeks before—a huge white carnation graced with a blue pipe cleaner twisted into the letter L. I'd picked it up at the florist's on Friday afternoon and kept it in the refrigerator overnight. The carnation was still cool when I lifted it out of its clear plastic box and pinned it to the strap of Monica's blue gown. She giggled when the back of my fingers rubbed clumsily against her pale hot shoulder.

At the old Civic Center downtown, Monica boogied with an explosive abandon. Released by the heavy beat of Billy Joe Royal's band, she shimmied her full hips and shook her pale shoulders with the self-aware sexual force of a fully grown woman, while I, practically tone deaf, shuffled to the beat. The narcissistic sexual power of her dancing left me behind, alone on the dance floor, and in truth I was relieved that she did not expect me to follow her.

After a few dances, Monica yelled above the music that she had to go to the ladies' room, and for fifteen or twenty minutes I stood by the stage, watching Billy Joe Royal sweat. He was famous for "Down in the Boondocks," which had reached number nine on the pop charts. The dance committee was very proud to have signed a name act—one even more famous than the Classics Four, who, a month before, had played their hit "Spooky" four times at the prom.

What was taking Monica so long? Had she lost me in the crowd? I pushed through dancers doing the pony, the frug, the bugaloo, and when I found people I knew I asked them if they'd seen her. Betsy, a girl in my French class, said Monica was on the other side of the room, dancing with some black guy.

I worked my way again through the crowd of dancers, moving cautiously this time, until I saw Monica and Luther, whom I had never met, dancing. The other dancers had pulled back from them, and Monica had seized the space they'd given her, throwing her hips loosely and aggressively with the music.

Numb, affronted, I circled the outside of the crowd and sat down on one of the Civic Center's old swivel-bottom seats. Because the seats were higher than the dance floor, I could watch Monica and Luther while I tried to think of what to do. I'd never even *heard* of a girl who'd gone off with another boy at a school dance. There were several iron-clad rules, rules designed to keep fighting to a minimum, and one was that you danced with the one what brung you, as the saying goes. And even with those rules fights broke out. You'd be dancing with your date, and suddenly a boy, rabbit punched, would careen backward through the crowd, scattering people, knocking them aside.

I just wanted to leave the dance and go home, but because we'd double-dated I didn't have a car. I had to wait at least three hours till the dance ended, then cadge a ride from friends. Sitting there, staring at the dancers, I knew I looked pathetic and dejected. The unhappiness that showed on my face was partly real, partly adolescent histrionics that I hadn't learned to suppress—and partly I was trying to make Monica feel guilty. But inside, to my surprise, I was strangely detached and pleased at how clearly I could understand what was happening. I could see that Monica didn't care about Luther any more than she cared about me. From the haughty sexual strut of her dancing and the gratified and determined look on her face, I could see she reveled in being the center of attention, reveled at being looked at because she was dancing with a black guy, reveled at thumbing her nose at her parents. She shimmied her shoulders so hard that the corsage flew off and skittered under the feet of other dancers. She laughed.

Was it more humiliating for me that she had dumped me for a black guy, I wondered. Nope. Same humiliation. I felt pretty good about my liberal humanism. But didn't it make things worse in the eyes of all the other people in this dingy civic center in the heart of the Deep South? Was I expected to stomp over to the dancing couple and punch him out? I might could have. He was about my height and skinny, with thick black-rimmed glasses. He was, I believe, a trombone player in the marching band. I actually tried to work up a little racial animosity. But, "My God, she's abandoned me for a black man" just sounded hopelessly self-aggrandizing. What really wounded me was another great southern passion: manners. Monica's using me as a beard and then ditching me without a word just seemed like plain bad manners.

What about the girl Luther must have brought to the dance and then dumped? Was she sitting somewhere, fuming? Should I try to find her and talk to her? Should I ask her to dance? But that would've taken more generosity of spirit than I could muster under the circumstances.

During the dance, friends stopped by to talk to me and to offer me rides home afterward. My friend Betsy, one of those preternaturally mature high school students who at seventeen is already a fully adult woman, stalked over to Monica during the band's second break, pulled her aside, and said, "Don't you know how unhappy you're making Andrew? *He's* your date."

"I'm not doing anything to him!" Monica snarled. "He can be miserable if he wants to be."

When Betsy reported the conversation to me, I laughed out loud. Even then, seventeen and miserable, I could hear in Monica's retort the delicious theatrical wickedness of an actress who loves playing the soap-opera vixen. It clarified the situation for me.

After that summer, I have seldom thought about the graduation dance except to marvel at my own young understanding that what happened had almost nothing to do with me. I date the beginnings of my emotional maturity to that evening. But now, thinking back on it, I'm puzzled at how, sitting for three hours on the rickety swivel-bottomed seat of the old Civic Center, I seriously pondered whether my failing to fight a black guy I had never seen before and have never seen since, over a woman I no longer even liked, might somehow mark me forever as a coward in the eyes of people amid whom I would probably live the rest of my life. And I am very happy that time and distance have left me puzzled by what I thought. Then, I understood it perfectly.

In the fall, I entered Huntingdon College, a small Methodist school about a mile from my father's house. I attended classes in the morning, and at noon I drove downtown to my job at Solomon Brothers, a dry-goods wholesaler that had been in Montgomery since before the Civil War, when cotton factors operated huge warehouses on the Alabama River. In the basement of Solomon Brothers, I cut cloth into squares and pasted them to stiff glossy paper, making sample cards for the sales reps. On breaks I'd walk around the decaying center of town—some struggling stores, empty storefronts, and the government offices and thriving banks that kept Montgomery from becoming a ghost town. On short breaks I'd dash to Capitol Book and News, the one good bookstore in town, where I'd flirt with books I couldn't afford to buy.

A year later, my wife and I would go to Capitol Book and News on our first date, and ten years later still, when our marriage was dying, I'd stand in the same bookstore, anxiously flipping through the books I still couldn't afford while I waited for her to get off work at a law firm across the street.

On Saturdays, when I worked all day, I'd punch out at noon, gobble lunch, punch back in at 12:15, and while everyone else was still eating I'd sneak out for a walk. Forty-five minutes at the minimum wage: I could make ninety cents as I hurried up Commerce Street to Dexter Avenue and then hiked up to the white, domed capitol building perched atop Goat Hill. Walking quickly, I passed Kress's dime store and H. L. Green's. Four years from now, during a summer stint as a Nabisco salesman, I'd slam Nilla Wafers, Ritz crackers, and Chips Ahoy! cookies on Green's dusty jumbled shelves and then race to the next store on my list.

On the corner of Dexter and Lawrence I always glanced down the side street, checking to see what kung-fu movie was playing at the Pekin Theater. I rushed on past the state supreme court building, where, standing on the marble steps leading up to the forbidding metal doors, my wife would be sworn in as an attorney in the blistering July sun. Across the street stood the Dexter Avenue Baptist Church, Martin Luther King's old church, which, not yet a tourist attraction, had fallen into shabby disrepair.

At the capitol, I always paused a moment and stood on the bronze star that marked the exact spot where Jefferson Davis stood when he took the oath of office as the first and only president of the Confederacy. On a high school field trip, I had pounced on the star with both feet and proclaimed loudly, "I feel the power to rip the Union asunder!" Miz Warr—that was her name—told me to shut up and get back in line—the very words that I would hear burst angrily from my own lips many times when I was, for one miserable year, a teacher at an elementary school here in town.

Behind the capitol, the green lawns dropped to Monroe Street. On flattened cardboard boxes I would soon slide, laughing, down that slope and tumble onto the sidewalk with my wife, who was not yet my wife, and eleven years later I would slide down them again, again laughing, with the woman I loved after her.

From the capitol I'd swing by the Little White House of the Confederacy, deliciously located on the corner of Union Street. Jefferson Davis lived briefly in the small clapboard house—now a historical shrine—before he and the capital moved to Richmond. After riffling my palm across the top of the fence slats, another ritual I always followed, I cut back to Dexter Avenue, walking downhill now on the other side of the street. The ancient battered city buses laboring up Dexter Avenue were as commonplace and dingy as the diesel smoke they fouled the air with. Dingy, commonplace—yet charged with history by Rosa Parks's famous refusal to move to the back of one and by the long boycott that followed. Now the buses were mostly filled with black women and driven by black men—a change that seemed so deeply historical, so saturated with ambiguous significance, as to be almost mythological.

Hurrying to get back to work before one o'clock, and sweating in the noon heat, I rushed past Belk's department store. My mother loved Belk's because there was one in her hometown when she was a child. "Belk's," she said, "is the only store that really has good sales"—a judgment I remembered in its exact wording every time I passed the store. At Belk's, she bought me for five dollars a pair of olive-green wingtips that I polished and polished and polished until they turned almost brown. I wore them to the Junior-Senior Prom and the graduation dance with the suit she bought on sale at Belk's for eighteen dollars—a shapeless black suit of the sort that street-corner preachers wear so as not to seem worldly. I was mortified by the suit, and judging from the look on her face when she first saw it, so was Monica Goldman.

On my very first trip downtown, when I was fifteen, I saw in front of Belk's a black man fry an egg on the hood of his Dodge Dart. The egg white set slowly in the broiling noon heat, and I was fascinated. I wanted to stay and see him flip the egg over. I wanted to see if any of the car's baby-blue paint flecked off on the egg. I wanted to be able to say confidently that I lived in a place where you could fry an egg on the hood of your car because I'd seen it done. But my mother hustled me out of the crowd and on to the next chore on her list, whatever it was.

Glancing at my watch, picking up my pace, I cut across Court Square, where, before the war, slaves were bought and sold. Here, Mary Chesnut, author of the famous *Diary from Dixie*, became physically ill—"seasick"—to see a bright mulatto banter from the auction block with the buyers in the crowd, confident of her fate. She already knew who would purchase her, and why. Mrs. Chesnut had to sit for a moment on a stool to "discipline" her thoughts.

At two minutes of one, I slipped back into the basement of Solomon Brothers, ahead of the people returning from lunch. When my boss returned to the workroom, he found me industriously gluing cloth to paper as if I'd been doing it unsupervised for the last forty-five minutes. At the end of my freshman year, Solomon Brothers up and moved to Atlanta, where everything goes, and within five years the empty warehouse was razed and the new—now old—Civic Center was slapped down in its place.

Years later I interviewed for a full-time job at Auburn University at Montgomery, where I'd been a part-time instructor for two years. I'd begun publishing poems in literary journals, so as the interview dwindled into conversation, one of the professors said, "Do you feel Montgomery has given you a sort of mythic landscape to write about or write from?"

I was almost thirty years old now, teaching part time and selling shirts the other part of the time, struggling to get by in a cultural backwater that I loved for being a backwater even though it was almost impossible to buy, say, books of contemporary poetry.

"Yes, absolutely," I said, lying. I needed the job.

But the more I've thought about his question—and I've thought about it a lot from that day to this—the more I have come to see that the professor was on to something—though I still quail at the word *mythic*. Somehow, without my entirely meaning it to, the town that I often hated and was seldom happy in wound its history into my life, and the intensity of my unhappiness and the desperation of my laughter have tightened my bond to the strange, fierce history of the state. Intensity has a way of being, well, intense.

Two years after I divorced and left Montgomery, I was standing on a street corner in Saratoga Springs, New York, waiting for a traffic light to change. Across the street, a policeman suddenly pointed his pistol at a young black man and yelled at him to lean against the wall of the Adirondack Trust. I crossed the street and joined a cluster of people who had stopped to observe the arrest. The cop patted down the man, handcuffed him, and marched him to the police car. Helping him into the backseat, the white cop delicately tilted the black man's head forward so it wouldn't smack the roof on the car, and the man said, "Yes man, thanks."

I carried that event in my head for a long time, mulling it over, because I didn't truly understand what I'd seen. I didn't know what the black man had done, or might have done, but, more disturbingly for me, I couldn't imagine, except in numb and useless clichés, what I had witnessed on that street at that moment in a town one thousand miles from home. In Montgomery, I thought as I stood there, watching the police cruiser pull away from the curb, I'd understand what I just saw. I might not like it, but at least historically, culturally, politically, personally, even spiritually, I could comprehend what was happening in front of me. Montgomery is the one place where I know what things mean, and I, for better or worse, now study the world with that understanding.

PHYLLIS ALESIA PERRY

The First Place

Nineteen sixty-five.

My mama's mother stands at the edge of the red-water pond. She is a rounded mountain of warm brown.

We have walked through the pasture to get here, past my grandfather's lazily drifting cattle. The woods make their noises and I dance around her skirt. I play with rocks and dirt. She plants her feet in the gummy Bullock County clay, spits on the red wiggler on her fishhook, and holds the line for bream and coyly elusive bass.

I am really small. Mama works in a not-so-distant town. Where my grandmother and I stand is not a town. It is a place, and one not created by geography alone. This community of trees and land and souls stamped on the Alabama map somewhere between Union Springs and Troy is the center of human perseverance. I don't know that in 1965. I only know that I can't remember a place before this place.

My mama and her five sisters were born here. They call it Perote. It whisks by almost unnoticed from car windows, only revealing itself in a corner-of-the-eye glimpse of a Co'Cola sign outside a crooked-board store. Or as gravestones rise on a hill planted with generations of dead white bones.

Departed black folk rest a little further on and off the road a bit, behind a screen of struggling pines and wayward weeds. A collapsing church ruin is a shabby honor guard for the dust of the ancestors. My great-great grands. My second-oldest aunt's two young sons lie there under short slabs. And Jeanette Hattie, my grandmother's mother. And more to come. But more dead folk than live ones here, where the glue that holds everybody in their place gets thinner with every drumbeat that sounds from the front lines of Montgomery, Selma, and Birmingham.

I ain't from here, if you want to just deal with the facts. Ain't from no place else, if you want to just deal with the heart. My mama left my birthplace and replanted me in the place from which she had sprung. It was like she knew. Atlanta is merely flash and clamor compared to the drawn-out hymn that is Perote. Atlanta is the noisy part of me; Perote is stillness and echoing laughter; it is old joy and old pain.

Nineteen sixty-one. My cue to enter.

Martin and Malcolm are still breathing—hard. JFK and RFK. Marilyn and Langston. Jo Baker and Louis Armstrong. Lester Maddox is stomping around Georgia, and George Wallace is stomping around Alabama, sharpening their words like swords, on the cusp of power. There has been much mourning; there is much mourning to come.

I have since returned to my unassuming and weary-looking birthplace on a surprisingly narrow Butler Street in downtown Atlanta. As if just looking at the place could give me any real clue to myself. Back then it was the hospital you went to if you were Negro and didn't want to go to the public hospital across the street. My father insisted that's where I would be born, although when the moment arrived he wasn't around to make sure his wishes had been obeyed.

He was born at the public hospital across the street, although it was a long time before I knew this. Only after I became forever angry about things he did not do did these kinds of miscellaneous facts appear. They often do after you decide on anger, after you have no use for them. So he was born at Grady Hospital, which also is where, thirty-something years and one first wife later, he met my mother, a nursing student with the glow of clean Alabama air still on her cheeks. Before all *that*. Before she came back to Alabama with her spirit beaten up.

Nineteen sixty-two.

I leave my grandmother's house and go to my grandmother's house. Daddy's mama probably doesn't know that when I leave Atlanta in my Aunt Bettye's arms for what is billed as a summer visit that I will be gone for good. But as the leaves begin to wither, my mother, the fifth daughter of six, comes home, too, with suitcases and resolve. I guess Daddy's sweet mama cries, missing us, even as Mama's mama embraces us.

Granddaddy doesn't like the whole business. A woman leaving her husband. But he's already taught her strength of will. There's nothing he could do about that now.

When Mama works, she lives in a room or apartment or something at the place she works. She comes down to Perote on her days off. Then we can stand together on our own ground.

Great-grandmama Jeanette Hattie bought the first piece of land from *them*. She insisted on it. She worked for the well-off proprietors of the cotton gin and lived in a house they owned on land they owned. Every day she cooked for them. They told her she could live in the house for the rest of her life. No, she said, I want it for more than the rest of my life. And so she left this little piece of the world for us. Granddaddy added more land, land where he drives his tractor, calls his cows, and feeds his bird dogs, where he worry-walks through his fields. In the summer his head bobs up and down between the corn rows sometimes softly singing. Sometimes, I guess, practicing one of his sermons in his head for Sunday or revival or some other opportunity to love and fear God.

"God ain't making no more land," he is known to say. Family and land, God and work. The world is just that.

Nineteen sixty-four.

Mama rents a basement apartment and takes me off to live with her. I still land in my grandparents' laps on the weekends while she works. My grandfather, who used to marvel at my infant accomplishments, is more distant now, more stern. "Every time I get attached to one, they leave," he said when my mother got ready to move me. He thought I was going to live there forever, fetching his glasses and chattering away at his feet.

"That's her child," my grandmother said. "Every child should be raised by their own mother if they can."

But still, on the weekends and during the summers (when cousins also arrive) I live a child's paradise, while they work. Mama and Granddaddy and Grandmama, too, who works all the time. Sometimes standing, sometimes sitting in her chair with her hands always on something, a needle, cloth, or peas that need shelling. Something. Sometimes calming the ladies in church. Sometimes fishing, when she seems to be doing something and nothing all at the same time.

She spits on the bait. Even when she baits the hook at the end of the smallest, lightest cane pole she can find and puts it in my hands. *Don't fall in that water!* I creep to the edge of things and place my offering beneath the surface of the muddy mirror. My plaits reflected there are spindly rays around my head, like ones I draw on Crayola suns.

I am really small and she is solid rock. And time doesn't move while we stand there doing our meditations.

Somewhere she still stands, I think, though I am a witness to that moment when she falls down forever.

Nineteen sixty-seven.

And it is January, I think. It is chilly and dark in a way that only winter in the deep woods can be. The house is cold, my grandfather away. She moves from the fireside, where she has been fingering needlework on her lap, and goes down the hall, complaining of a headache, leaving her work on her chair.

Somewhere she still stands, though it is true I hold her head in my child's lap while she dies, slowly, her brain being starved by years of delicious death in the form of fatback and such. It was stroke, I learn much later, that caused her to fall down like that. I find her and kneel and hold her head. She murmurs almost soothingly, her heavy skull squishing my skinny thighs. I don't dare leave her.

She still stands, though Granddaddy finds us when he returns from Perote store, an eternity having come and gone. The brown mountain and her little one sprawled together on the new bathroom vinyl. Me long since weary of calling her name, her long since weary of trying to answer. I believe Granddaddy put that new bathroom in himself, when he decided an outhouse was too tedious for a modern man such as himself. Just as he and his brothers had built, years before, this house we will all now mourn in.

Not yet six, I see my mama's mother finally made small by death, shrinking there in the casket at the front of Perote Baptist Church.

But when my mind and heart wanders looking for her, it is usually at the muddy pond that I find her. Sometimes little me is with her as she stands, her hat tilted against the sun, her eyes intent on the cork bobbing in the water, her hard-life fingers around the long, supple cane, waiting for the jerk on the end of the line.

Two thousand.

Last time I see that pond, young pines have edged up to the rim. The old pasture has become a mini pulpwood forest punctuated with knee-high grass. Best to navigate it wearing hard, tall boots and stomp through to warn the snakes as you approach. You don't see that muddy water until you almost step into it, one foot on the bank and one suspended over the gently rippling surface.

And the air smells the same, but we are all different. People you love fall down and sink into the hard ground, rising again in dreams.

Granddaddy joined the ancestors in 1993, and we laid him right there beside Grandmama. But he visits me sometimes when I sleep, a much happier man than the one I used to know.

Life is motion. Love in human form moves away from each other, then comes back together. And the beloved ones return to you, but not as the people you knew before. They are not the untouchable, the all-powerful, the almost supernatural beings you remember. Even as a child, I wondered about everything that was inside of them all. Everything that was inside of every person, dead or alive, who survived it all, whether I knew them or not. I wanted to know things about them that they didn't know themselves. Childhood is decades gone, and I still grope with the tips of my fingers, with the edge of my consciousness, for who they are and how they became me.

I don't remember when I began to *feel* stories about people I've never met. Who knows if they're real or not—the stories or the people? As much as I love facts, somehow I know that facts don't matter as much as truth. The desire for truth is the gift that has brought family closer. It has made me understand that the separations of time are only shadow.

So I learn to listen and to watch for whatever signs present themselves. I watch the cork bob on the surface of the water, even when the surface seems still, and know that all stories move in a circle, forever rippling out from some unknowable center.

No, I ain't from here. I belong to many places both "real" and imagined, both tangible and mythic. But sometimes when I close my eyes in the quiet I'm in Perote, as close as I come to being somewhere called home. And it's from home—good or bad—that all stories come.

R O D N E Y   J O N E S

A Half Mile of Road
in North Alabama

Briefly, I would like to illuminate the community where I grew up: small houses about a quarter of a mile apart, of whitewashed or unpainted clapboard, each with a well and outhouse, the larger houses with barns, chicken coops, toolsheds, and smokehouses. These were the late fifties and sixties, and we were small farmers and day laborers, mainly self-sufficient, mainly of Scotch-Irish, English, and German descent, with perhaps a faint and legendary tincture of Cherokee blood. Here and there, some farmer, like my grandfather, might have endured the eighth grade and learned a little Latin, but the larger part of our learning came across the fence and from the other side of the bucksaw. Culturally, we saw ourselves as pioneers as much as southerners or Alabamians. Neither much money nor light had arrived, and for every six automobiles, there would come a horse-drawn wagon, often trailed by a great gawky colt.

The Nesmith house, where we lived until I was six, had evolved from a log cabin to a dogtrot, and then the dogtrot had been boarded in to make a hall between the west side's living room, kitchen, and pantry and the east side's two bedrooms. Stone chimneys stood at each end of the house, and above us an attic, rich with miscellany: a spinning wheel with spavined and missing spokes, a warped sidesaddle, boxes of wood tools, gaiters, spectacles, dried gloves, and shoe lasts. You got to the attic through a kitty-holed door that opened off the front porch, which was a few feet from the well house and the well, into which, it has been told, I once dropped a Persian cat.

Under us, my great-grandfather Nesmith had excavated a rectangular space where he kept in a large wooden cask his wine bottles. The cask and bottles remained, testament to one who had survived that era when the hard-shell feminism of the great Protestant revival had quarried from saloons and brothels legions of southern infidels and restored them to their families. "God dammit," he had said once when a neighbor invited him into a ditch to take a swig, "I ain't never hid to take a drink in my life, and I don't intend starting now." Although my folks were teetotalers, they admired Tom Nesmith and kept the instructions that he left for his funeral service (no preachers) and burial (in the plain cedar box that he had made).

They cared less for that remnant of customers who would occasionally void a decade and show up drunk, but such visits only bolstered his continuance in our lives. In that space under the floor, I constructed my first roads and cities, and whatever consciousness I possess spreads outward from there in a tentative, grappling wonder. Just east of the house his vineyard of small, sour grapes still clung to the rusting baling wire strung between rotting fence posts. Behind the house and chicken house, his outhouse stood like a sentinel. There was a garden and a smokehouse where hams, shoulders, and side meat lay buried in separate salt bins, and west of the smokehouse, the barn, and then the hog lot. We were on a little foothill of a larger wooded foothill, which we thought of as a mountain.

A dirt road in front of our house stretched east and west of us alongside that mountain. To the west, it went downhill around a curve and passed the old Jones schoolhouse on the left, which had been turned into a residence after the county had consolidated the schools. There were still holes for the school toilet in the woods east of the house. As a boy, my cousin Leroy, a sheep-farmer and preacher whose visionary preelection sermons portended the religious right, had fallen in one of those holes and had to be rescued with a rope. It was a story that my parents delighted in, one of many of the old schoolhouse. Now the Flowerses—Coyd and Martha and their children, Junior, Linda, and Jenny—lived there, and just beyond them, across the garden, there was a clay-floored shack, where an old man whittled and hummed and every so often slung his head abruptly to the right to eject his chaw.

I do not recall the year when the old man and the shack vanished, but then as now, the true way through the valley was not by road but by story. It extended to the remotest parts of thickets between fields. The form of the story was a mystery, and it was not exactly handed down, but added to and subtracted from and totaled differently by each citizen as the sum and account, so that it could be further revised and debated. The story went on inside each solitary head, as beans were strung and hay was baled and it never ceased, never went away, or located itself precisely on the sorts of oratorical occasions and in the places that scholars would like to imagine as the mainstays of the oral tradition.

If one were to dig up a pistol so clotted with dirt and corrosion that it was barely identifiable as a pistol, that pistol would be reunited with its owner: first as the toy of a dead second cousin, then as the real pistol of a man named Quattlebaum. If one were to gaze out over a pasture and make some meaningless remark, one would hear how, during the Second World War, as a plane had passed over that pasture, a leather satchel had dropped. James Hardin, working in the pasture at the time, had thought it a bomb and sprinted toward safe ground, but, when the satchel did not explode, he had returned and brought it home, and the next day the pilot had come out and claimed it.

The story jumped time. It was variegated and layered. Some parts traveled only among men in the rough discourse of men, others more subtly and enigmatically among women: at quilting bees, Ladies Home Demonstration Club and Missionary Society meetings. We young overheard what we were not capable of interpreting, but the truths of fiction were hardening in us like bone. The story was the road that traveled almost to the interiors of lives, the human presence in what was still held to be a wild place, and its scenes were the ones that we knew.

At the top of the mountain near the right-of-way for the power lines, my cousin Raymond and his brother Anthony had seen a mountain lion in the late thirties. In a grown-over field west of the creek, a scion of the valley had once come upon a widow-woman and made a thoroughly indecent proposal. She had paused for a moment and then said, "Beats hoeing cotton, I reckon." It is a little-known anecdote, but I allow it. The story was of vulgar and biblical rootstocks, but the two strands usually grew side by side and did not mix.

A part of the story came from song and another part from prayer. Sunday morning benediction was an event, for each potential supplicant wore different rhetorical finery. Most spoke in an antique register, thou and thying with the diction and syntax of the King James English that the master himself spoke. Some wept as they prayed. Everyone employed codes. For thorn in the flesh, read menopause. For burden, read imprisoned son. Certain prayers we dreaded. Leroy's election-season benedictions sometimes stretched for half an hour. Though chickens were plucked for frying, sweet pies waited in ovens, and Leroy's political visions veered far to the right of most, these prayers were generally tolerated, for they were given with a measured glory and seemed in substance and artfulness the stuff of literature, a story that was almost as graven and eloquent as a poem.

The story was so vast that it occupied every moment of barter, and it impeded the ever-encroaching money economy, for no payment could ever occur without an exchange also of stories, and a good enough story, droned out with sufficient relish and on a low enough frequency, might be accepted as currency. In full story drawl, augmented by chaw or cigar, a man might tweak and torture a single vowel for six seconds. In fact, the slowness with which a story was told added to its value, for the story and the song were essentially dilatory, forms of shade and respite from the heat of the midday sun. And later, when men and women were done with a day's work and were offered pay, the customary refusal occasioned another story, the one that leaned into the dusky-dark and made supper late. Then, of course, the money was paid, and the story about the story got told at the supper table, and the next morning the road was there in the very place we lived.

There by the whittler's shack, if you followed the side road to the south, you would come to the Jones home place, now the domicile of Leroy and his mother, Aunt Dilly, and finally to the cemetery, which offered the best view of Fairview. But if you continued west, you passed a renter house where Jim Watts, his wife, Alma, and their children, Gene, James, Shirley, and Larry, lived. My Great-Uncle Freddy and Aunt Ella had raised their family there before moving south to Cullman County, but we called it the Monk house, for a Monk had built the house. After my uncle had lived in the house, he sold it to a man named Vada Laney, who sold it to my father. It was like that there. Each house had a history and two names: the name of the original inhabitant and the name of the current resident. Between the two names and before the names there was the story back to the clearing of ground.

I imagine the valley now because it has disappeared or been transformed, time-doctored and decimated. I do not know of any natural, waking imagination other than memory, fear, hunger, and desire, and each focuses mercilessly. A state like Alabama is too large, but I hold part of that road like blood. A black dog growls. The blind piano tuner passes with his driver. Nineteen fifty-four weds 1967. The life of the mind travels beyond the known ridges and enters the habitation of rumors. In the near distances lived possum eaters, snake handlers, and bootleggers. I did not doubt it. Nor that the angel of death had only a few years earlier ridden a white horse to the house where Nancy Cooper lay dying and taken her soul. My grandfather's father was there and saw it.

The road led west like the sun, and I usually went that way, too. Beyond the Monk house, you crossed on a plank bridge a creek that had once meandered through the fields and pastures but that had long since been channeled to control flooding. Once, when we dynamited a stump on the bank of our swimming hole, we came back to find the water roiling with snakes. My father shot one, a large female cottonmouth, and cut it open. Forty-eight young wriggled out, but this did nothing to defer play. At the bridge, you stood in the center of the community, with the mountain southeast, south, and west of you, so that the ground of the valley felt like the grounds of a stadium.

Farther along, my grandparents' house and barn sat on the right and the Fairview Church of God on the left. My grandparents' house was a neat, square two-bedroom house with green shutters. There were always cats in the yard, for my grandmother fed them freshly squirted milk each morning and evening, and in the barn lot, Charlie and Nell, the elderly horse team that my grandfather had purchased as yearlings in 1938, still held court over the seven or eight milk cows. That house stood a little in front of the concrete porch of their previous house, which had burned in the early fifties. The church, too, was connected with disaster, as it had been moved from the southwest corner of the valley after a tornado had blown away the old church. Some still connected the tornado to the controversy over the appropriateness of makeup and earrings.

We attended the church three times a week, twice on Sundays and once on Wednesday night for prayer meetings and Bible study. To my mother, who had been reared Methodist, the church needed finesse and a more dignified service, free of foot washings, of amens and say-its, but her spiritual negotiations remained open. She studied what she heard and read and took what heartened her as gospel, but she did not condone all opinions or Scripture. Especially, she disliked Paul, whose pronouncements on marriage, sexuality, and divorce struck her as so fanatical as to be almost diabolical. She suggested to my sister and me that, ultimately, we should not be instructed in religious matters. The honest heart would tell. Nevertheless, salvation was expected of us, and this troubled me.

Most young people in our area were saved at great countywide revivals, where not only a duck-tailed and pomaded evangelist but also selected all-conference halfbacks witnessed and professed their Christianity, and where altar calls might yield as many as three hundred souls a night. But my family did not attend those revivals, and it took more mettle to be saved at the Fairview Church of God. One had to kneel before the entire congregation and weep heroically as one repented one's sins. The less theatrically inclined often declined the call. Occasionally, the storms of puberty or alcoholism might spirit some particularly wayward soul to the altar, but usually we went home as we had come.

Not that we were not saddened to the task. A good country evangelist has been seasoned in the very rhetoric of the tear ducts. His discourse migrates ever so gently from Saul, who was struck blind and did see, to the days of his own alcoholism, to personal recollections of young men and women who had felt the conviction of the spirit and almost made the decision to accept Jesus on the last night of a revival but did not heed the call. These died. Invariably. Horribly. Usually in head-on collisions that left a profusion of limbs scattered and burning among the fumes of alcohol. A few survived the ambulance ride. The evangelist would arrive at their bedsides just in time to hear the last words, "Brother McGuire, why are my feet so hot?"

These were only appetizers. The main course did not materialize until my grandmother began navigating on the old upright "Softly and Tenderly Jesus Is Calling." The region high in the back of my throat, which I had identified as the soul, would begin to salt and cramp. "Do you feel the presence of the Lord?" the evangelist would query. And, on this cue, certain of the saved and sanctified would mobilize and ever so softly and tenderly creep toward the known sinners in our midst: the cussers, drinkers, and smokers; those who were weary from all-night moonshine coonhunts; those that delighted in filthy jokes and crap games. These had been drawn to the social lights of the revival, and now they were hemmed in, with a kindly hand tender on their overall straps and a pious murmur soft in their ears.

The evangelist would now instruct my grandmother to play more softly. "I feel the conviction of the spirit moving among us," he would say. Concomitantly, the voices of the faithful would lower and sweeten, the minor chords take on a nearly funereal quality, so it would seem to the poor sinners that their own mothers and stillborn infants were serenading them from beyond the River Jordan. For anyone who has not witnessed it, there is a great beauty to that moment. Still, mostly these entreaties failed. "Don't harden your hearts," the evangelist would caution. He might revisit the aftermath of the automobile accident or some moment of his own life on skid row, how a blind woman approached him one day . . . and still, when no one came, the evangelist would change his strategy and establish what purchase he could find.

"Now, with every head bowed and every eye shut, I want to see the hands of you out there that feel the conviction of the Lord but aren't yet ready," and after an interlude of silence and brethrenly amenning, "Yes, I see that hand, yes, amen. He's calling. Yes, amen. . . ." Sometimes I would steal a look through squinted eyes and see either no hands or the hands of fugitive masturbation, and abusive marriages, and terminal diseases lifted furtively. Then the sermon would decrescendo. The children would be running frantically between the cars in the gravel parking lot while the adults wonderfulled the evangelist or chatted amicably of recipes and football.

By Wednesday night the hardened sinners would be driven away. The evangelist might attempt a healing or two, the rumor of which would swell attendance for the coming nights. Then the pressure rose again, but this time directed toward the vulnerable young. Much talk was given to "the age of accountability," that unspecifiable age when a child became magically eligible for eternal perdition. Almost invariably the emphasis of the sermon would be on the nature of that perdition: how God would hold the saved in one hand, the unsaved in the other, and cast the unsaved into a bottomless darkness, whence a terrible wailing could be heard.

I slept uncomfortably with that image, but I feared salvation at the altar as others feared the outcome of a biopsy. The act seemed not only a personal humiliation, but a surrender to a group that disturbed me. One Sunday school teacher suggested that black people were the Children of Cain, and I, a great admirer of Martin Luther King Jr., argued, but what power could my arguments have? I was either unsaved and therefore one of the damned or a child who could not be held accountable. Yet my desired conversion stuttered and halted when I thought of the altar. The thief on the cross who had been saved at the moment of his death struck me as a worthy example, as did my mother's brother, Bill, who had been asleep in his pew one Sunday morning when the minister made a call for new church members. When the man beside him rose and walked to the front, Uncle Bill had gone with him. He had joined the church in his sleep.

But Bill Owen was a Methodist. One did not "join" the Church of God. One got saved or burned, and, with the passing of each year, the flames intensified. "When are you going to get saved?" my Grandmother Jones would continually ask, and my Aunt Polly, the only college-educated member of our immediate family, might join in with stories of the salvation of various children of her knowing. Briefly, I had the idea that knowledge of Scripture might substitute for salvation and memorized scores of Bible verses, but sermon on sermon proclaimed only that one gate by which one might enter that kingdom whose citizens agreed on the five unspoken directives: "Don't smoke, don't drink, don't cuss, don't screw, don't go with girls who do."

The years seem to stretch through those days and interminable services like a smooth gray thread through a multicolored blanket. Hay was cut, fence wire was stretched between black locust and cedar posts, and graves hollowed out of the flinty clay. Across the Atlantic, the Beatles were making a stir, Kennedy had taken office in Washington, and violence was erupting at lunch counters in North Carolina, but in Fairview our daily life continued to move around hard work, from which no child or woman was released. I was a morbid child, and as I hoed cotton or cleared brush from a thicket, I would happily dream of being buried alive, scrambling and scratching at the lid of my casket, but inevitably the question of my mortal soul returned and I would despair.

Then, by virtue of what I still take for divine grace, I was given a portal. One night in a testimony meeting, a woman said that she had been saved not in a church but in a corncrib. A few weeks later, at Wednesday prayer meeting, the devotional leader announced that on this night each member of the congregation was to testify, telling how long and under what conditions they had been saved. One by one, the members stood, made an account, and went to stand in the place reserved for the choir, until I alone sat in the pews. I waited, with my neighbors, grandparents, mother, and sister in front of me, carefully averting their eyes from mine, and then I stood and walked to the front of the room. "I was saved in a cornfield two years ago," I said. So it came to pass that Brother Ralph Alexander lowered me backward into the holy water and, in the presence of family and neighbors, I rose as a new creature.

I am often told that I lack a spiritual dimension, and it must be true. When it comes to religion, I close my eyes and see not Jehovah and the angels, but an airbrushed, toothsome family from an old Sunday school quarterly. They ride along in their shining car, trying very hard to look beatific. I make every effort not to look beatific. I have an unnatural fondness for skepticism and more toleration of outright sarcasm than most Alabamians would brook. By my own dim lights, which my mother recommended, I have grown certain of uncertainty, suspicious of the possibility of any common under-standing of a deity that can be brought to utterance, yet I cleave to the existentialist wisdom of Ecclesiastes and the first verse of the first chapter of John, and the rhythms of the King James Bible stay with me, too, and the attitude of prayer. More important, I locate myself around that church, with the first known faces.

Such a community, in which a single place is not only before one but the central obsession of personal vision, may exist now, but I doubt it. We are residents of information zones and discourse communities, technological nomads who, with the twitch of a finger, may bring into focus disasters and sporting events from the other side of the planet. Such distance provides moral convenience. What is missing is our own involvement, our proximity, and relationship. The hard labor behind our ease remains anonymous. The very chickens we eat are strangers. While Fairview lacked range, its residents knew the sources of everything they touched.

Past the church there was the parsonage, then Louise and James Hardin's house, and, finally, at the intersection, Cousin Henry Hardin's store and house. Two Shell pumps stood in front of the store. Once my great-grandfather Jones had run a sorghum mill and sawmill, but now, aside from farming, the store was the only commerce. Cousin Henry, as befit a storekeeper, was preternaturally friendly, a bald country aristocrat with two fine sweet-spirited bald sons, Limuel and Noel. It took me a year when Noel returned to the valley from Detroit to tell them apart.

The Hardins were the western branch of my father's family. Cousin Henry's mother had been the sister of my great-grandfather Jones. Geneva, the oldest daughter, called "Jibba" by her nieces and nephews, lived with Cousin Henry and cared for him. Once a man from the next county began courting her and they became engaged, but one night at the door he asked for a kiss and she broke off the engagement. The younger daughter, Ola Mae, lived just south of the intersection with her husband, James McCarley. The Hardins were mostly known for their laughter, and the Joneses for making the Hardins laugh. Both branches of the family sang, and often you could hear the voice of Jibba or my grandmother, Daisy, working the refrain of "What a Friend We Have in Jesus" as they bent in the fields across the valley.

It felt as if we were all kin there, and mainly we were. Neither did kinship stop at the edge of the valley. It only diminished. Third cousins diminished to fourth cousins, and fourth cousins to fifth cousins until we were at a marriageable distance from home, which was the distance our fathers had traveled to court their girlfriends and wives, though the homely might have to go farther. My father, a handsome man, seemed to know all the country families in our county and half the families in the counties to our south and west. This was true of both black and white people. If he met people he did not know, he would ask about their mother's maiden name and keep shimmying the family tree until he found a branch that extended to a neighbor or himself.

To be a rural Alabamian of my age and era is to be inured to the long, slow view, the one in which the cemetery is ahead and our lives behind. It is no doubt a negative of vision to many, but it persists as mental occurrence. I go backward through the years and light on the earliest memories. Of all the qualities of that place and time, darkness is the one that I remember best, not the sort of darkness in which one stumbles from vague outline to vague outline, but cave darkness, space darkness, the kind of darkness that renders exact blindness. The windows would fill with it minute by minute, and then the sounds of night predation would begin. Snakes crept among the nests. Foxes slithered toward the hen house, and evil that had filled the sermons began to sap from the black books and the stories that the old men told.

How absolute that first light. How magical the extrusion of our waking hours and the hosannas of those shining appliances: electric ovens and heaters, well pumps, refrigerators. Where once they had played rook with neighbors, now my parents would sit up late, reading and listening to radio dramas and country music. My father wired our barn, and soon he took a job at Wolverine Tube in Decatur, Alabama. He purchased our first new car, a blue and white

1955 Chevrolet, tore down the Monk house, built a new ranch house there, and gave over the Nesmith house and the farm to sharecroppers. The money was as dizzying as the light. The centrifugal motion of the water in the toilet enchanted and terrified me. Suddenly and unpredictably, we felt almost indecently modern.

Yet my parents would not buy a television set for five more years, so my sister and I read and were encouraged to read real books. Dickens's London and Twain's American West were as real for me at ten as Henry Hardin's store and the Fairview Church of God. Books filled my head when I picked cotton or hauled hay, and books caused me to run the tractor through the fence in front of my father and the county agent. My most recurrent dream was that the place I lived in was not truly my home.

Today Fairview might be any rural neighborhood in southern Indiana or eastern Maine. The road is dotted with tract houses, no horses ever pass, and cars rush by on the pavement at eighty miles an hour. Electricity brought a greater music, a more masterful athleticism, an intelligence, and physical beauty, but it diluted what was near. To walk with my father in the woods was to learn the names of trees, bushes, and plants and the calls and plumage of birds. He was finely attuned to the sort of knowledge that is based in local talk and practicality and that seems most ancient. I have grown into the sort of man who knows both the names of trees and the images of trees but who does not put them together well.

Some few of us still alive in this country began with that darkness and in that sort of community that was so confident and complete in its locality that it seemed to defy the very idea of region. By the time I became aware of the concept of Alabama, it sickened and shamed me, for it seemed a place where knowledgeable people colluded with buffoons to promulgate an intolerable society based on racism and narrow, xenophobic interpretations of Scripture, yet I do not wish to resolve anything with that thought. The stupidities and brutalities of one age become the theater of the next. The paradox of region is that it is too large to produce great art. The port of the novel and painting is one room or one field. The actual scene inevitably surprises.

Place once whispered something unimpeachable and anomalous about a human being, and it still does, but it is damned odd. I have seen fishermen dancing to Herbie Hancock in El Salvador and known black Catholics from northern Minnesota. One of them, Georgia Yorama, told me that in a tribal village in Nigeria, on the wall of her husband's grandmother's room, she discovered a photograph of Dolly Parton. I delight with heartbreak to think of that, as if the cultural virus of my own Fairview had been incubated. Junior Flowers, the first of us to really take to broadcast, has gone into the ministry. As a boy, he worshiped Buddy Holly and Picasso, and when he was not beating on a guitar, he was painting huge unwieldy abstractions. They hung across from a pot-bellied stove in the living room, a foreign currency in our historical colony, but I remember them to this day. "I will remember you," he would say if I stepped on his foot or loaned him a pencil, "when I am famous."

WILLIAM COBB

When the Opry Was in Ryman and We Still Believed in God

Cletus Hickey was the most terrifying bully I encountered in my youth. He wore overalls without a shirt and was a head taller and fifty pounds heavier than anyone else in the fourth grade at Demopolis Elementary School. I have no idea how old he was. I only know that he could high jump over the large fifty-five-gallon black metal drums that trash was burned in, sometimes while the flames were licking up over the rims. I don't think he lasted the whole year. For months back then he haunted me every day, threatening me with his incessant gaze. And now he haunts me in another way, and I think it will be for a long time.

During those vaguely innocent days at the old tan brick school on south Main Street with its packed-dirt playground and its swings and monkey bars, he would stare at us much smaller boys out of narrow slanted eyes the color of pecan shells. His face was red and flushed, round as a dinner plate, and his hair was close cropped and seemed highlighted in a mossy pale green. He never said much. He would push in line, and sometimes kick. I would rush to get out of his way. Once he grabbed my arm and twisted it behind my back and forced me face down into the mud of the playground. I thought I was a goner. My friends would not come to my rescue. He finally let me up, and I was humiliated by my tears. I had to wear the mud, the badge of my shame, for the rest of the day. Everyone knew it had been my turn and it would be someone else's the next day, and we all hated him for it.

He had a younger sister, Maybelle. She was in my class, so for that brief time around 1947, they were in the same class. She was quiet, rawboned, and shy, with freckles and stiff blond hair. She was in my class on into high school, long after Cletus had faded away and disappeared into whatever hardscrabble and doomed life he may have led until the day I encountered him again. Maybelle may have even graduated with the class of 1956, but I don't remember. I don't remember ever hearing her say a word. What I do remember is that the boys in my class used to tease each other about her. We would get each other in a hammerlock—very similar to the one that Cletus had put on me that day on the playground—and not let each other up until we shouted for everyone in earshot to hear that we loved Maybelle Hickey. It was the most awful thing we could think of to make someone say. She must have heard us at one time or another. Surely she did. We didn't care. It never occurred to us that we were hurting Maybelle, not each other.

I forgot about both of them until one day in 1974—I was long gone from there, in a whole new life—when I picked up some clippings from the *Demopolis Times* and saw those pecan-shell eyes staring at me from a fuzzy picture on the front page. Cletus had raped and murdered a nine-year-old girl and left her naked and broken body on the river bluff. He led the local police on an extended chase, but they finally caught him. They caught him and put him in the Marengo County Jail. And he eventually went to prison. I stared at that picture. I felt guilty and ashamed. I had known his sister, had sat in the same overheated classrooms with her when *she* was nine years old and I was, too. I had known Cletus. I could still smell his sweaty hard body as he forced me to the ground. I can still see his eyes, to this day.

When I was nine years old like the little girl who Cletus raped and killed, my paternal grandfather died. I have only two clear memories of him: walking with him out to the stockyards to watch the cattle auctions, Grandpa carrying a dark-stained wooden cane, buying me Cokes and peanuts while he sat with his cronies with his belly straining the buttons on his white shirt buttoned at the neck, his cane resting across his knee. I remember the sounds and smells of the stockyards, the trickling loud rattle of the auctioneer, the manure and hay and sunshine. And the other memory of him is shortly before he died, over at the old Cobb home place in Sumter County, sitting in a chair carried outside on a sunny Sunday noon at a family reunion and barbecue, on the lawn near the pear orchard. The black women from the place were standing behind the long table laden with barbecue cooked all night and potato salad and cole slaw, swishing the flies away with willow branches. My Grandfather Cobb, sitting in the chair wearing a vested suit, started to cry. The tears rolled down his cheeks; I stood flatfooted and watched him. I knew he was going to die. Maybe that was the first time I had realized that people die. I was touched by some sorrow so deep that I knew I could never understand it. I ran away to play with all the other cousins.

The memories of my maternal grandfather are much more vivid. He lived long into my mature life. He was a rural mail carrier by vocation and a mule dealer by trade. As a small boy I rode with him on his route, all over the red clay hills of southern Choctaw County. When I was nine he drove a 1939 Ford coupe, generic dark gray, the color of all cars then except for the astonishing cream or white or red of some models that we saw only in magazines. The people would come out to meet us all along the route, all up and down those curving sometimes chert, sometimes gravel roads, and my grandfather would chuckle when he would see them. He would chuckle at the heavy-hipped women and the tall, toothless men sucking on their pipes or leaking their tobacco juice down their chins. They lived in cabins back in the hollers, subsisting on corn planted on the slopes and a few hogs and milk cows. They all knew my grandfather, of course, and he called them all by name. We would stop at a store in a tiny crossroads hamlet called Moseley's Bridge and he would buy me a Grapette, and he would talk about the weather or the world situation with the men gathered around the stove, chewing and spitting and laughing. Always laughing.

I looked into those haunted, starving, dancing eyes, all along the route and sitting in the cane-bottomed chairs in the store. We sat amidst the smells of woodsmoke and cinnamon, peppermint hard candy and cheese, the sharp chemical smell of new rubber boots hanging from the ceiling. My grandfather's restrained laugh was low and guttural, and it was a protest of delight at these people. They seemed strange and country to me, but he *liked* them all. They made him laugh, and finally they made me laugh, too. Sometimes we laughed *at* them and I learned from Pa-Pa that that was all right. My grandfather *appreciated* these people, and that he did was as natural and unselfconscious as breathing. They were comical and they were dirt poor and they were his neighbors; he was their window on the world, and they grasped the new Sears and Roebuck and feed catalogs hungrily and gratefully, like starving children. It was life as raw and hard as it could be, and my grandfather taught me to laugh in the midst of it, because *they* did, too.

My grandfather's post office was in Gilbertown, Alabama, and on those Saturday nights I would spend with them we would gather around an old upright Philco radio and wait anxiously as Pa-Pa gently—with the delicacy of a safe cracker—moved the knob fractions of an inch at a time until finally there would emerge from the crackles and the buzzing static the clear high greeting of Minnie Pearl, "Hoowwdeee!" and Pa-Pa would emit that prolonged shaking that was his laugh, his eyes sparkling, and for three hours we sat around in the living room, the grown folks' rocking chairs creaking on the old boards of the floor, the coal fire popping and snapping in the fireplace. I heard Ernest Tubb and Maybelle Carter and Granpa Jones and Jimmy Rodgers. I heard Lester Flatt and Earl Scruggs and Little Jimmie Dickens. I imagined them all to be like the people we saw along the mail route and the store at Moseley's Bridge.

I could never stay awake. The sounds would fade until I could only hear the music as though from a great distance. I would be soothed to sleep by the rhythmic creaking of the rockers and the crackling of the fire, warm in the safety of that rambling old wood-frame house in that little sawmill village that was just a rail stop along the Mobile Short route, with nothing but a string of five or six brick stores facing a gray depot and a lumberyard across the narrow two-laned highway and railroad tracks. The town had that one paved street and two churches—a Methodist and a Baptist—an elementary school, and, of course, my grandfather's post office, a tiny wooden building hardly bigger than a playhouse. My mother, the youngest girl (she was called "Sissy") and the second youngest of five children, went to high school in Silas, fifteen miles through scrub piney hills to the south, toward Mobile and the Gulf. The air was full all day of the ripe, clean smell of sawn lumber, and you could hear the high whine and shriek of the sawmill from the first light on.

The last time I went back to Gilbertown, four years ago, was to bury my mother's oldest brother, Buck Land, on the hill behind the whitewashed Methodist Church, which, to my astonishment, had a woman minister. We sang "How Great Thou Art" and put him in the ground without too many tears. He had lived a long life. The big old house that had been my grandparents' was gone, and built on the spot was an arts center that was doing a performance of *The Sound of Music*. Across the sandy street, paved now, what had been my grandfather's barn and mule lot was a parking lot. There was no sign of the sawmill or the lumberyard, and the old depot was boarded up. The post office was a new red-brick building with Gilbertown, Alabama, and the ZIP code—36908—spelled out in metal letters on the front. It was not my grandfather's post office, and it should not have been.

My father saved all the clippings about Cletus Hickey for me back in 1974 because I had moved away and didn't even subscribe to the *Demopolis Times* anymore. "Billy," he said, "you ought to write about this."

"I guess I will," I said.

"Well, are you going to write about Cletus Hickey or not?" he asks now, just the other day, sitting in his reclining chair, his eyes as bright and sharp as a boy's. I drive down there now to see about him. Only his lost hearing and his bad leg betray him. I don't point out to him that I've already written about Cletus; he was the model for Bud Squires in *Harry Reunited.*

"Yessir," I say, "I'm going to. Soon."

In 1974 my father took me to the place on the bluff where the body of the girl Cletus Hickey murdered was found. Nineteen seventy-four was the year my own daughter was born, a year of the future for me, a bright year in the midst of darkness. We stood in the lime-rock patches between the railroad tracks and the river near the old Riverside Cemetery. My father's leg was not bad then and he could hear and he was spry, and we walked along the bluff looking out over the thick green swamps to the west. He stopped walking after a while. "Do you suppose," he asked me, "that that boy believed in God?" My father has never talked about God much. He is a lifelong Presbyterian. And I was raised one. The Presbyterian way is to be a little bit embarrassed about talking about God, except of course on Sunday mornings at eleven, safely inside a church.

As a child and a young man I had believed in God because I was afraid not to. By 1974 I didn't know what I believed in, or if I believed in much of anything except maybe flower power, whatever that was. I no longer believed in the "Old Southern Way of Life." Which meant segregation and rejection of all things new. I was working on my first novel. I had published enough short stories that my father finally accepted the fact that writing was not simply a hobby that I would outgrow, like stamp collecting or model trains. He still thought it was useless and a little shameful if you didn't make much money at it, but he accepted it. As long as he didn't have to talk about it much.

I was surprised at his question. "I don't know," I said. I thought for a long time. "I think maybe Cletus does believe in God. And I think maybe he is mad at God. You would have to *believe* in something to be mad at it, wouldn't you? Maybe he is still mad at *me*," I added.

"*You?*" my father said. "Why would he be mad at you?" His graying eyebrows were arched on his forehead. "I didn't know you even knew him."

"I didn't," I said. "Not really. He probably wouldn't even remember me at all." The afternoon sun was hot on my head. "But I remember *him*. I don't think I'll ever forget him," I said. "Not now." My father was staring at me. Those bushy eyebrows looked like question marks. I cleared my throat and coughed. "Do *you* think he did?" I blurted.

"Of course he didn't!" my father practically shouted. "Of course that boy didn't believe in God! He was a murderer!" And before I could blink he had turned around and was walking back to where we had left the car.

Was it God who rested in my heart like a cold stone in those following days and months that became years whenever I thought about Cletus and Maybelle? Why couldn't I forget either one of them? Where was God during those long elementary days when we taunted that girl, and where was He during the long time that followed? Time that Cletus filled up with whatever hopelessness and pain finally led him to do what he did? Why was I as connected to those two people—I had not laid eyes on them, as far as I knew, for almost thirty years then—as I was to my two grandfathers? And remain so, so that they form the other point in the triangle, the part that completes the base. Why are they more real to me even now than my other classmates and friends? Because they have come to represent God to me. They have come to answer the question.

The God instilled in me back in my childhood was a cold, distantly intellectual God, a God drilled into me through catechism by a stern minister with a doctorate, a man who had retired from a huge church in Little Rock, Arkansas, and come to Demopolis to take a small-town church in retirement. He was a little man who wore severe dark suits and preached long dry sermons, and his pastoral prayer went on sometimes for what seemed like days to a child. There was little laughter in the church. Everything was so frighteningly mysterious that we dared not ask questions about it, much less laugh in its presence. "God" was harsh and judgmental, and I couldn't quite put Him together with Jesus, who didn't seem to be at all. I kept my confusion a secret, because everybody else in the entire world that I knew seemed comfortable with it all. But to me, God seemed absent, gone. We wore stiff Sunday clothes, and the most memorable thing about those years to me was the appearance every Sunday morning of an old black woman in motley rags who came to ring the church bell. Her name was Carrie Winfield, and she had a big gold tooth in the middle of her mouth, and she could not have come in and sat down with the rest of us because we were white and she was not. I cry now when I remember the happiness with which she accepted the few coins. I think I knew even back then, in my confused adolescent heart, that if God was ever in that church then He came in with Carrie. And left when she left.

Years later I would walk the streets of Nashville, Tennessee, on a Sunday morning—because someone told me that walking was good for a hangover—and I would pass by Ryman Auditorium, listening to the church bells ringing all over the city, and whenever I heard them—even now when I hear church bells—I would think of Carrie Winfield and that single gold tooth and her bright-colored, ragged clothes. Ryman, where I might have been the previous night with graduate school buddies or drinking in the bars along lower Broad Street, and I would think about those Saturday nights when I was a child listening to the Opry, sprawled in my grandmother's lap. My grandmother played the mandolin, and she used to strum along sometimes with the songs on the Opry. She left me the mandolin when she died because I loved it so. I am not musical and could never play it, but I have it still, propped on my mantel. The Opry was still in Ryman then, when I lived in Nashville, before it moved out to Opryland into all that slick, sterile tackiness. We would get drunk and go to the Opry on Saturday night and those old church pews would take us all back to our own private memories of our lost youths, and we would go out afterward and get drunker.

I drank heavily then, and in the years to come, with the ferocity and fierceness of the newly converted. I became a certified, first-class drunk. A lost soul of a rummy. I had the love of a good woman. So I was not searching for love. I knew my restless search was for something else, for a God who had been absent from my life for a long time. I didn't know where to find Him. I knew where He *wasn't*, but I couldn't find where He was. My demons drove me down long dark passageways full of hopelessness and pain. I looked in books, searched in poetry and the theater, gazed for hours into the bottom of a bottle or a glass. I wrote into the night, raised hell with loud music, partied for days, and hugged my share of toilet bowls. I did a lot of things that it took a really good woman to forgive me for. Though I managed to lose most of the decade of the seventies in some vast drink- and drug-induced blackout, almost losing that good woman and my daughter, I was still somehow fumbling down the right path. Though I was a driven soul, haunted and empty, I was on the right track and didn't even know it.

I wound up in an alcoholic treatment center in the hot summer of 1984. In treatment they strip you of everything, tear you down completely, and begin the process of making you over again. Long afternoons of group therapy with street people spaced out on cocaine, professional men like me, country boys who wanted to fight at a sideways glance and often did, truck drivers and cowboys, everybody at their own particular version of rock-bottom dragged-down hopelessness. Guys who were there to stay out of jail or were headed to jail as soon as they got out. Guys who had lost everything: jobs, families, self-respect. I was in there for more than a month. Not counting my detoxification, which had begun in a locked and barred ward of a hospital in the city. I had hit total, seemingly unredeemable rock bottom.

"I miss my country music," Cowboy said to me one evening. He had tears in his eyes. He was young, and he was from "Candem," he said. *Camden,* I knew. I had never heard such an obvious dyslexic pronunciation in my life. We could not listen to the radio. We had no newspapers or magazines or television, only video tapes of old movies two nights a week. There was much roughhousing and laughter. There was fighting, bloodshed, and fury. But there was always laughter.

"You can't listen to that shit when you get out," Country Boy said. He was redheaded, barrel-chested, and strong. He was mean. He looked around, daring anybody to contradict him. "Can't nobody listen to that shit without drinkin' beer."

"Hell," Politician said to Cowboy, "you come from so far back in the sticks ya'll don't even *git* the Grand Ole Opry till *Tuesday* night!"

"I got to have my country music," Cowboy said. "That and Jesus." He cried all the time. He missed his parents.

Camden is down near Choctaw County, not all that far from Gilbertown. Cowboy had told his group that his greatest ambition was to go to Nashville and go to the Grand Ole Opry. Cowboy was in Family Week with me, the last week, the culmination of all the therapy, when our significant others came. His father wore overalls and his mother wore cotton Mother Hubbard dresses. They could have been some of those people I saw on Pa-Pa's mail route all those years ago. They seemed totally dumbfounded by their son's alcoholism. Cowboy had driven his fist through a plate-glass window and didn't even remember it. My wife came. She looked terrific, with a new kinky perm. She was cool and reserved, not very trusting at first. I understood, but it cut deep into my heart. I was sober for the first time in a long time, and the world was clear and focused, and I couldn't pretend not to see my own naked soul anymore. The week was hell. It was confrontation time. It was time to be even more raw, even more naked. There were enough tears to float a tugboat and pushing and shoving and screaming and walkouts. And there was laughter. Wild and fierce laughter. We were some comical lost souls, all right, and we laughed at ourselves way into the night.

It was about dying and being born again. About dying to your old life. And they are right, your life—your childhood, your family —passes right before your eyes like a movie. And you mourn, and you cry, and you laugh. In the midst of it, you laugh.

Toward the end of Family Week things began to connect. I don't know when it was that I first became aware of it, but gradually I came to believe that God was right there in that room. That this was where God had been all along, all those years. That Jesus Himself was there, right where He always promised to be, among the lowest dregs and sinners you could expect to find most anywhere. And then one day toward the end of the week I saw Him, just as clearly as I've ever seen anybody, saw Jesus Himself just hovering there looking at all of us, at me. With eyes as familiar as my thumb. It took me a while, but I finally placed those pecan-shell eyes. Because Jesus was looking at me out of the eyes of Cletus Hickey, and He reached out and took my hand.

"Peace, *brother*," He said.

FRYE GAILLARD

The Heart of Dixie

The human heart in conflict with itself . . . only that is worthy
writing about, worth the agony and the sweat.
—William Faulkner

There are memories now of the Alabama summers and a farm in
rural Montgomery County, a rolling piece of Black Belt prairie
where the Muskogee people hunted buffalo and deer. In the 1950s
it was a tamer place as I came to know it—nearly two thousand
acres near the Lowndes County line, where the white-faced cattle
grazed on the hills and every so often there were stands of pine that
slowly gave way to blackwater swamps. As a boy I roamed every
inch of the place, learning to ride with the help of old Mack, a
swaybacked bay nearly thirty years old. He was an animal wise in
the ways of young children, gentle and sure, not much given to

stubbornness or fright. We scouted the range for outlaws and Indians until one fine day, on the strength of his teaching, our cowboy games gave way to the real thing.

The work was hard—long days in the sun chasing steers or cutting hay, sometimes castrating the newborn calves. But with my uncles and cousins and the other hands on the place, we managed to find a little time for adventure.

One hot afternoon after a morning in the fields we went to fish at a pond behind the house. On the distant bank we saw an old canoe—a dugout that my uncle had carved from a tree. There had been a storm the night before, and the boat had obviously blown loose from its moorings.

It lay upside down in the mud, waterlogged and in need of repair. I agreed to paddle it back across the lake so we could pull it out at the dock. At worst, I thought the canoe would sink and I would simply swim ashore. But as I moved out sluggishly toward the middle of the water, I realized it was not going to be that easy. The canoe listed badly to the starboard side, and no matter how I paddled, it tended to veer in that direction.

I was cursing it silently when all of a sudden, to my absolute horror, a rifle shot rang out from the shore. The bullet hit the water not a foot from the boat.

"My God!" I screamed. "Have you gone crazy?"

"Just keep paddling," my uncle replied, taking new aim. I thought of diving for the safety of the water as a second shot thudded into the side of the canoe. But then I saw my uncle's target—or multiple targets, to be more precise—for I had apparently paddled through a nest of water moccasins, and they were swimming purposefully in the direction of the boat. One, in fact, was slithering inside when the second rifle bullet split him in two. It was a situation so appalling, so completely terrifying and absurd, that I had trouble for a moment believing it was real.

I paddled furiously for the next several minutes, which seemed like days, while my uncle continued to fire away at the snakes.

Finally, just as I thought I might have it made, the canoe ran aground thirty feet from the shore. Swept away by a new wave of panic, I jumped out and ran, my feet barely breaking the surface of the lake.

For years after that, my uncle told the story, and it became enshrined as a piece of family lore—the day a mere mortal walked on the water.

And so the summers unrolled through the years, with each adventure a little more grand, until boyhood suddenly ended with a jolt. Before I really knew what was happening, I was compelled to deal with a set of contradictions—the rich ambiguities of the human condition—that left little doubt that I would be a writer.

Those were dark and dangerous times in Alabama, as they were in much of the American South, for there was a revolution underway, and many of us in the 1950s were not at all sure we were on the winning side. The way we understood it at the time, the whole thing started in the city of Montgomery, when a black middle-class preacher named Martin Luther King made a speech to a rally at a Montgomery church. King was only twenty-six years old, fresh out of graduate school in Boston—a young upstart, many white people said, who wanted to tear things apart.

We had no way of knowing when we first heard about it that on December 5, 1955, just before his speech, King was so overcome by his doubts—his sense of inadequacy for the task that lay ahead—that he put his trembling pen aside and prayed that God would help him find the words. Such images were invisible to white Alabamians. What we saw instead was an insurrection, reaching far beyond the modest demands of the bus boycott taking shape in Montgomery. Embedded in the majestic sweep of King's sermon were intimations of a shredded status quo—a radical recasting of the southern way of life, with blacks leading the way on the road to redemption. And the most disconcerting thing about it was this: Despite his secret fears on the same afternoon, Martin Luther King seemed to be so sure: "We are not wrong tonight," he proclaimed.

"If we are wrong, the Supreme Court of this nation is wrong. If we are wrong, the Constitution of the United States is wrong. If we are wrong, God Almighty is wrong . . . If we are wrong, justice is a lie."

I still remember the response of my family—their rage at the impudence of this young black preacher, who may have been raised in the state of Georgia but had picked up some funny ideas in Boston. As a child, I didn't know what to think, but then I saw him one day in Birmingham. I think it was the spring of 1963. I had come to the city on a high school trip, and King was there as the civil rights movement was rushing toward a peak. He was afraid of Birmingham in a way. He thought it was the place where he might be killed, for this was the city of Eugene "Bull" Connor, the infamous commissioner of public safety who regarded brutality as a necessary tool. But for the civil rights movement that was the point. King and the others intended to show that segregation in the South had never been benign—that it was not simply custom or polite separation, as many white southerners preferred to pretend, but an ugly stain, violent at its core. They hoped Bull Connor would not disappoint them.

The skirmishing began in April of 1963, just before Easter Sunday. I happened to be there as King was arrested, and at the moment it didn't seem particularly historic. The crowd of marchers was small, and by the time I wandered onto the scene, a bewildered bystander, it was almost over. Somebody told me there had been some demonstrations at a lunch counter, and then the march, but the police now had it under control. They were hauling King away to a paddy wagon, and even to the whites who had learned to hate him, he didn't seem especially threatening anymore. He was a smallish man in blue overalls, with an expression that betrayed neither anger nor fear but a stoicism that seemed to shade into sadness.

The sympathy I felt for him came in a flash, almost involuntary at first. I don't remember thinking of segregation or civil rights but simply that I knew who the underdog was—the victim of a cruelty that grew more vivid in the next few days as the snarling Bull Connor turned loose his dogs and aimed his fire hoses at the crowds of demonstrators. It was not always that simple and pat, for there were blacks who showered the policemen with rocks. But Connor and his troopers made no distinction between those who were violent and those who were not. The images flashing across the country were awful—German shepherds tearing at a teenager's flesh while another person was knocked from his feet by a hose and blown along the ground like a piece of tissue paper.

It was exactly what Martin Luther King had hoped for—a demonstration of the violence at the heart of segregation—and yet he brooded about it in private. Some years later I interviewed his daughter, Yolanda King, who remembered her father's anguish when Birmingham's white citizens blamed the problems on him. Even the most moderate ministers in the city issued a statement condemning the protests, charging that King's nonviolence was a mockery at its core, for violence, after all, was precisely the point, the drama that kept the movement in the headlines.

King recognized the grain of truth, especially in September of 1963, when dynamite exploded at a Birmingham church. It was 10:29 on a Sunday morning, and the crowds were beginning to gather for worship. Four teenaged girls—Carol Robertson, Addie Mae Collins, Cynthia Wesley, and Denise McNair—were especially excited on this particularly morning, a late summer's day with the sound of church bells and the singing of birds. They were junior high school students who had been invited to participate in the service for adults. They had gone to the ground-floor restroom to primp when the bomb went off and ripped through the wall, killing all four in a cascade of bricks. Dr. King was in Atlanta when the phone call came, bringing with it the grisly details—four murdered girls who were killed for one reason: Their church had been a base of operations for his movement.

The members of his family had never seen him so depressed. This was segregation laid bare, but he had never quite dreamed there would be such a price—the blood of four children barely older than his own. Was it really his fault? The irony of the question was nearly more than he could bear, but whatever the answer, he also knew there was no turning back. He was the personification of the movement by now. A few weeks earlier, in the most triumphant moment of his life, he had spoken to a remarkable march on Washington, delivering the most powerful address that many of the people in the crowd had ever heard. It didn't start out that way. He was plodding at first through the printed text, almost reading, when he got caught up in the excitement of the day. The crowd was huge, maybe 200,000 people, a fourth of them white, spreading out from the base of the Lincoln Memorial. As he moved through the text, gazing out across the mass of jubilant faces, he remembered a passage he hadn't thought to include. He had used it before, and it had gone over well in Birmingham and Detroit, "and I just felt," he told his biographer, David Garrow, "that I wanted to use it here." So he pushed his printed text aside, and simply let the words pour out in a rush:

> I say to you today, my friends, even though we face the difficulties of today and tomorrow, I still have a dream. It is a dream deeply rooted in the American dream. I have a dream that one day this nation will rise up and live out the true meaning of its creed—we hold these truths to be self-evident, that all men are created equal.
>
> I have a dream that one day on the red hills of Georgia, the sons of former slaves and the sons of former slave-owners will be able to sit down together at the table of brotherhood. . . . I have a dream today!

It was a vision that became his gift to the country, an antidote to the tragedies of Birmingham and other places. And for some of us growing up in those times, it became an image that we couldn't put aside.

For me, however, the final conversion on the issue of race, the moment I knew there was no going back, came a few years later at Vanderbilt University. I was a history major, class of '68, which happened to be the first at that particular institution that contained a smattering of black undergraduates. The first group was impressive, some of the brightest young people I had known, and I found it hard to explain to the student down the hall, making A's in calculus while I was fervently praying for a D, why his race was inherently inferior to mine.

The epiphany, however, came later in the year, when George Wallace arrived to speak on the campus. In 1964 the governor of Alabama made a run for the presidency, and although he came up short, the people back home were proud of his spunk. There was a theory circulating among the members of my family that Wallace was not really talking about race—that even his stand in the school-house door, a symbolic barrier to two black students who had been admitted to the University of Alabama, was simply a principled defense of states' rights. In retrospect, it was pure nonsense, but at the time it was a theory that I wanted to accept—a gesture of loyalty, I suppose, to the family. Wallace, however, made the truth very clear.

On the day of his speech, there were blacks in the crowd—a handful of students from Fisk University, well-mannered and brave, who had made the trip across town to see if he was really as bad as they had heard. One girl rose to ask him a question, a tremble in her voice, and Wallace interrupted her question in the middle.

"What's that, honey? You'll have to speak up."

She tried again, and Wallace again cut her off with a sneer, the sarcasm dripping from the edges of his voice. "You're mighty pretty, honey, go ahead with your question."

Many years later, George Wallace would change. Long after the murder of Martin Luther King, after he, too, had been crippled by a would-be assassin, Wallace paid a visit to King's church in Montgomery. Ray Jenkins, one of Alabama's great journalists, described the remarkable moment in the little brick chapel, barely a block from the Alabama state capitol, where Jefferson Davis had taken his oath and "Dixie" had been chosen as the battle anthem of the South. Wallace, still governor but confined to a wheelchair, spoke of the redemptive power of suffering and the ability of God to change a man's heart. As he was wheeled down the aisle at the end of the sermon, the choir sang "The Battle Hymn of the Republic," and the people wept and a hundred black hands reached out to touch him.

But all of that was well hidden in the future, and what we saw at Vanderbilt in 1965 was a demonstration of spite, the racism elemental and pure. And all we could feel, my friends from Alabama and I, was a deep sense of shame that this man was one of us.

Visits home were harder after that. I remember one particular occasion when I was lecturing the family on the latest outrage. There had been a killing up the road in Lowndes County. A civil rights worker named Jonathan Daniel, a white Episcopal priest from Massachusetts who had come south on a voter registration campaign, was murdered in the sleepy little town of Hayneville. He was torn apart by a shotgun blast, and there were a couple of witnesses, both of them black. But the killer's lawyer made a simple defense: Jonathan Daniel, he said, was a rabble-rouser from the North who had gotten pretty much what he deserved. His death was a warning, a declaration of war against those who would tamper with the southern way of life, and it was the jury's duty to let the killer go free.

The jury agreed. The twelve white people quickly voted to acquit, and I told the members of my family at the time that it made me ashamed to be from Alabama. I was sitting in a small rocking chair as I spoke, lounging back comfortably, when an uncle from my mother's side of the family decided suddenly that he had heard enough. He bolted angrily across the room and with both hands braced on the arms of the chair—his face only a couple of inches from mine—he called me a traitor to my family and the South. I called him a race-baiting son of a bitch, then pushed him aside and stalked from the house.

For me, at least, it was a moment of hurt. I was fond of my uncle and knew him as a good and decent man. He was a courageous veteran of World War II, having survived the fighting in the Ardennes Forest—the Battle of the Bulge, the Americans called it—when the German army rallied for one last assault. The struggle for a while was nearly hand-to-hand, scarring the survivors with memories that were often too vivid to recount. My uncle certainly never talked about it much, but he brooded sometimes in a world of his own as he puttered around his Montgomery farm, the site of many of my boyhood adventures. He was shaped, I think, by the spirit of the place, which was worked in the 1950s and 1960s by a group of black people who lived in small and unpainted cabins without electricity or indoor plumbing. A few of them turned their jobs into art—cooking, training horses, performing with consummate pride and skill the functions that were necessary to the farm. Others, however, merely tried to get by, putting in their time until nightfall finally brought a reprieve. Those of us not part of that life never knew very much about the nights—what mysteries lay concealed in the black people's cabins—though a small boy could lie in his bed and wonder.

That was particularly true on the night that Savannah came screaming to the house. "Mr. Ned!" she cried. "Mr. Ned, Mr. Ned! You gotta help me, Mr. Ned. The man's gonna kill me." Savannah was a cook who worked at the farm, and she was fighting that night with a man at her cabin. We never knew why. An infidelity perhaps? Attention withheld? Those were some of the points of speculation, but whatever the case, Savannah was drunk and afraid for her life and she had fled across the fields to the only haven she knew.

"I'm staying here with my white folks!" she screamed. Out in the car, the man yelled back, threatening more harm if she didn't come out. My uncle surveyed the whole scene calmly, then shook his head and strolled toward the car.

"We don't need any trouble," he announced. "You better move on." And he knew when he said it that the man would obey.

My uncle's conception of the issue of race was shaped, of course, by moments such as that, while mine was shaped by the civil rights movement. The gap between us should have come as no surprise.

But on an April afternoon in 1966, I was back at college and thinking about those family estrangements when a professor of mine, who knew of my budding ambition to be a writer, handed me an essay by William Faulkner. It was a speech that Faulkner had delivered in the fifties, when he was accepting the Nobel Prize for literature. He had been asked, apparently, to define good writing, and this, in part, was what he had said:

> The young man or woman writing today has forgotten the problems of the human heart in conflict with itself which alone can make good writing because only that is worth writing about, worth the agony and the sweat. He must learn them again . . . leaving no room in his workshop for anything but the old verities and truths of the heart, the old universal truths lacking which any story is ephemeral and doomed— love and honor and pity and pride and compassion and sacrifice . . .
>
> The poet's, the writer's duty is to write about these things. It is his privilege to help man endure by lifting his heart . . . The poet's voice need not merely be the record of man, it can be one of the props, the pillars to help him endure and prevail.

As I read those words, I suppose I was stirred by the poetic elegance, and even more by the message—the notion that the only fit subject for a writer was the human heart in conflict with itself. As a young man coming of age in Alabama, I thought I knew what Faulkner had in mind, for the conflict seemed to be everywhere, not only in the hearts of individual people, but also in the collective heart and soul of our place.

It was easy enough in the 1960s for a journalist to find himself drawn to that story, and there was something about the vantage point of Alabama. There were those horrible moments like the day in May of 1961 when the Freedom Riders came through and the Montgomery police made a bargain with the Klan. In his remarkable book *The Children*, journalist David Halberstam offered a chilling account of that agreement: We'll give you fifteen minutes, the police officials said. Whatever you want to do to these people, make sure it happens within that time. And the Klan, of course, accomplished much of what it set out to do.

In interviews with Halberstam, and some of the rest of us, too,

John Lewis remembered the late-morning stillness as the bus pulled into the Greyhound station, an eerie quiet, stark, unnatural, holding the promise of the violence just ahead. Lewis was the senior member of the group, not in age but in the level of his commitment to the civil rights movement. He was a young Alabamian who was a student in Nashville and had been a leader in the sit-ins. He had established a reputation for his courage, and it was tested that day on the streets of Montgomery as the crowd of white people closed in around them, armed with clubs and pieces of pipe.

"Stand together. Don't run," Lewis called to the others as the beatings began, and for the next several minutes he assumed he would die. But then a couple of shots rang out as Alabama's commissioner of public safety, Floyd Mann, who had heard about the Faustian bargain with the Klan, fired his pistol into the air and declared emphatically enough for everyone to hear: "There will be no killing here today."

For many of us in the years after that, it was satisfying to write about the heroes—John Lewis, Floyd Mann, and all of the others—and it was easy to write about the villains in the Klan. But there were also the thousands of people in between, those like the members of my own family, who were angry and bewildered by the civil rights movement but who were also moved—perhaps at a level that they wanted to deny—by the fundamental righteousness of the cause.

All of that left a writer, who was beginning his work in the 1960s, with instinctive understandings about the nature of the craft and the nature of the story that was there to be told. There were rich and inexplicable ambiguities that seemed to be the essence of the human condition. If most of us were doing the best we could, struggling with the values on which we were raised, it was a writer's opportunity to celebrate his place, with all its heroism and its flaws.

Then, as now, the Heart of Dixie held plenty of both.

Sena Jeter Naslund

Thunderhoof and the Mantel Clock

I was a scabby child, one who played hard and sometimes got in bit-ing, hair-pulling fights with other girls; with my brothers' friends, I wrestled, raced, and occasionally had my hands laced into maroon, junior boxing gloves for a round or two. *Wearing seersucker trunks and no top, in this corner . . .* One of my brothers was my coach, the other the referee. Aside from a few fights, the neighborhood, Nor-wood—Birmingham, Alabama—was full of free-roaming girls and boys who mostly had a wonderful, unsupervised time. All day we tore across unfenced yards and through alleys; half the long summer nights we played under the street lamp at the corner of Fifteenth Avenue and Thirty-sixth Place North, where the U.S. mailbox was "home" for hide-and-seek.

What a magic ring we formed within the circle of light: all our fists stuck forward to count potatoes to determine who would be It:

"one 'tato, two 'tato, three potato, four . . ." It was an enchantment of language, words strong enough to send us out from the circle to find hiding places in the dark. And what did it mean to chant "Red Rover, Red Rover, send Sena right over," followed by a mad charge toward the line of the other team? Who was Red Rover? The words of London Bridge: "Take the keys, and lock her up, lock her up, lock her up . . ." whispered of long ago. Sling statue, played on a soft lawn, seemed an artistic game to me; ringing doorbells was mischief just over the line, but it was so thrilling to be chased home, flaunting your speed, by an irate adult. Sometimes it was necessary to lie to stay out of trouble.

Night games had about them both mystery and excitement; whoever came out to play was included. And yet throughout my childhood I felt marked as an "outsider." Not so much in action, but in conversation I felt myself to be different. While I describe what in many ways was certainly an idyllic childhood growing up in Alabama, it was a childhood haunted by my feeling that I was not quite a part of things.

When I was very young my mother told stories to us after lights were out to ease the transition into sleep, or I sang, flat on my back:

A little star creeps over the hill
When woods are dark and birds are still
The children fold their hands in prayer
And the love of God is everywhere.

I slept beside her, my two brothers in two double beds in the adjacent room, easily within earshot of her stories: Bitsy Mary, Epaminondus, Little Black Sambo surrounded by a ring of tigers who chased each other till they turned to butter. My brothers fell asleep; my mother snored. Our father was away doctoring in Laredo, a coal-mining town on Buffalo Creek in West Virginia.

Unlike good children everywhere, in spite of the incantation of dark woods and still birds, when I tried to sleep, insomnia seized me. The mantel clock bonged through the Birmingham night—a single bong for 12:30, 1:00, 1:30—time to continue my story. And

so I entertained myself with tales of two pioneer boys, my own cre-
ations, Nathan and Jonathan, moving west, or my own version of
Peter Pan sailing a ship that resembled the full moon.

If I told myself stories, I lay not restlessly but quietly: no one
knew I was too wicked to fall promptly to sleep, a girl of fights and
lies, explosive temper, and an occasional small theft. And beyond
those transgressions, a girl who wanted to be good, felt that her
failure made her different, not normal: too strong, too wild, too
clever. Odd.

Those early dreams! Terrifying: a rehash of Tom Sawyer attending his own funeral, but it was I, and I was really dead. Of having to
pass through an underground corridor where a giant spider lurked.
Of needing to cross Al's park, a flat stretch of Norwood Boulevard
where my brothers, John and Bubba, played baseball and I brought
them and their friends water with floating ice cubes in an aluminum
pan, but now the grass was littered with nightmare snakes and I
couldn't run. Of invasion, first the Germans in the houses of our
neighbors, coming closer to our house, then in later years the Rus-
sians. I tried to learn how to distinguish between dream and reality
while I dreamt.

With the reoccurring invasions, the narratives of fear pivoted
repeatedly on a moral choice: did I save myself or put myself at risk
trying to save my dawdling family? The terror of that choice always
made me wake up before I could decide. The narrative of Nathan
and Jonathan, pioneer boys, was propelled by another tension:
which character type did I prefer? Nathan, the younger, fun and full
of high spirits, getting into trouble; Jonathan, the older, quiet and
studious, reliable. Not being able to decide kept the story going;
new episodes tested my hypothetical choices.

Bong! Only the sound of the mantel clock seemed to separate the
narratives of insomnia from those of dreams.

On summer nights, when I was too young to read well, Mama
and I lay on the bedspread while she read aloud—all the Laura
Ingalls Wilder Little House books. The bed was pushed against the

double windows, and the attic fan pulled in the cool night air. When I begged for another chapter, she read another. And another. Sometimes her nose would wrinkle and she would say, "Polecat!" which was her word for *skunk*. But I couldn't detect the odor as distinct from the rest of my world, and I thought what a fine nose she had that could tell the difference.

To get those books we rode first the streetcar and in later years the electric trolley from Norwood to the Birmingham Public Library, next to what was then named Woodrow Wilson Park. Above the bookshelves in the children's department was a long mural depicting fairy tales. I didn't like fairy tales; I preferred realism, but the magic of the murals made the place enchanted. Beyond the children's room was the Main Reading Room, with gigantic figures from other mythologies and cultures: Brunhild, Lancelot, Confucius, David with his harp, Pegasus, Pocahontas. The room was a metaphor for the adult mind—lofty, vast, myriad. And could I ever belong there? On the balcony was a bronze statue of twin boys—Romulus and Remus—suckling a she-wolf. To belong on the balcony I would need to confront strange wildness, the sexuality implied by *suckling*, that cities might spring from feral origins.

Did I think those things? Yes, though not quite with that vocabulary. Perhaps I should write I *felt* those things. I feel now a gratitude to those city fathers and mothers who planned and built and paid for such a temple as the library.

I am grateful, too, that those solemn stone exterior walls included display cases which could be admired from the outside. I could see that the display cases had small doors in their backs, and I felt pleased that there was an unusual passage from the inner world to the outer. Those almost hidden little doors were emblematic of the possible exchange between the sunlit world and the life of the mind.

When I admired the library from the outside, I also loved gazing up at the stone frieze—you had to look up and see the sky, too, to see the words of the frieze—sacred words: Philosophy, Poetry, Plato, Dante . . . Shakespeare—I'd heard of him, perhaps I'd learn the other names incised in stone just below the sky. The library was the crown of human achievement and those names were the jewels in it, fit to be close to the blue of heaven.

And my thanks (to the sky, to the air, to time, to all the powers that be) for the park, especially for the large, shallow ponds with the beautiful stone borders where one could sit and quietly feed the large goldfish, swimming among the lily pads, with crusts of bread brought from home. And for the annual children's art show held among the trees, next to the library. There at the foot of Twentieth Street, a trolley ride from Norwood, was an Arcadia.

When I was about ten, one hot summer day, I sat reading to myself in the living room—no air conditioning, and you don't run an attic fan during the day—reading a description of a blizzard in one of the beloved Laura Ingalls Wilder books. Suddenly I came out of the dream of the narrative to notice that I was shivering! Yet it must have been ninety-five degrees in the room. *Why am I cold?* Then I articulated the answer: "These words, just this language, made me feel cold." And then I thought, "I want to be able to do that." And that was the first time I consciously thought of becoming a writer. I wanted to have the power to transport not just myself but others through the medium of language.

My earliest writing was sheer play: my brother John and I constructed a cowboy newspaper, complete with a cartoon across the bottom. (Reading the *Birmingham News* funnies, spread flat on the living room rug, us kids—Bubba, eight; John, six; and Sena, four— on our knees, hunched over, shoulder to shoving shoulder, was a nightly ritual.) Our cowboy newspaper was an outgrowth of our play where John and I saddled the long black piano bench and the shorter chestnut dresser bench with sofa cushions, fashioned stirrups from the straps of binocular cases, and spoke our adventures as we rode. I think Bubba—Marvin—would have been on the sofa, reading *The Iliad*, occasionally using the collegiate dictionary he had asked for for his sixth birthday.

Writing began in play; writing became a tool for preserving the moment. Birmingham had fierce thunderstorms, which suffused me with romantic excitement, and, at a somewhat older age, I wrote little paragraphs trying to perpetuate that glory; I wanted my language to conjure up again the thunder and flash, the drone of rain and the sweep of wind. And I also wrote descriptive paragraphs to capture the thrill of the spectacular sunsets (air thick with particulates from the steel mills) observed from the western end of our front porch. Though this was the city, nature came to it with the weather and season change, the rhythms of night and day. Every morning I loved the shadows of catalpa leaves on the yellow shades pulled down beside the bed.

I knew I needed beauty, and I found it in the architecture of the library, in Woodrow Wilson Park, in Norwood Boulevard, in weather, in certain dresses—my green dress with the circle skirt and red rickrack sewn around the hem; my mother's oversized magenta velvet beret with the gold medallion on it; her black patent leather high-heeled sandals; her navy blue eyelet housedress, which my brother John drew her wearing. Then I admired not just her but his talent.

Mama's pies, chocolate piled high with slightly browned meringue or the cherry ones crisscrossed with a lattice of crust, were beautiful to look at as well as to eat, as were the delightful irregular bulges of chocolate chips or raisins in fresh-baked cookies. (I had a nose for them.) But most of all I lived in the beauty of the music she played on the piano, several hours, surely, every day—Beethoven, Chopin, Schumann, Schubert, Bach, Brahms, Debussy, Grieg, Bartók. I conceived a dislike for Mozart—imagine that!—and considered him "sissy." A great deal of my writing as an adult has tried to capture something of that source of transcendence in my growing up.

Across the red clay driveway was another six-room bungalow, almost the mirror image of ours, and there lived my father's two sisters—Kumi, who taught math at Phillips High School, and Pet, who was an invalid—and my grandmother Sena Sewanee Carter

Jeter (for whom I am named). Aunt Pet was my particular joy, for she told stories of mad dogs in south Alabama (the family came from a farm in Crenshaw County named Helicon down around Shady Grove and Petrey, south of Montgomery), and of haints, and of gold buried on her grandfather's property. Aunt Pet could draw anything she wanted to, make exquisite doll clothes, a whole rag doll three feet tall for me; she fashioned roses out of folded toilet paper secured with a bobby pin, the torn edges reddened with lipstick—which I sold door to door. Pet loved the colors red and pink and wore them constantly. She kept a supply of chewing gum for me and let me squirt myself with five different kinds of perfume and cover myself with her costume jewelry.

Hers was the realm of license. I never heard Aunt Pet speak a critical word of anyone. As she lay prettily dressed on her bed, she delighted in her visitors, shared all that she had. I think I learned from her the lesson of kindness.

Aunt Kumi was the source of individualistic opinions: she told me there should be no statues of old Julius Caesar, who had made war, but instead of Louis Pasteur, who had done some good for mankind. She told me about the horror of the Holocaust. She told me that if there were another world war, the family should have no part in it but hide in the woods of Helicon, which they should never have left in the first place. She baked tea cake cookies, sprinkled with nutmeg, a most mysterious ingredient, and, just for me, a little yellow cake in a tiny scalloped pan.

Kumi had a charge-a-plate for Loveman's department store and could buy on credit. She showed me a woman could be economically independent, have a job, own her own car, take care of her mother when she was old. Kumi bought *Little Women* and gave it to me, inscribed, for Christmas, and in Jo March I read how a girl could become a writer. When I won a poetry recitation contest at Norwood School, Aunt Kumi brought me the most beautiful bracelet I had ever seen: pearly beads spaced in a loose circle from which dangled a small golden basket of pearls with ruby and emerald cut glass mixed in.

Although my father was a doctor, we were not wealthy; he gave away his services and doctored for free when people couldn't pay or had just a chicken or a bedspread to offer. Small baubles of luxury—Kumi gave me a bowl with a china red rose on top of it as well as the bracelet—added much color and joy to my growing up. My father's bed had a puffy comforter—green satin on one side and pink on the other—and I felt proud of it and that he deserved this special warm but light cover. One day Nice, the black tomcat, was sick on Daddy's comforter—I could scarcely believe that the order of the world could have allowed such a desecration. I'd learned to read in that bed, nestled in the crook of my father's arm.

Besides the neighborhood group games, my childhood relied on acting out stories with my best friend, Nancy June Brooks. About age three, she and I once struggled over who would carry a glass of water to Aunt Pet, but our imaginative games were a rapture of accord. We took over characters we knew from the radio—the Lone Ranger (whom we called the Long Ranger) and Tonto, the ranger's nephew Dan Reed; from the black-and-white movies we took Tarzan, Jane, and Cheeta the monkey and made up new adventures for them. (Two of my published novels *Ahab's Wife* and *Sherlock in Love* are rooted in such play.) Sometimes Nancy and I enacted the characters I had made up when I couldn't sleep—the pioneer boys or detectives. Using the nooks and crannies of our houses and yards, particular tree clusters and bushes, and my playhouse (first white-washed and later painted red), Nancy and I pretended, acted out, created, day after day. After Nancy moved away, every month or so her mother, Myrtle Brooks—dear soul—would ferry us across town in their big black Cadillac so we could continue to play. To this day, Nancy and I revel in our friendship—it's lasted more than fifty years, with no break—and she cheers me on in my imaginings.

When I was older, age ten or so, I shared reading books—*Anne of Green Gables, Rebecca of Sunnybrook Farm, Little Women*—with two sisters, Janice and Juanita Lewis. We discussed the parts we liked on long walks and while sitting in a favorite tree near their house close to the railroad tracks. The actual reading was done separately, at night, but after the sisters' father got them a tape recorder, we took parts and read aloud, with musical background and sound effects, our favorite passages—Beth's death, I particularly remember. When one of us had to read a male role—I was Mr. Alladin from *Rebecca*—Juanita and I dissolved into giggles and would laugh uncontrollably again when we listened to our recorded fits of glee.

Their house, a little apart from the rest of the neighborhood and down a dirt road, was an enchantment of its own, with pear trees and lilacs, giant rosebushes, blackberry brambles, an enormous grassy lawn. I felt liberated when I entered their realm; it was like reading a book to go there: a whole new world. In the shade of the Chinese elm throughout the summer, we lay on a bedspread to play Clue, Parcheesi (which Janice always won), and Chinese checkers.

On their spacious lawn, under the cumulus clouds, we played croquet and badminton. Perhaps best of all was the twenty-foot swing their father fashioned with a steel cable to be sure it wouldn't break while we flew. For a treat on hot days, their mother let us sit around the kitchen table and have ice cubes in our water. These were not simply enjoyments. Such pleasures as I had in their company made me want the language to capture it forever.

Their father made them wooden stilts, on which we could walk for blocks, three feet higher than usual; we could climb steps, have jousts on the stilts. At this point, I renamed myself Thunderhoof the Magnificent. Now I was high and mighty. When dogs barked at me, I would bark back at them.

At Norwood Elementary School, in the junior first grade, I really learned to read and write from Miss Mary Barnett. We read Dick and Jane, and she made it as easy and natural as breathing. One day she asked us a surprising question: "Do you know what my favorite word is?" I had no idea, but more startling was the implication that one could have a favorite word, like a favorite dress or color. Her question changed the ontological status of language for me, forever; words had being in and of themselves. They were not mere conveyances. Her favorite word was *help,* and I was struck by the generosity of her choice. She was there to help us learn. And that was the attitude of all my teachers in the Birmingham public schools.

I loved and do remember every one of them—their first and last names, their handwriting, their clothes, some of their jewelry. I could write a book about them—often unmarried, bright, responsible, proud to be teachers, and dedicated to the work—but here I'll mention only a few of the lessons that I learned that relate to my having become a writer.

Another memory of Miss Barnett, thin and red-haired: she printed a story on the board for us to copy about one of our classmates, Bill Eason, who had ridden on a float in a Christmas parade. And with that, Miss Barnett showed me that we each have our own stories, that stories are not just about the Lone Ranger or imagined pioneer boys. In senior first grade, elderly Jesse Scruggs *told* us stories so ornate with imagery that I lost my prejudice against fairy tales: she made them vivid. She discovered somehow that I could stand before the class and tell stories, and I was sent back to regale the junior first-graders with a legend that my mother had read to me from *Jack and Jill,* a children's magazine we subscribed to.

In third grade, round and beautiful Miss Mable Dowling read *Uncle Wiggley* aloud to us, and I learned the joy of seeing every face shine with the pleasure and fun of it—a community of listeners. I felt less odd in my love of language and stories. In the fourth-grade classroom (on the second floor!), Mrs. Vivian Hood kept a set of books we might read ourselves—Childhood Days of Famous Americans, bound in orange, illustrated with silhouettes. And when reading a book of our choice, we were allowed to leave our regular seats. I sat close to the large, elaborately framed print of Renoir's *Madame Charpentier and Her Children,* which I wrote about decades later in a short story of the same title.

Norwood School had a number of beautiful art prints, nicely framed, in the halls, and I studied them every time we walked by in our orderly lines from classroom to classroom: Goya, Grant Wood,

Monet, and others. Those hallowed halls! Painted two tones of green; I wanted them to remain unchanged forever and resented it when new paint of a slightly different shade was applied.

By this time, perhaps from grade four on, I suffered with the knowledge I did not fit in with the lunchroom gossip groups; on the playground I still wanted to run and play kickball, not discuss hair or nail polish. My interests were different from the others; I felt respected but not "popular." They loved "I Love Lucy," a show I thought was silly and degrading, an embarrassment, not truly funny. I tried to conceal my snobbery. I relished the teacher-organized school or church experiences that dissolved the differences among us, playing cello in the orchestra, being in plays. I loved it when everyone in the upper grades strolled the halls singing Christmas carols and jingling bells. I watched each newcomer to see if she would like to become my special buddy, and finally there was talented Wanda LaRue, who was allowed to draw reindeer on the windows and could stand on point in ordinary shoes.

The most wonderful room at Norwood School was that of Mrs. Gladys T. Burns, who taught science and later geography to grades three through eight. Each grade had map projects, and the room was lined with our understanding of rivers, the location of cities, crops, topography, maps we worked on in small committees. She called our books our "magic carpets" because they took us to distant lands. When I outgrew my beloved *Jack and Jill*, she recommended a subscription to the *National Geographic*. Mrs. Burns not only had imagination; she was beautiful, a *lady* who was a model for grace and kindness—to all her students.

Everyone adored her. Occasionally she would lose her voice, and then we were all quiet as mice to show our respect for her, since she couldn't gently correct us without her voice. But someone always asked at such times, knowing she had no children, how many children she had, and she would fling up all her fingers over and over to show that we were all her children. We nearly sobbed in gratitude. Without the word for it, I experienced the heartbeat of *paradox*.

Mrs. Burns's best friend was Miss Claudia Huston, who had

been a WAC in World War II and would eventually become principal, after E. B. Calhoun. I adored Miss Huston, too, my fifth and sixth grade teacher, and often contemplated the differences between those two teacher friends, as I had with Jonathan and Nathan. Miss Huston offered us moral guidance, often through illustrative stories, and she helped me to steady my somewhat high-strung and nervous personality. By this time, with my bookish interests (which Miss Huston encouraged and endorsed; she *expected* me to have already read *Little Women*), I felt more certain that I was not like the others—not because of wickedness, now I never lied, I controlled my temper, never fought, tried to be nice—but because of my intrinsic, immutable essential self. Sometimes Miss Huston and I exchanged a thought about another student just with a mere glance. She told my mother at parents' night, "What Sena has is *understanding*." As an outsider, the idea comforted me: at least I had *something*.

I also had a boyfriend—Joe Cardwell—who lived down Thirty-sixth Place, and we studied together, played with his chemistry set, loved watching *Lassie* and *Disney World* on his black-and-white TV. His parents took us to the glorious Alabama theater to see a re-release of *Gone with the Wind*, and I fell in love with the scope of epic. Joe got Jack Daily's father to make me a steel cuff bracelet with my name on it (which I still have); soon Mr. Daily made one for every member of the class, and, for a while, I was one of them, with a boyfriend and a bracelet.

The teacher who most directly encouraged my writing as well as my reading was Mrs. Grace Montgomery, who was the music teacher. She played the piano while we sang from songbooks appropriate to grade levels three through eight, but she also helped us in the library and required book reports. She admired my descriptive writing, encouraging me to make pictures when I wrote. I particularly remember my report on the travel writer Richard Halliburton and his moonlight trip to Italy's blue grotto near Capri.

And I must mention our auditorium teacher, Mrs. Maude Hardy Arnold, who read to us, with much expression, Helen Keller's *Story of My Life* and the novels *Two Little Confederates* and *Mrs. Wiggs of the Cabbage Patch.* (It gives me such pleasure that I have just bought a hundred-year-old home in Louisville, on St. James Court, a few doors down from where Alice Hegan Rice lived. I wish I could invite Mrs. Arnold to visit the street that gave birth to Mrs. Wiggs.) Mrs. Arnold had us memorize poetry and put on plays, using our little stage with the marvelous velvet curtain. Now, when I read aloud on book tours, I can hear Mrs. Arnold coaching me on diction, rhythm, *expression.*

Playing the cello and attending for six summers the music camp held at the Northington Campus of the University of Alabama, Tuscaloosa, bridged the passage for me from elementary school to high school. I was curious about how it had been possible for these other kids to grow up in places other than big Birmingham, and I loved the sounds of places they named as home—Bay Minette, Troy, Ardmore, Mobile, Florence. My particular friends were the gifted Jan and Betty Lowi, violinist and cellist from Gadsden, whose father was shot in the hand by a terrorist attacking their synagogue; and Barbara Geissler, violinist from Huntsville, whose father had been a rocket physicist in Nazi Germany.

At Phillips High School I took classes as often as possible with Janice Lewis, with whom I had walked on stilts and discussed books; her friendship in the school setting gave me an affectionate connection to a congenial mind and spirit, and we were closest friends among many kids who seriously studied at Phillips. I think I've never studied harder or been more weary from carrying big loads of books than I was in high school—not even in Ph.D. studies at the University of Iowa. Besides our reading, Janice and I discussed our lives—our hopes and ambitions, what we thought of the world, our religious beliefs and confusions. I treasured my friendship with Janice.

The halls of Phillips were lined with the heads of animals shot on safari by the Comer patriarch (builder of what was Birmingham's first skyscraper, the Comer Building), and there were large plaster reproductions of the *Venus de Milo* and the *Winged Victory.* The biology room had a human skeleton in a locker and models of the interior organs of humans. More than any other place, Phillips High School showed me the world was wide.

As a freshman, I wrote a book report on Melville's *Moby Dick* (borrowed during the summer from the Birmingham Public Library), and the teacher, Miss Anne Ellis, asked, in a patient, kind voice if those ideas in the report were my own or those of some "art critic." She quickly believed my reply, but her question had opened up new vistas for me: there were *art critics* and some day I might find and read what they had to say. And, a novel, then, must be a *form of art.* I gloried in its new status. To be a writer might be to be an artist of sorts.

Also, as a freshman, thanks to Miss White, my speech teacher and the debate coach, an import from the North, I learned in a definitive way that racial prejudice was irrational and untenable. Before, in my progressive family, I was unaware that race was an issue. My father delivered babies in the Quarters (it didn't occur to me, but I think it did to Bubba, my smart older brother, that the word was short for *slave quarters*); my father treated whoever came to the door, considered Zeke Bell, the handyman, a valued friend. Black leaders, singers, scientists, athletes were spoken of with respect in my family. We had nothing to do with the fact that black people sat at the back of the bus; but I had accepted the order of the day.

I remember Miss White's intense question, pointing to her white arm, saying, "How can people think that the color of their skin, the pigment in their skin in any way makes them superior to any other human being?" I thought simply, *She's right,* and I felt a great flood of joy that with this clear idea the world could become better, more just. I could hardly wait to get into the hall to exclaim over the glorious clarity of her thought with my classmates. But for most of them, the scales had not dropped from their eyes; they backed away.

When the Reverend Mr. Fred Shuttlesworth was beaten outside Phillips for trying to integrate the schools, I became aware that racial prejudice was a terrible issue. I expected the law of the land would be enforced the next day—I was excited to think that everything was about to change—but it was many years before Birmingham schools were integrated. I became self-conscious in my politeness with African Americans; I hoped they knew that I was different, that I believed in our equality. For the first time, I felt proud rather than ashamed of being an "outsider."

Also as a freshman, I met for the first time a teacher who, I was sure, knew a great deal more than I did: white-haired Mrs. Edith O. Craig, the general science teacher. For the first time, I realized that I could not learn all that Mrs. Craig knew about humans, animals, plants, machines, chemistry, or the mechanics of physics as she lectured without notes, a wild Einsteinian look in her eye. Mrs. Craig inspired me to study as I never had before, and the world of science began to challenge me. I worshipped the flamboyant parrot tulips she brought in for her desk.

But my greatest inspiration was Miss Leslie Moss, whose love of literature and ability to instruct were infused with transcendent imagination. When she gave me the opportunity to write a scene referred to but not present in *Julius Caesar,* I wrote eighteen pages depicting Portia's death ("She Swallowed Fire"), and Miss Moss gave me an A++++. I didn't know such an animal existed. So there was a world beyond A+, and I must try to attain it. Miss Moss believed in me as a writer. Those pluses were like the wake of a shooting star. Now I was Thunderhoof sniffing along Shakespeare's trail.

When I wrote a Christmas story, as the sponsor of the school newspaper, *The Mirror,* she ran it above the fold, all across the front page. I took the title from a carol, "Then Pealed the Bells, More Loud and Deep," and after that I thought more seriously that my calling might be literature, to study it and to write it. I did not particularly like journalistic writing, but I worked on the newspaper so I could work with Miss Moss. When my father died, when I was fifteen, she was particularly understanding and comforting. Those days I sometimes went out with James Eaton, a ballet dancer, who was also one of Miss Moss's special pets and who also introduced me to the novels of Virginia Woolf, although I was not ready to appreciate Woolf fully then.

Perhaps because of my father's death I matured more slowly than others, and I graduated from Phillips and began study at Birmingham-Southern College more or less as a large child. At Southern I found a whole community that revered both art and science. There I had friends who read poems and novels as though their lives depended on understanding them.

I think it was Nietzsche who wrote, "The essence of all beautiful art, all great art, is gratitude." Whether my writing is or ever will be beautiful or great, I do not know. But I do know that the attempt to make it so is rooted in gratitude to my home place. For me, the names of family members, friends, teachers reverberate as deeply as the bongs of the mantel clock. These people, and many more, meant Alabama to me, meant a rich and bold intellectual and artistic ambiance, meant I had grown up ready to venture forth.

CHARLES GAINES

Growing Up in Alabama

A Meal in Four Courses, Beginning with Dessert

We are made who we are by our appetites and how we indulge them. Don't *ever* let anyone tell you that is not one of the truest things you can know: on a par with character is fate. In fact, I'll marry the two of them for you right now, like the cheddar and bacon in one of my favorite omelets: Appetite is Character.

Growing old is as much a shrinking portfolio of appetites as enthusiasms, and in that way can we sometimes, by the grace of God, become reduced to more pungent versions of what we were before—*demi-glaces,* if you will, of our former selves. (We can also, of course, become the burnt crust on the pan, but that wouldn't be you or me who doesn't know when to turn down the heat.) With a certain kind of empathy—love, call it—one can sip a mature person as one would a *pot au feu,* pulling air into the taste, and identifying many of the constituent ingredients—the salient hungers with which that person has recipeed himself since childhood.

Personally, I tend to create and locate myself by what I eat. Though not the most clamorous of my appetites, eating is the most defining one I own and always has been. Perhaps like you, I feed the person I am becoming at any given time, according to how I am the hungriest; then I am what I eat until some new hunger changes me again.

The single most perfect meal I have ever eaten was at the country inn and restaurant *La Mere Charles* in Mionnay, near Lyon, a place then owned, cheffed, and commanded by the great Alain Chapelle. This was autumn, in the year of our Lord 1978, and it was very easy to believe that all the world was a Brittany oyster I was lifting to my lips. Indefatigably hungry at the time for richness and variety, for orchestrated charm with oaky overtones of meaning, I ate this meal in the company of my wife, Patricia, and three male gourmands, two French and one American, who were as hungry for all of that as I was. No one meal could possibly have satisfied our appetite (in fact, two weeks of one- to three-star lunches and dinners every day on an orgiastic eating tour of France only whetted it)—but this one might have if we had only known better. Fueled by it, we all charged on for years with orchestrated charm, our lives rich and various with an overtone of meaning here and there; but that was not the meal's fault.

We drank four bottles of '76 Chevalier Montrachet and three of Bonnes-Mares '72. We ate a salad made of lobster, lettuce, and white truffles, sauced with the green tomalley of the lobster; and then *gatteau de foie blanc*—a mousse of young poultry livers in a yellow sauce of crayfish tails and truffles; and then a pearly fleshed fish called a *bar,* exquisitely cooked with a spicy tomato/basil sauce and stuffed with miniature green peppers and Jerusalem artichokes; and then a vegetable course of local white spinach called *cardons,* truffles, and *gratineed* beef marrow sauced with duck juice, the red wine here a white-gloved traffic cop directing us stylishly to three well-hung partridges that were carved rare at the table and served with *foie gras* on toast; and finally a cheese board fit for Falstaff, a dessert tray fit for Aphrodite. . . .

My three friends and I finished up in the bar with fi*nes de Champagne* and Montecristos lit with slivers of blond wood; then Patricia and I walked into the courtyard and stood for a while without speaking, irked at each other for some reason, under a willow big enough to shade an elephant, looking up through its branches silently at a black sky. I remember that meal with reverence, and I would eat it again tonight, I suppose, if I could, but I am not hungry for it, and never will be again.

How much longer can this man prattle on about French food, you wonder? Is this or is this not an essay about growing up in Alabama? Assuredly it is, and I beg your pardon; if I could I would uncork a bottle of good Sauterne at this very instant to direct you more gracefully than I to the first course of that improbable meal.

First Course: Dessert

A cake it was. One I made at eight years old with my younger sister's reluctant help in the basement of our parents' house in a good-burgher Birmingham suburb of self-satisfied yards, houses, pets, and people. Outside the basement was an asphalt driveway banked with a high stone wall. It was hot—early summer, maybe: thunderheads towering in the sky, the smell of rain, the steamy, edgeless afternoon lassitude that to this day I associate with desperation. Famished for it, I mixed my cake covertly on a table against the wall, out of sight of the woman who was paid to watch over my sister and me, and it felt like stirring up a revolution.

I wanted to put into this cake everything I liked and aspired to like. I wanted firecrackers in it, Gene Autry and Champion, fishing at Watts Bar Dam, the underwear of my sister's best friend. I wanted it to be bright and excruciatingly beautiful to look at as well as delicious, so I used Jell-O mixes of different colors and fruit juice. I made the frosting banana yellow with stripes of cherry red and plum and pepper green and set it to glittering with a full half pound of sugar crystals. When my sister Hansell and I finished overbaking the cake in the little stove in the maid's room, it was disappointingly formless, so I hacked away at it with my pocket knife until it was more or less the shape of a toaster, then slathered the frosting over it with my hands.

My cake weighed maybe two pounds and sagged. It was inedible, but I ate most of it anyway, and I was sustained for years by all I had put into it and by my first taste of transubstantiation. On that same afternoon, I believe, my friend Ashby Bouleware and I were finally able to mix other things in such a way as to blow up a chemistry set I had been given for Christmas.

Recipe for Cake

Cake mix, eggs, cornmeal, a can of soup, orange and cranberry juices, muddy water from Shades Creek, Jell-O powders. Frosting: eggs, maple syrup, sugar, Kool-Aid powders, sorghum, eight to ten little bottles of food coloring.

Second Course: Cereal with Banana and Cream

My grandfather Paschal looked a bit like God, I thought when I was ten. He was a well-loved, successful man with a head like Daniel Webster's and a tender heart who would literally pine himself sick when one of his children or his wife, Caroline, went out of town. He lived in a stone house just south of Birmingham at the top of a hill overlooking the city. He built the house when Highway 280, presently four ugly lanes of bedlam, was dirt, and his children grew up there during the South's last period of grace in an idyll of pony carts and pet roosters, of buttermilk and secret gardens.

On "the mountain," as everyone in my family called it, were turkeys and chickens, a huge vegetable garden, Jersey cows and Tennessee walking horses in the pasture. There would be eight or ten family members around my grandmother's dining room table for Sunday dinners of fried chicken and green beans and turnip greens

and rice with gravy and sliced tomatoes and onions, all of it but the
rice and the ambrosia for dessert raised or grown by my grandfather.
He would sit at the head of the table, say grace, then tip the horn of
plenty, and what spilled from it tasted of an earlier time and place
than when and where I lived down off the mountain. The honor in
it tasted like when you put your tongue against a piece of old silver.
I didn't know their names, any more than that of anise or car-
damom, but at that table I learned the tastes of iron discretion and
allegiance to family, generosity, inerodable optimism—more tastes
than I can name, and they made me hungry for an antique, regional
way of living with dignity, control, and symmetry that was as out of
reach to me then, at ten, as it has continued to be.

But my biggest appetite was for my grandfather's cream, which
the cook produced each week, along with butter and buttermilk,
from the milk of his beloved Jersey cows.

I would be spending the night at his house, and we would meet
for breakfast before he dropped me off at school and went to his
office as he did *every* day, including Sundays and holidays (driven
there by his chauffeur, Donald, in an ancient, beautifully kept black
Chrysler), up to within weeks of when he died at ninety-six. In his
early eighties now, he would come in to breakfast freshly showered
and shaved, dressed in a striped Brooks Brothers shirt, a paisley tie,
his suit jacket folded on the arm of his rocking chair in the living
room, his gold pocket watch chain gleaming below his belt. We
would sit across from each other in the breakfast room, and he
would read the morning paper until the maid brought our break-
fasts. His began with a bowl of cornflakes and sliced banana; then
he went on to eggs and bacon, grits with butter and pepper, and
toast. I began and ended mine with the cereal, sometimes three or
four bowls of it, because I could not get enough of the cream I
poured over it.

I'd offer the pitcher to my grandfather first and he would wave
for me to go ahead, still reading the paper, his face austere and
remote as one of those romantic mountains in N. C. Wyeth illustra-
tions, his glasses glinting like ice. Willful, spoiled, unpopular, and

hungry as a horse, I would tilt the pitcher and hold it there for a second or two before the yellow cream began to run, thick as ketchup, over the noisy, weightless flakes of cereal, quieting them, soaking them up like a benediction.

On those days, I would go to school steeled by cream into believing there was life after the fifth grade, and that I myself might reach at least the foothills of it eventually.

Recipe for Breakfast Cereal with Cream
Cereal. One banana, sliced. One full pint of cream from a Jersey cow, which when it is struck dead by lightning one morning will have a completely achieved man, nearing ninety and wearing a business suit, stand over it and say its name.

Third Course: Fried Bream

I am tempted to tell you about the enormous, Jughead-like hunger I developed for hamburgers at around twelve years old—about how hamburgers seemed to feed my very soul then when I was chubbier and more self-absorbed than I would ever be again, and would sit by myself in the breakfast room on Southwood Road on Saturdays and be served *four* of them for lunch by Ethel, our maid, whom sometime in that year I ran over with a lawn-mower-engine car my father had built for me at his sheet metal shop (she lived, and we got along better after that)—but I have never understood that particular appetite very well.

I believe I do understand the one I developed a couple of years later for club sandwiches covered in Durkees dressing and eaten, sometimes two of them, with iced tea at a place called the Mountain Brook Country Club between, say, golf in the morning and tennis in the afternoon, two appetite-enhancing exercises of privilege. That was a hibernating hunger like bears have in the fall, feeling in their bones that they are about to enter a coffin-like life of uncertain duration and storing up energy to deal with a long tedium in the dark.

But important as club sandwiches were, they were not half so defining or raging an appetite for me at that age as bream. Bream— as my father cooked them at nine or ten o'clock at night, after we had fished all afternoon and evening at the lake he owned thirty minutes outside of town and then returned home to the help gone and my mother in bed, to a quiet, dark house—was like manna from Heaven, like milk and honey, like a fatted calf, to me in the summer of my fourteenth year.

My father would explore the kitchen looking for what he needed and had no idea how to find: scaler, frying pan, cornmeal, lemon. We would scale, behead, and gut the red-chested little panfish. Then he would pour a swallow more of brown whiskey into his glass, roll the fish in egg, dress them in cornmeal, and drop them into a cast-iron skillet popping with bacon fat. His *pièce de résistance* was half a lemon squeezed onto each fish and nutmeg sprinkled over them before he served them up on whatever plates or platters he could find.

My father was himself a man of prodigious, sometimes debilitating appetites who loved the clean, tightly focused life of the outdoors as much as any man I have ever known, but at that time he lived largely an indoors one, hard and begrudgingly at work for my mother's family. He knew exactly where the soul freedom second only to God was found, and during the last two decades of his life— self-shorn of lesser, no longer defining appetites—he went there often and died a happy, fearless man; but at the time of our bream suppers he was ridden hard by work, an ulcer, booze, and other scoundrels with spurs. To say that I was not the least of his problems would be to understate, but we always got along well in a fishing boat and famously over those bream, for whose sweet ivory flesh it was hard to say which of us was hungrier.

We would pick the meat off one side of the fish, then lift out the backbone and ribs and fall on the clean slate of the other side, talking about oceans and rivers and lakes that he had fished and that I yearned to: about the time he had to cut the treble hooks out of Jake

Secor's back; Rainy Lake; Walker's Cay; his world-record king mackerel that was disqualified because a shark hit it as it was being gaffed.

I had just made a pig's breakfast of my first experience with prep school, one in Alabama, and was about to go away to Connecticut, where he and I both knew I would probably make the same of my second experience—but neither that nor any other offense that one of us might have dealt the other was fair consideration on those nights when the whole house smelled of bacon fat, when moths threw themselves against the kitchen screens and the breakfast table grew a pile of bream carcasses between my father and myself big and bold enough to seem the leavings of a Viking crew on its careless way to fish some northern sea.

When we finished, I would go to bed shark-full and fortified to keep on swimming upstream, knowing for certain where my next real meal was coming from.

Recipe for Fried Bream

About a dozen bream for two. Lemon, nutmeg, cornmeal, bacon fat. Cut slack and dreams of a vagabond life on water to taste.

Fourth Course: Mixed Vegetables

I was famished for the hallucinogenic cactus peyote for a while in my middle teens and was the only person I knew to order it, legally I think, from a mail-order distributorship in Arizona and raise it in a Mountain Brook flower garden. I and certain friends also hungry for escape had read Aldous Huxley's *Doorways to Perception* and thought for a brief while that those doorways might as readily open to us as they did to southwestern Native American mystics and shaman. Why not? We were perfectly nice boys.

So we ate and drank peyote, puked our guts out, and had a few Technicolor visions that we didn't understand. No matter how we diced, toasted, fried, and blended it, the tit-for-tat little cactus always made us sick before delivering up its unintelligible secrets, and inside a few months that emetic appetite fell through a hole in my pocket somewhere in downtown New Orleans and was lost for good.

One reason I couldn't handle the vomiting, I think, was that I had started lifting weights, was eating enormously, and wanted everything to stay inside and metabolize into cantaloupe deltoids and grapefruit biceps. Pumping iron, mingled with eating into one consuming appetite, was the first means I had found to occasion noticeable change in myself—to become, by design, something bigger and better shaped than what I was. It seemed a sacramental thing at the time, and I came shortly to recognize it and its mysterious interaction with the mind as my symbolic ticket to ride—out of what I wanted out of and into what I wanted into.

I can honestly declare that I have never been as hungry for anything in my life as I used to be for vegetables at Morrison's Cafeteria after a workout at the old Magic City Health Studio. Joe Disco, Richard Coe, Peewee Suits, and I, say, would swing out of the gym around one o'clock into the sweltering, cottony air of downtown Birmingham, feeling clean, as if all our blood were new, and very fresh and clear in the head. Bulging and protean, we would lat-walk down the sidewalks to Morrison's and there fill two or three plates apiece with black-eyed peas, turnip greens, lima beans, carrots, beets, mashed potatoes, okra, squash, stewed tomatoes. . . .

"My glutes hurt," Peewee might say, using a spoon to eat with because it got the vegetables into his mouth quicker than a fork.

Another vegetable eater: "That's because them little bitty calves of yours caint pull their share of the plow on your donkey calf-raises."

Another: "Your left calf looks like it's been in intensive care for about six months. If I'm lyin' I'm dyin', Peewee."

Another: "Like a snake in a sock. And I'm your *friend*. Are you gonna eat the rest of those butterbeans?"

And I have never since felt as full—with an inarguable sense that I had eaten the world and that life from then on would be just a matter of digesting it—as following those vegetable feasts, particularly after Patricia and I met, before I was twenty, and I started bringing her along to the cafeteria and sometimes, with Joe Disco, to Joy Young's Chinese Restaurant. One night after one of those lunches I took Patricia out to dinner at the Catfish King in Ensley, and in, I think, some idiosyncratic expression of love and readiness for anything that happened next with her, broke a longstanding record there by eating twenty-two chicken breasts *and* all the vegetables that came with them.

When, shortly after that she and I and our first baby left Alabama, I was finally, more or less, the size and shape I believed I needed to be. And I couldn't have eaten another bite.

Recipe for Mixed Vegetables

Vegetables—all you can eat, then more, followed by a walk on the streets of some city you are ready to put in the rearview mirror.

JUDITH HILLMAN PATERSON

Coming Home

I left Montgomery in 1980, shaking the dust off my feet. Never wanted to see the place again. Alabama was backward, a bad place to be a woman, and too damned hot. Never mind that I'd spent the first forty years of my life there and didn't have a soul anywhere else on this earth who loved me.

If at that time somebody had asked me what I thought about the famous southern sense of place, I'd have said I didn't know a thing about it. Whatever it was, I didn't have it. There is, of course, the way that soft coolness falls around you in the late afternoon, when the smell of tea olive floats on the slightest breeze—as if tiny infusions of lemon and apricot had been mixed with honey and sprayed into the air. The sweetness seems strongest at twilight.

But I wasn't thinking that sort of thing in the summer of 1980. Not me. I was storing my furniture and packing my Chevette hatchback—the worst automobile ever made—and heading to Washington, D.C., to seek my fortune. A little late in life, or so I thought at the time, and I was pumped, also scared. Not so scared of what would happen to me in the nation's capital as of what I feared I'd become if I looked back.

Friends who had gone to Washington with Jimmy Carter's administration said there would be no shortage of jobs for women like me when the president was reelected in November. That's what everybody thought in July. But, as all the great fairy tales and legends of history show, folks who go seeking their fortunes usually find something different from what they went looking for—often of a spiritual nature and of much greater value. They also tell us that, as T. S. Eliot put it, "the ways [will be] deep and the weather sharp, / The very dead of winter."

And so it is that, in life as in legend, most of us have to travel through the dark valleys in order to get to the green pastures. The journey always starts with the place and the parents God gave us. My particular heritage is complex.

My mother died of a terminal combination of depression and addiction when I was nine and she was thirty-one. Her love for my volatile father only made matters worse. He was alcoholic himself, though he suffered a less rampant form of that dreadful disease than my mother did. He too had depressive tendencies to grapple with. Under the influence, he had a violent, unpredictable temper that could be triggered by anything. Sober, he was on the intellectual side, a born nurturer, destined to be the great love of my life as well as my mother's. One of my earliest memories is of sitting on my father's lap while he read aloud from the *Montgomery Advertiser*, attempting, I suppose, to keep me quiet and read the newspaper at the same time.

For a long time, the story line of my life seemed to be governed by the doomed marriage of my parents. Among the options offered by that plot, I chose a combination of physical presence and emotional escape. What can a nine-year-old do when her mother dies and her father sets out to drink up all the liquor she left behind?

From as soon as I could make out the words on a page, I read . . . and read . . . and read. I doubt it's a coincidence that troubled families produce more than their share of readers and writers. Compulsive reading still seems to me the most constructive—certainly the least destructive—of the plethora of escape hatches human beings have devised.

I especially liked a series of books called The Childhood of Famous Americans, patriotic, primary-colored little hardbacks that fit like a nest of pearls in the hands of a child in search of meanings not to be found at home. As I remember it, the famous Americans were as likely to be girls as boys. Children's books always have morals and messages, and I was looking for guidance as well as escape.

I loved schools from the moment I set foot in Miss Simpson's first-grade classroom at Cloverdale School—new playmates, new books and games, all those predictable and well-behaved adults. I can still smell the chalk dust and see the moats floating in sunshiny air. Miss Simpson seemed very stern and looked older than my grandmothers. She pulled her hair back in a tight, gray knot and wore long, straight dresses of a silvery, gunmetal color that matched her hair. Despite such a formidable first role model, I was probably destined by nature and circumstance to become a teacher.

By the time I started packing my Chevette, my proclivity for burying my head in a book had gotten me a Ph.D. in English from Auburn University and a satisfying job as a writer and professor at Auburn in Montgomery (AUM). I loved everything about that job. Imagine getting paid something close to a living wage for reading, writing, and talking about books all day to a captive audience. My personal life was, on the other hand, a shambles. Anyway, no looking back. Montgomery was driving me crazy.

"My parents came from families about as different from one another as two families that had been in Montgomery for several generations could possibly be." By the time I wrote that sentence in 1996, I knew that what was driving me crazy had more to do with my family than with where we happened to be located. Or did it? In my mind—and perhaps in actuality—Momma, Daddy, and Montgomery, Alabama, were part and parcel of the same thing. From a certain angle my heritage looks like a chimpanzee took the most intense hues from the palette of Alabama history—cotton, coal, iron, land, slavery, race, class—and flung them against a canvas.

Momma's people had been big slaveholders: Black Belt planters on the one side and industrialists in Kentucky and Birmingham on the other. For as far backward and forward as I can see, her family tree is heavy with veneration for the Lost Cause and problems with addiction and depression.

Montgomery had quite a few families like my mother's. But, in all my research and travels, I have never come across another southerner descended from people like my father's grandparents.

Coming their separate ways, William Burns and Margaret Flack Paterson arrived in Alabama in the 1870s, part of the stream of missionaries that came south to educate African Americans set free by the Civil War. When Reconstruction ended and the other missionaries (mostly Yankees anyway) fled, my ancestors stayed and made a place for themselves against all odds. They raised five talented children and established Alabama State University plus a successful nursery/florist business called Rosemont Gardens.

They were Christians, reformers and true believers in equal opportunity and the American dream. They were also, as you might imagine, teetotalers. Yet, looking back, I see evidence in their bloodlines predisposing their descendants to sadness and to drink. Their second son, my grandfather, married a teetotaling, salt-of-the-earth, Southern Baptist from Wilcox County, whose family turned out to bear similar tendencies.

Birds of a feather? Like drawn to like? Too much inbreeding among the homesick, whiskey-loving, Celtic-blooded clans that settled the state? Too much bacon grease and not enough fish oil in the diet? Who can say? Is Montgomery more afflicted with such failings than other places, or does my imagination run away with me?

For all the differences in the way their families had come there and what their histories had been, Momma and Daddy both thought Montgomery was the plain-as-day center of the universe. People not born "around here" came from "away from here" and were not to be trusted. Not that the poor things could help it. To tell the truth, when I'm asked where I'm from, I still get a little thrill from saying Montgomery, Alabama, as if I had been born in Paris or Hollywood or somewhere like that and didn't want to sound too conceited about it.

After Momma died, Daddy married the widow of one of his Wilcox County cousins. By then, Dorothy Moore McNeil (a native Virginian no less) had lived in Camden for twenty years and become more devoted to Black Belt ways than Mr. Boll Weevil himself "just lookin' for a home." More loyal even than Momma's plutocratic Aunt Bessie, whose father had been wounded at the Battle of Chickamauga—stepped on by his own horse, actually. Still, he had been there and paid some dues.

Daddy's country cousins were no less inclined to weep in their beer and enjoy a splash on occasion than those I already knew, but Wilcox County was different from Montgomery. The image that lingers is of driving past civilization's last outpost at Selma and seeing the land grow darker, the woods thicker, and the people more scarce. The kind of people who were the most scarce, come to think of it, were white people. And the people of African descent were truly black, not the many shades of light to dark brown I saw in Montgomery.

A tiny handful of whites (mostly kin to me) controlled everything. I saw black people being treated with more condescension and disregard than I had noticed at home. The vague unease (more surprise than anything else) of that realization is my first recognition of the degrading nature of the racism that permeated my world—degrading to the white people who practiced it as well as the black ones who endured it. I still connect that moment of childhood awareness with the hovering rural darkness of the place.

Thanks to the way consciousness willy-nilly links the external with the internal and the forgotten with the remembered, I also associate that day with the way certain images collected around a secret pool of anguish inside me—Momma's death, Daddy's marriage to a woman I didn't know, and the way drink transmuted my father's tenderness for his children into contempt.

That type of recollection is what I call a "bubble of memory" because of the way such moments erupt into consciousness as colorful, brightly lit circles of related impressions forever still-shot inside a single moment. No matter how poignant or disturbing the other content of a bubble may be, it usually also contains an almost unbearably sweet recollection of the sights, sounds, colors, odors, and temperature of the surrounding landscape. Pink daybreak. White sunlight. The sharp, dusty smell of a pine forest. Stillness. Heat.

It's those bubbles, I now believe, that have preserved my most vivid and precious memories as well as the sense of place I thought I didn't have. Memories can no more live cut off from the place that gave them birth than the body can function free of the brain that runs it.

A few years ago, a friend asked me if I missed Montgomery, and I said, "No . . . but sometimes in the summertime in Washington, I'll open my door on the early morning damp of a day that is going to be very hot . . . and suddenly I'm wrapped in the warm, still air of home. No matter how hard I try to hold the feeling, it slips away."

My friend said, "You're describing nostalgia."

Maybe. Still, who can say why heat, silence, and tranquillity come to be so closely linked to the memory of a place in the mind of one person and not another? I think of nostalgia as a longing for a time that is gone and a spot that is no longer as it was. A sense of place, on the other hand, reflects how the nature of a certain location combines with our own tendencies and the circumstances of our lives to make us who we are. It suggests, too, that people from a place with a distinct nature are apt to be similar in some ways and deeply connected both to that place and to each other.

Thanks to my stepmother's association with the Wilcox County side of the family, I have vivid memories of the rural Alabama Black

Belt and a part of my own heritage that would otherwise have been lost to me. My father relished the absurdities that appeared in the *Wilcox Country Progressive Era* and never called the newspaper anything except the "Progressive Error." He claimed his Camden cousins rejected the idea of outside industry by saying, "We've got enough strange people around here already. The last thing we need is more strangers." It was to that part of the state—Greensboro, Selma, Marion—that my Paterson ancestors came in the 1870s as do-gooding outsiders of the most unpopular sort.

The thing I liked most about my summer sojourns in Camden was the free run of the county that we children seemed to have. My Wilcox cousins drove cars, smoked cigarettes, drank beer, and skinny-dipped at a much earlier age than my overprotected friends in the big city of Montgomery. Children of all ages just seemed to come and go as they pleased.

Looking back on it, I realize that the whole town had an eye on all of us at all times. When any young person did something that was truly out of line, the news traveled faster than e-mail along an invisible grapevine of adults. Anything communicated by telephone was known countywide within minutes, since all calls went through a central operator and "central" was always listening. Infringements worth reporting tended to fall into three categories: sexual involvement with someone inappropriate, any deviation from racial mores, and destruction of property.

The place was tiny and crawling with tattletales. Drug-related murders and carjackings could not have been imagined. The blue-gummed nigger who was the bogeyman of all their tales, now that was a fear you could sink teeth into. He was real, for all I knew. Things were that strange down there.

Somewhere along the way I learned to dance the dance between what I knew and what I said. Perhaps I had known it since the first time my mother told me to keep something secret from my father and I understood that I could decide whether to do it or not. I didn't tell my friends in Montgomery what I got away with in the wilds of

Wilcox County—mainly for the fun of it. Some secrets were more serious than others.

I liked my eighth-grade English class because Mrs. H. allowed open discussions on Friday. On one memorable day, she had been talking about religion and was trying to make sense of the sins of the fathers being visited on the heads of their children and all the generations to come.

"Good Lord! What nonsense," I thought before blurting out, "That's the stupidest thing I ever heard of."

To tell the truth, God had already given me several opportunities to question His ways. Having Momma and Daddy marry each other, for starters. I sure didn't want the sins of those two visited on my innocent head any more than they already had been. Certainly not on the heads of my as yet unimagined children.

The face of the ordinarily placid Mrs. H. went suddenly fierce. She rose stiff as a board out of her chair, leaned forward and shouted, "It's in the Bible. You call God stupid? You?" Then in halting words almost too low to hear, "Don't . . . ever . . . ever . . . say . . . anything . . . like . . . that . . . again. Understand?"

Nothing like this had ever happened to me in school before. I was stunned and also furious. Something inside me went stubborn and still as night. She hadn't given me time to explain what I meant. To hell with that Sunday school prim old bitch. The other students looked away. I made my face into an mask of adolescent outrage and said nothing.

"Do you understand me?"

Nothing.

"Do you understand me?"

"Yes, ma'am," I finally said, emphasizing *ma'am* in a way that I knew she would consider impudent. She let it go.

Leaving class, Patsy Graydon said, "You certainly got a rise out of her. I never saw that before." I thought she was trying to comfort me. I didn't need comfort. I hated people telling me what to think.

By then I had already grown careful of what I said at home.

Daddy's heavy so-called social drinking had become cyclical. Fairly long periods of sobriety were now followed by binges so terrible they shook our world and could have killed him. On the other hand, they left him sober for long periods of time, during which he nurtured us and encouraged us to think for ourselves. I, of course, had no understanding of addiction. Nobody much did in those days.

I thought a binge could be set off by something someone in the family said or did. With that in mind, I had assigned myself the big-sisterly task of controlling everything that happened in my father's presence. Fat chance of success I had, considering the volatility of the household and the unruly nature of my three younger siblings. Before that incident in English class there had been two places where I thought I could say what I pleased—my grandmother Paterson's house and school. Believing firmly that actions spoke louder than words, Gram generally took what people said as little more than hot air. Her plain little house with its open gas heaters would always be a haven to me.

As far as I was concerned, the two best days in the year were two Sundays, one a month before Christmas and the other a month before Easter, when the Patersons opened their greenhouses to the public. Because he (like his father before him) had grown up on that side of the family business, Rosemont Open House was also a very big day for my father.

The mud, the hoses, and the everyday clutter of growing flowers under glass were all cleared away. The place was spotless. Roses bloomed in splendor, row after row. Poinsettias signified one season. White lilies the other. The air inside was dewy with humidity and the earthen aroma of dirt mixed with chemicals and compost. That smell plus the tobacco from his Camel cigarettes were as much a part of my memory of Daddy as the way he spoke and gestured and moved.

During the week before open house, we watched the weather like pagan priests and wondered how the day would dawn and how many people would come. In memory, the weather was always resplendent and a little bit chilly. Daddy was cold sober all day and utterly happy.

The cottage my grandmother and grandfather built as newlyweds stood close to the greenhouses. Friends, relatives, and admirers streamed through their house all day, praising the weather, the flowers, the Patersons and all they stood for.

They stood for civic duty, camaraderie, education, racial moderation, and good sense. On this day nothing lingered of the ostracism their parents and grandparents endured. The Patersons were one with the place, and I was one with them. Still, there were so many of them by then, and what they stood for had grown more complicated. Even as a child I saw the sadness in them and noticed how much they drank.

Although Alcoholics Anonymous was founded in 1935, knowledge of it was not widespread until 1939, when the *Saturday Evening Post* ran an article praising the practices and philosophy of life that made sobriety possible for many people. Though seven more years would pass between 1939 and my mother's death from an overdose of alcohol and barbiturates, I doubt she would have considered joining the groups that met in Montgomery, since few women did in those days.

She had been dead more than thirty-five years by the time antidepressant medication began helping people with severe clinical depression and related disorders. Looking back, I see her illness as so complex and the symptoms (depression, agitation, paranoia, insomnia, anorexia) so extreme that I have to wonder if even the most expert modern treatments could have helped her.

Daddy did, eventually, achieve intermittent sobriety in AA. My stepmother would always be torn between believing my father's alcoholism stemmed from a disease that required help from outside the family and believing that, with enough determination, she and he could lick it together—alone. His four children reacted to the situation in many different ways. Like so many firstborns in troubled families, I played the bossy peacekeeper at home and the over-achieving, keeper-of-the-secret away from home. In the mystifying way that families have of assigning roles, I became the child who went into the world to prove we were doing just fine. It's a seductive assignment, and I did it in spades. The role has obvious perks—attention, praise, good grades, success in the eyes of the world. Its dark side includes workaholism, compulsivity, guardedness, and constant fear of exposure.

I don't know when or how I learned that certain things were not to be acknowledged—much less discussed—either inside or outside the family. My mother's death was one of those things; my father's drinking was another. I have no memory of being told not to talk about those things and have come to suspect that all families have hot spots that nobody wants to touch. Each member seems to feel the impact of the emotional content and knows at least some (but not all) of the facts believed to be hidden.

Spoken or not, "Shussh . . . don't say that" stays with us forever. I suspect I preferred silence to either hurting my father or risking his anger. There were times when my very existence seemed to rest on his moods, his whereabouts, and what he thought of me. Only when things were stable at home did I feel free to pursue my own activities and interests. When there was more tension in the air than I could bear, I read or studied in my room. Contrary to all the laws of common sense, it turns out to be fear rather than joy that binds us too inflexibly to the ways of our families.

By the mid-1950s, when I was at Sidney Lanier High School in Montgomery, AA was familiar to most people. Though the companion twelve-step programs—Al-Anon for the families and friends of alcoholics and Alateen for their teenaged children—were also in existence, they were much less well known. If Daddy was already attending AA meetings at that time, I didn't know it. In those far-off days before the phrase *self-help group* existed, I certainly had not heard of either of the other organizations.

One day I was standing in a crowd at recess outside the school. The bell rang. Someone hung back to tell me some kids with alcoholic parents were meeting that afternoon to talk about their families. I could come if I wanted to. Nobody would know. It was anonymous like AA.

The idea of exposing the trouble at home and throwing in with strangers went into my mind as pure madness. My two sisters already showed signs of the depression and/or alcoholism that would plague them for life. They were damaged, I believe, as much by our mother's heavy drinking during her pregnancies with them as by our genetic heritage. It did not help that family dynamics were dominated by my father's drinking and what we now think of as shame, denial, and enabling. For me to admit weakness either in myself or my family seemed out of the question.

I could not have been more horrified if the person standing before me on that sidewalk had said the group was getting together to discuss the efficacy of human sacrifice. Such a group, I concluded, must surely be for kids much worse off than I was—and much more reckless. Crazies. Losers. What could we possibly have in common? Anyway, nothing in that school was anonymous.

I still wonder what difference—for better or for worse—it would have made if I had responded differently. That memory marks for me one of the hundreds of (mainly forgotten) choices we make every day. We take one road or another and each road taken branches into two more—one taken, one refused. And those tiny, semiconscious decisions amount to our destiny.

One day in the summer of my junior year I looked up from my reading and my ruminations long enough to hear a young woman a few years older than I singing the praises of Hollins, a liberal arts college for women in Roanoke, Virginia. I had never heard of it before. I knew I'd had enough of splitting myself between being a good student and acting the straw-brained southern belle so many of us were raised to look like in those days. Enough, too, of being the beard for a family imploding behind closed doors. A college for women seven hundred miles from Montgomery struck me as a very good idea. The school took the education of women seriously, she said, and valued the intellectual and emotional growth and ful-

fillment of every student who went there. In one surprising jolt of
adolescent impulsivity, determination, and insight, I made up my
mind to go there.

I left home for college in September 1955. Three months later
Rosa Parks refused to give her seat to a white man on a Montgomery city bus. Because of the way they had come to Montgomery,
the Patersons had always held progressive views on racial matters,
especially equal opportunity. Still, by the time I was born they were
deeply committed to the ways of the community that had finally
accepted them.

As long as the issue was seating on buses, most of them sympa-
thized. But with the expansion of the movement and the spread of
rumors about promiscuity and communism among the activists,
their sympathy went underground. Some believed one thing and
some another. They had to get along. After all, they were in the
business of selling flowers, mostly to white people.

The Hollins faculty was staffed in those days by an enthusiastic
set of youngish male professors and an older generation of intellec-
tually liberated women who had been the suffragists and reformers
of their day. I was hardly settled in, it seemed, before I was reading
W. J. Cash's *Mind of the South,* C. Vann Woodward's *The Strange
Career of Jim Crow,* and learning about Thorstein Veblen's theory of
conspicuous consumption.

A girl named Angela on my hall went home to Richmond one
weekend during her freshman year, showed her parents her books,
and told them that her professors were saying things about race,
gender, economics, and religion very different from what she had
learned at home. She returned just long enough to pack her bags
and go. In my last memory of her, Angela stands nervously in the
doorway saying goodbye and trying to explain. I think, "What a fool
to tell her parents."

In memory, I see my mind opening in one great gulp of common
sense. Although the process must have been slower and more considered, I remember it as a single moment in which I looked at the
assumptions I had been raised with in Montgomery and thought,

"Why in the world did I ever think that?" If Negroes and women were not inferior to white men—and I had my own reasons for believing they weren't—if the democracy I had been grilled in since kindergarten meant what it said—then the way we lived in Montgomery in those days made no sense at all. Suddenly, everything was up for grabs, including the fundamentalist view of God that pervaded the very air we breathed.

Thorstein Veblen's description of the leisure of women as little more than prostitution, just another way for men to display their wealth, stopped me in my tracks. I had seen my mother die trying to live the myth of the leisured southern woman on a pedestal. I knew that strong women had borne the brunt of survival on the Alabama frontier and in the wreckage of the Civil War. I had seen my stepmother throw herself across her bed and weep because she had no way of supporting herself if she left my father. I knew, firsthand, my father's penchant for controlling his children with money and condemning all opinions contrary to his own. I made up my mind never to be financially dependent on a man again for as long as I lived.

All that was in my head. My heart, on the other hand, was a scrambled mess of love, resentment, and fear—with my only bloodparent at its center. Daddy was forty-two years old the year I went to college. His athletic body had grown a pot belly and his once handsome face was red and puffy with drink. He suffered an attack of Bell's palsy that year and had a deep-seated cancerous tumor removed from his lower lip. He stopped drinking for a while and started using a long, ivory cigarette holder for his Camels. The next year, after a weeklong binge, he had an esophageal hemorrhage—the result of liver damage—that almost killed him. I was angry with him most of the time, going to college year-round in order to graduate in three years and get out of his house for good.

But I happened to be home the day of the hemorrhage and heard him hit the bathroom floor with a thud that sounded like furniture falling. I found him on the floor spattered with so much blood that I could smell its hot stickiness. My stepmother was in the bedroom calling an ambulance. I was on the floor with Daddy, holding his head in my lap, caressing his face as if he were my child or a lover. Neither of us knew what to make of this moment of tenderness that arose so unexpectedly out of the anger and resentment that now connected us. And neither of us ever forgot it. The doctor told him to stop drinking, another hemorrhage would kill him.

Although he got serious about AA after that, the intermittent binges never stopped. For the rest of his life, every time he fell off the wagon he climbed back on again. Interesting thing about the people in AA is how they always take you back.

My major professor at Hollins wanted me to go to graduate school. I had scored well on the Graduate Record Examination. He said I could get scholarships. I had never known anybody who went to graduate school, male or female. Teachers were the only professional women I knew. "Career women," as we called them in 1958, were considered hard, driven, sexless—even pitiful, because they had to work. Neither my parents nor my community (minus a few of those teachers) expected me to grow up to be anything other than an accomplished and well-educated wife and mother. My imagination failed me.

In hindsight, I suspect the umbilical cord that attached me to my father and my troubled siblings had never intended to let me go. Anyway, I wouldn't have been caught dead asking Daddy for another dime. Instead, I decided to go home and marry my high school sweetheart. Even as I did it, something beneath the surface said, "Educated to make her father look good. Kept by a husband to make him look good." That damned Veblen.

My relationship with the man I was about to marry had begun in a moment of youthful compatibility and playfulness when I was in the ninth grade. He didn't drink at all at the time and seemed so unlike my father. Yet almost from the beginning, the relationship had been off-again, on-again in a way that reflected our shared ambivalence about love, interdependence, and family. To make matters worse, college had changed us both in ways we did not admit to each other.

My decision to go home in that way came to me in one of those out-of-the-blue flashes that I have come to associate with my most radical and fruitful choices. In the beginning, however, and for many years afterward, I saw it as a failure of courage. Finally, now, after eighteen years of marriage and twenty-four of divorce, I've come to see it differently.

Deep down, I was dying for a strong, happy family of my own. In believing I could create one simply by avoiding the mistakes my parents had made, I had reacted in a way so common it has become a clichè. Little did I know how hard it is to replace ingrained patterns of family behavior—or how much those patterns long to repeat themselves.

Some people say we women marry our fathers. Others say it's our mothers. Some insist we marry our essential unresolved family conflict in order to take another shot at it, hoping, this time, to get it right.

I married a man who was as destructively bound to his troubled family as I was to mine—and equally unsure of what he, left to his own devices, might have wanted to do with his life. The birth of a daughter and then a son bonded us deeper and opened veins of feeling in us and between us that neither of us knew how to handle. Predictably, he and I grew more and more depressed and dissatisfied with each other and with ourselves.

Major bubbles of memory tend to come back to me whole and in the vivid present tense we often use for retelling our dreams. Like this one, which occurred in the late winter of 1964.

President Kennedy is already dead. Betty Friedan's *Feminine Mystique* has just been published. There's a new dance called the twist and a new way of dancing. The Beatles are about to replace Elvis. A childhood friend of mine is about to be shot out of the sky in Vietnam. My childhood is so dead to me that I don't even go to the funeral. The civil rights movement is exposing an underbelly to Alabama that is darker than anybody I knew would have admitted if we hadn't seen it on television every day. Hoses. Dogs. Sunday school girls murdered in church, as demonic and poignant as if Shakespeare—or the Devil himself—had dreamed it up.

I sit in a dark-paneled den in a small suburban house outside Montgomery. My spirits are as dark as the room where I sit. I've never heard of either Betty Friedan or her book. But there she is, a disheveled-looking woman on a black-and-white screen describing a life of despair and ennui that mirrors my own.

Whether the reasons are personal or political or both or neither is of little consequence to me. I am twenty-eight years old, unable to believe that my six-year-old marriage has little chance of long-term survival, unwilling to admit that the depressive bent that has dogged my family for generations has now taken a bite out of me.

I worry about my two-year-old son and five-year-old daughter compulsively and mostly without reason. My feelings for them and for my husband toss between love and fear of loving in a way that alternately saps my energy and blows my heart to bits. A few miles away, troubles grow like weeds around my father's house. When I can find nothing to worry about in my own family, I worry about his.

I go outside to fetch my daughter home from play. The sun sets behind her. The air is unseasonably warm. Something cracks inside me and what flows out is not the despair I expect, but joy and a sense of being profoundly connected to my children, myself, the landscape, and God. I am struck by the familiarity of the feeling and its long absence, which had been like a death.

This moment, fleet as it was, constitutes the great bubble-memory and turning point of my adult life. In retrospect I see how deeply landscape and a sense of place are connected to my experience of the holiness at the center of existence and of all that is most important in life. I mark that day in 1964 as the day my spirit came back to me.

In some symbolic way that was the day I began to come home, not only to the place of my birth but also to what Paul Tillich called the ground of being. Awareness of that ultimate ground (a word that can also mean place) first came to me as a child responding to the natural world around me. Even now, knowing how long and steep the journey forward from that sunset was going to be, I think of it as a road sign pointing "this way."

Within a year of that day I did what had always worked for me in times of crisis. I went to school. It was also around that time that my husband and I discovered a magical backwoods vacation spot on Soldiers' Creek behind the Mobile Bay and began taking our children there every summer. Something about the combination of stillness, woods, water, and the rhythmical sound of waves kissing the shore awakened creativity I didn't know I had and triggered a set of poems that became my first attempt to express the meaning that memory, place, and family hold for me. Ten years later I had a Ph.D. and the job at Auburn in Montgomery.

A few years after that I was divorced. Daddy was diagnosed with lung cancer. My children were growing up. There was nothing I could do for my siblings. The way I saw it, I could either stay in Montgomery and preside over the collapse of my father's house or I could run for my life.

And that's how I came to be driving my Chevette into the sunset in the summer of 1980, humming "the blues done caused me to pack my bags and go" the way Bessie Smith sang it. Not only was Jimmy Carter not reelected in 1980, neither were a lot of other Democrats. As soon as the election was over, the blues started causing just about everybody I knew in Washington to pack their bags and go. Government jobs for yellow-dog Democrats were as scarce as hen's teeth.

The next few years were financially and psychologically challenging beyond anything I could have imagined when I started making the decisions that took me to Washington. With nothing but a rusty hatchet at hand, I had finally taken a swipe at the umbilical cord. Through the blackest depression of my life, I simply hung on. For five years, I got by financially off a combination of freelance writing and teaching that miraculously landed me a position in the College of Journalism at the University of Maryland.

Back home, my father's physical health worsened, as did the

mental health of my brother and two sisters. My father was also dead broke from a lifetime of mismanaging money and throwing it at the problems of his two youngest children. My stepmother had weakened and aged under the strain. Daddy died on February 5, 1985. I went back to Washington the Sunday after his funeral and attended my first Al-Anon meeting. I was still numb to the loss I had suffered and half relieved that my father was gone..

For thirty years I had remembered that conversation outside Lanier High School. Gradually, I had come to understand the kind of group it must have been. Still, it wasn't until Daddy was safely in the ground that I started to investigate what the "family disease of alcoholism" (as Al-Anon literature calls it) can do to families.

Twilight in Washington. Flakes of blowing snow stung my cheeks. The depth of my loneliness sank in. I followed a young woman with a knapsack into the basement of a Lutheran church near the capitol. Though the nave of the church was rather grand, the basement beneath it was as bare and stark as the Baptist Sunday schools I attended as a child with my grandmother. Colorless, plain, and achingly familiar.

Fifteen or twenty people sat in a circle of schoolroom chairs. They seemed unnaturally calm and joked in a way that struck me as odd. A woman who looked like a nun said a higher power was restoring her to sanity. "I choose to call that power 'God,'" she added, "as I understand God."

I thought, "What the hell am I doing here?"

For the first time in my life I heard people talking about alcoholism and other problems in their families. Some of them were recovering alcoholics themselves. The group was three-fourths women, some black and some white. Their faces looked strange to me and suddenly beautiful. They reminded me of Quakers at a meeting.

"Your family life is bound to improve," someone said.

"Mine could hardly get worse," I mumbled. "One half's crazy and the other half's dead."

Nobody laughed. Alcoholism kills people, maims them, costs

them their children, their marriages, their jobs. Lands them in jail, the nut house, the cemetery. The effects on the family are everlasting. It can always get worse. And also better.

The meeting ended. I felt awkward. But somebody said, "Keep coming back," and I did. Soon I found meetings like that one all over the Washington area. Starting there, I began to look at the harm the family psychology had done to me—and to start letting go of the stoic, super-achieving, and lonely role I had always played, at least in part, to please my father. Slowly I learned patterns of behavior more satisfying and productive than the ones I had learned at home. Patterns that—for all my determined independence—I had not, Lord knows, been able to teach myself.

On the first anniversary of Daddy's death, my forty-one-year-old brother suffered a fatal stroke. With his death the life went out of our stepmother.

I spent the summer of 1987 moving her into a nursing home, where she died in September, broken in health and defeated by forty years spent loving my father and trying to fix all the things that were wrong with him and his family. She wanted me to come home to look after my two alcoholic, now mentally ill, sisters.

In our last meaningful conversation, she said, "Do what you think best with the house. Your Daddy loved it." I took her words as a blessing and a kind of permission to live the rest of my life by my own lights.

In the years since that terrible concentration of grief that saw the passing of my father, my brother, and my stepmother in a short nineteen months, I have come to think of them almost altogether as they were in happier times. My mind returns less and less to the shrunken images of themselves they became near the end of their lives. No matter how much we grieve the death of those we love, they often free us to live out something shackled by the very bonds we mourn.

My father's death set me free to begin loosening the grip of the family psychology. After the death of my stepmother and brother were added to his, I cleaned out and sold the home place we had all loved. I returned to Washington with a car full of family photographs, clippings, and letters and began a family history project the likes of which had never crossed my mind before.

By the spring of 1987, I had begun driving my car across the Deep South and into Ohio, Kentucky, and Virginia to search courthouses, local archives, and the attics of strangers for stories and information about three generations of my family. Soon I was calling long-lost relatives and friends of my parents. Not all of them welcomed me with open arms, but no one refused to see me. Some of them had pictures, scrapbooks, and letters. All of them had memories. All of them listened, and eventually most of them talked.

Everywhere I went, big towns and small, Ireland and Scotland as well as America, I found twelve-step meetings for people whose lives and families had been touched by addiction and despair. Gradually, through a process that is still mysterious to me, the history of my family and my efforts to change my life and the way I related to other people began to come together.

When I wasn't teaching or traveling, I was combing the National Archives and the genealogy room at the Library of Congress for references to my ancestors. When I could find the time, I worked at writing what I thought would be the story of how the two sides of my family came to Alabama and became part of its history. It was on such a day that I sat down to write history and, instead, wrote my memory of the day my mother died. Suddenly there it was, the whole thing, in a form that could be read by someone else and understood.

Over the next few months, I came to realize that the story of my family cried out to be told from the point of view of my own childhood. I saw, too, that the bubbles of memory produced images more vivid than anything I had ever written before. Soon the scenes were coming faster than I could write them down, and every sensation reminded me of home. I began to see how sweetly even my saddest memories were mixed with the joys of childhood and the beauties of a landscape so native to me that, in memory, I can hardly tell the air around me from my own skin.

The combination of traveling, remembering, writing, talking to people who had previously been silent, and learning the history of America, the South, Alabama, and my family brought me home to myself, my country, and my region in a way that I could not have imagined when I unpacked those boxes of memorabilia in the fall of 1987. Thomas Wolfe not withstanding, I suspect the urge to be reconciled with home and heritage may be universal. And that urge may lie at the heart of the flood of memoir and autobiographical writing that has come upon us amid our turn-of-the-century rush to move on.

My own sense of place and the need to go home to it follow not Wolfe but T. S. Eliot, who tells us, "The end of all our exploring / Will be to arrive where we started / And know the place for the first time."

ALBERT MURRAY

Epilogue

Regional Particulars and Universal Implications

As a very ambitious writer who would like to create fiction that will
be of major interest not only as American literature but also as a
part of contemporary writing in the world at large, I must say I am
not primarily concerned with recording what it is like or what it
means to be a southerner or even a down-home grandson of slaves.
My concerns are more fundamentally existential, which is perhaps
to say epical, if by epic we mean to suggest an account of a hero
involved with elemental problems of survival rather than with social
issues as such. In any case, my stories are really about what it means
to be human. They are concerned with the life of human feeling.

Which is most certainly not to say that I am not at all or even
only a little concerned with being a southerner, for it is precisely by
processing the raw materials of my southern experience into univer-

sal aesthetic statement that I am most likely to come to terms with my humanity as such. The condition of man is always a matter of the specific texture of existence in a given place, time, and circumstance.

But the point is that the regional particulars—the idiomatic details, the down-home conventions, the provincial customs and folkways—must be *processed* into artistic statement, *stylized* into significance.

Art, as André Malraux points out in *The Voices of Silence,* is the means by which form is rendered into style. And art is also, as Kenneth Burke has said, fundamental living equipment for our existence as human beings. What these two notions suggest to me is a concern with the quality of human consciousness. Which might also be said to be the basic concern not only of education, whether formal or informal, but also of religion and of all ceremonial occasions including holidays, red-letter days, and pastimes as well.

Applied to literature, this becomes, for me at any rate, a concern with the adequate image, by which I mean the image of the hero or effective protagonist, that personification of human endeavor, if you will, which most accurately reflects the complexities and possibilities of contemporary circumstances or indeed any predicament, and also suggests its richest possibilities. Perhaps one could say that an indispensable function of such an image is either to inform or remind us of these possibilities.

As for a working definition of *adequacy,* why not measure it in terms of its statistical validity, reliability, and comprehensiveness? It must yield a solid deduction. It must work time and again, and it must have broad applicability. It must work in the world at large; otherwise it has to be rejected as too exclusive, too narrow, or, to get back to the theme, too provincial. Too southern. Of some down-home significance, perhaps; if you like that sort of thing. But not of very much immediate use elsewhere.

So, yes, it is precisely the regional particulars that the storyteller as full-fledged artist processes or stylizes. But it is the universal statement he should be striving for. Beneath the idiomatic surface of your old down-home stomping ground, with all of the ever-so-evocative local color you work so hard to get just right, is the common ground of mankind in general.

The storyteller either says or implies as follows: *Once upon a time in a place far away or nearby or right on this very spot or wherever, where people did things this way or that or however, there was whoever who was in whichever situation (to wit, et cetera) and who did whatsoever. Once upon a time. But perhaps also time after time after time and so on up to this time and this very day. So take note.*

In other words, as a serious writer and also as an engaging and entertaining storyteller, you are always concerned with what Kenneth Burke calls the *representative anecdote,* which I take to be that little tale or tidbit of gossip, that little incident that is in effect definitive in that it reflects, suggests, or embodies a basic attitude toward experience.

Ever mindful of the guidelines suggested by Malcolm Cowley in *The Literary Situation,* you approach your anecdotal tidbit not as a symbolic action per se, but rather by treating a basic southern occasion as a basic American occasion, which is in turn a basic contemporary occasion, and thus a basic human occasion. According to Cowley: *"If it isn't real, it isn't a symbol. If it isn't a story, it isn't a myth. If a character doesn't live, he can't be an archetype. . . ."*

Another definition. Art is the ultimate extension, elaboration, and refinement of the rituals that reenact the primary survival techniques (and hence reinforce the basic orientation toward experience) of a given people in a given time, place, and circumstance, much the same as holiday commemorations are meant to do.

It is the process of extension, elaboration, and refinement that creates the work of art. It is the *playful* process of extension, elaboration, and refinement that gives rise to the options out of which comes the elegance that is the essence of artistic statement. Such playfulness can give an aesthetic dimension to the most pragmatic of actions.

It is indeed precisely play and playfulness that are indispensable to the creative process. Play in the sense of competition. Play in the sense of chance-taking. Play in the sense of make believe and play also in the sense of vertigo or getting high. Play also in the direction of simple amusement, as in children's games, and play in the direction of gratuitous difficulty, as in increasing the number of jacks you can catch or the higher distance you can jump, and as in the wordplay in *Finnegans Wake* or soundplay in a Bach fugue.

Incidentally, implicit in the matter of playful option-taking extension, elaboration, and refinement is the matter of the function of criticism in the arts. For wherever there is extension, elaboration, and refinement there is the possibility of overextension, overelaboration, and overrefinement, and, as likely as not, attenuation.

Perhaps the very first function of criticism is to mediate between the work of art and the uninitiated reader, viewer, or listener. As mediator, the critic decodes and explains the elements of the game of stylization and makes the aesthetic statement more accessible. Then, having indicated what is being stylized and how it is being stylized, the critic may also give a "professional observer's" opinion as to how effectively it has been stylized and perhaps to what personal and social end. In doing all of this, criticism proceeds in terms of taste, which is to say a highly or specially developed sense of the optimum proportion of the basic elements involved and of the relative suitability of the processing. But all of that is a very special story in itself.

To get back to the matter of the representative anecdote. My primary vernacular, regional, or indigenous, or, yes, down-home source is the fully orchestrated blues statement, which I regard and have attempted to define and promote as a highly pragmatic and indeed a fundamental device for confrontation, improvisation, and existential affirmation: a strategy for acknowledging the fact that life is a low-down dirty shame and for improvising or riffing on the exigencies of the predicament. What is that all about if not continuity in the face of adversity? Which brings us all to the matter of heroic action and the writer to the matter of the heroic image.

I don't know of a more valid, reliable, comprehensive, or sophisticated frame of reference for defining and recounting heroic action than is provided by the blues idiom, which I submit enables the narrator to deal with tragedy, comedy, melodrama, and farce simultaneously. Obviously I do not hear the blues as a simple lamentation by one who has not loved very wisely and not at all well; and certainly not as any species of political torch song. I hear the music counterstating whatever tale of woe (or worse) the lyrics might present for confrontation as part and parcel of the human condition.

The ancient Greek playwrights, remember, addressed themselves to tragic happenings in one form, dealt with comic confusions and resolutions in another *(even on other days),* and for satiric and farcical matters they used still other forms. I associate melodrama with medieval romance. The great Elizabethan tragedies, to be sure, did come to include comic relief sequences as a matter of course.

But the fully orchestrated blues statement is something else again. Even as the lyrics wail and quaver a tale of woe, the music may indicate the negative mood suggested by the dreadful, or in any case regrettable, details, but even so there will also be tantalizing sensuality in the woodwinds, mockery and insouciance among the trumpets, bawdiness from the trombones, a totally captivating, even if sometimes somewhat ambivalent, elegance in the ensembles and in the interplay of the solos and ensembles, plus a beat that is likely to be as affirmative as the ongoing human pulse itself.

There is much to be said about the literary implications of this aspect of my down-home heritage, and I have written not only in direct terms of it in *South to a Very Old Place, The Spyglass Tree,* and *Train Whistle Guitar,* but also in no uncertain terms about it in *The Hero and the Blues* and in *Stomping the Blues,* both of which may be read as being, among other things, books about literary terminology and as attempts at a functional definition of improvisation as heroic action, as a way of responding to traumatic situations creatively. So I will reiterate only in passing that (1) blues lyrics should not be confused with torch songs, which wail the heart-on-sleeve frustrations and yearnings of those rejected or discarded ones who still love not wisely and not at all well; and (2) that the improvisation that is the ancestral imperative of blues procedure is completely consistent with and appropriate to those of the frontiersman, the fugitive slave, and the picaresque hero, the survival of each of whom depended largely on an ability to operate on dynamics equivalent to those of the vamp, the riff, and most certainly the break, which jazz musicians regard as the Moment of Truth, or that disjuncture that should bring out your personal best.

The point of all this is that your representative anecdote also provides your representative man, your *hombre de época,* your all-purpose protagonist, whose personal best is exemplary. Incidentally, speaking of the South as such as a locus of motives, as a context for heroic action, I read fellow southerner William Faulkner's great novel *The Sound and the Fury* as a story about the absence of truly heroic action. Neither poor Benjy, sad Quentin, nor mean Jason can riff or solo on the break or set a personal pace for a truly swinging ensemble. They are all stuck with stock tunes that only add up to sound and fury, signifying a big mess.

But for all the restrictions that you inherited as a southerner during the days of my coming of age as an apprentice in literature, being a southerner did not automatically mean that my mind, my interests, and my aspirations were limited to things southern; moreover, it is not at all unsouthern to read a lot. In any event, it was in a down-home library that I discovered the Joseph in Thomas Mann's *Joseph and His Brothers, Young Joseph, Joseph in Egypt,* and, *Joseph the Provider,* who as I have suggested in *The Hero and the Blues* is a hero whose playful creativity is his stock in trade, and also the salvation of his people.

My attempt to suggest an image of the hero as improviser is Scooter, the first-person narrator of *Train Whistle Guitar, The Spyglass Tree,* and *The Seven League Boots,* in which I try to make the literary equivalent of an Ellington orchestration of a little blue steel and patent leather down-home saying that goes *my name is Jack the Rabbit and my home is in the briar patch,* which for me is only an upbeat way of saying *"woke up this morning [with the] blues all around my bed, . . ."* which means that Scooter could also say *I live in a land menaced by dragons and even Grand Dragons, and that's why I have to be as nimble in brain as in body—or else!—and must either Find or forge my own magic sword and be heroic or nobody.*

All of this is nothing if not down-home stuff. Which brings us to our out chorus: it is precisely such southern "roots" that will dispose and also condition my protagonist to function in terms of the root-lessness that is the basic predicament of all humankind in the contemporary world at large.

Afterword

The way sunlight casts shadows on the ground through the dying leaves of September reminds me of the languid days of the summer's end. A certain smell evokes memories of my mother's room and how her perfume drifted and lingered there. The incandescent glow of a firefly gives me pause to remember the sound of bare feet rushing through a meadow. The taste of butterscotch creates a bittersweet memory of my family gathered together at Christmas. And that certain sound that only the creak of a wooden swing can make carries me back to the arms of my father as he pulled me close to him on the front porch swing to tell me a story. I can smell his Old Spice and see the laughter in his blue eyes when I asked him to tell me another story, and to make it long, and to tell it slow. For it was not just the words that were important, but the sense of well-being I felt just having him there with me.

The Remembered Gate: Memoirs by Alabama Writers is not only about the words you have read. It is about those memories, some of joy and some of pain, but all bound up in the tangible world that makes us who we are. And it is about the sense of well-being that we experience knowing these words are a gift to us all.

These memoirs can be a passageway for Alabama's children—to learn about their history, their community, and how their home state has shaped the lives of nineteen widely acclaimed Alabama writers. There are not as many porch swings for our children as there once were. This fact challenges each of us who care about the personal legacy we will leave to make sure the wonder of a firefly or the sweet taste of butterscotch will one day inspire our children to tell their stories.

The Honorable Mark Kennedy

President, Board of Directors
Alabama Corporate Foundation for Children

Contributors

MARY WARD BROWN was born, raised, and still lives on a farm near Marion, in the Alabama Black Belt. She is a graduate of Judson College and studied creative writing at the University of Alabama and by correspondence at the University of North Carolina. Her collection of short stories, *Tongues of Flame,* received the PEN/Hemingway Award for Best First Fiction in 1987. Subsequent stories are included in anthologies such as *The Christ-Haunted Landscape; Downhome; God, Stories; A New Life, Stories and Photographs; Many Voices, Many Rooms;* and *Alabama Bound.* Her new collection of stories, *It Wasn't All Dancing,* will be published by the University of Alabama Press in 2002. She received the Governor's Award in 1993 and the 1997 Distinguished Career Award from the Society of Fine Arts, University of Alabama.

WILLIAM COBB grew up in Demopolis, Alabama. His novels include *Coming of Age at the Y, The Hermit King, A Walk through Fire, Harry Reunited, A Spring of Souls,* and *Wings of Morning.* His short-story collection, *Somewhere in All This Green,* was given the 2000 Book of the Year Award by the Alabama Library Association. The volume includes the widely anthologized "The Stone Soldier," which was first published in *Story* magazine and given its top prize nationally the year of its publication. Cobb is the recipient of fellowships from the National Endowment for the Arts and the Alabama State Council on the Arts. He lives in Montevallo.

FANNIE FLAGG is a native of south Alabama who has enjoyed a distinguished career as an actress and public figure and as a writer. Her novels include *Daisy Fay and the Miracle Man, Fried Green Tomatoes at the Whistle Stop Café, Coming Attractions,* and *Welcome to the World, Baby Girl!* The Alabama State Council on the Arts awarded Flagg the Distinguished Artist Award for 2001. Her script for *Fried Green Tomatoes* was nominated for both the Academy and Writers' Guild of America awards and won the highly regarded Scripters Award. Flagg narrated the novel on audiotape and received a Grammy nomination for Best Spoken Word. She lives in Santa Barbara, California, but makes regular visits to Alabama and is an active alumna of Birmingham Southern College.

PATRICIA FOSTER grew up in Foley, Alabama. Her edited books include *Minding the Body: Women Writers on Body and Soul; Sister to Sister: Women Write about the Unbreakable Bond;* and *The Healing Circle: Narratives of Recovery.* Her memoir, *All the Lost Girls: Confessions of a Southern Daughter,* was published in 2000. Foster is the recipient of a PEN/Jerard Fund Award and a Florida Arts Council Award. Her fiction and nonfiction have appeared in *Prairie Schooner, Virginia Quarterly Review, Gettysburg Review,* and *Southern Humanities Review.* She received a Ph.D. from Florida State University and an MFA from the Iowa Writers' Workshop. She is currently an associate professor in the MFA program in nonfiction at the University of Iowa.

A native of Mobile, FRYE GAILLARD started his career covering the South for the *Mobile Press Register* and served as a staff writer and later managing editor of the award-winning *Race Relations Reporter.* Gaillard became the southern editor of the *Charlotte Observer,* where he covered the Charlotte-Mecklenburg school busing controversy, the rise and fall of Jim Bakker and PTL, Jesse Jackson's presidential campaign, and the presidency of Jimmy Carter. Among his more than sixteen books are *The 521 All-Stars: A Championship Story of Baseball and Community; As Long as the Waters*

Flow: Native Americans in the South and East; The Heart of Dixie: Southern Rebels, Renegades, and Heroes; and *If I Were a Carpenter: Twenty Years of Habitat for Humanity.*

CHARLES GAINES's books include *Dangler; Stay Hungry* (nominated for the National Book Award); *Pumping Iron, Staying Hard; A Family Place: A Man Returns to the Center of His Life;* and a memoir, *The Next Valley Over: An Angler's Progress.* He is the recipient of two Cine Golden Eagle Awards for television writing, an Emmy for television writing, and a Writers' Guild of America Annual Award nomination for film writing. He is special correspondent for *Sports Afield* and a contributing editor to *Men's Journal.* He divides his time between homes in Nova Scotia and Birmingham, Alabama.

ANDREW GLAZE was born in Tennessee and raised in Birmingham, Alabama, where he eventually returned to work as a reporter during the civil rights struggle. His first major poetry collection, *Damned Ugly Children,* was a runner-up for the Pulitzer Prize. His *Someone Will Go On Owing: Selected Poems, 1966–1992* received the 1998 SEBA Poetry Book of the Year Award. Glaze received the Bruce P. Rossley Literary Award (Boston) in 2001.

WAYNE GREENHAW is a native of Town Creek, Alabama. He has written novels, nonfiction, and plays and has worked in public relations. Among his thirteen books are *The Golfer; Hard Travelin'; King of Country; Tombigbee and Other Stories; Beyond the Night; The Making of a Hero: Lt. William L. Calley and the My Lai Massacre;* and *Alabama: Portrait of a State.* Greenhaw's awards include Travel Writer of the Year (Southeastern Tourism Society, 1995); numerous state, regional, and national citations for his reporting; and a 1972–73 Nieman Fellowship at Harvard. He has been director of the Alabama Department of Travel and Tourism, a magazine editor and publisher, associate publisher of Black Belt Press, and a teacher at several central Alabama universities. He lives in Montgomery.

JAMES (JIM) HASKINS is the author of more than one hundred books for adults, young adults, and children. He has been honored for individual books with Coretta Scott King, Carter G. Woodson, Alabama Library Association, the English-speaking Union, and ASCAP Deems Taylor awards; and the *Washington Post*/Children's Book Guild has recognized him for his body of work in nonfiction for young people. Haskins was a member of the National Education Advisory Committee of the Commission on the Bicentennial of the United States Constitution. He serves as general editor of the Hippocrene African Language Dictionary series and was general editor of the Hippocrene's Great Religions of the World series. Haskins's latest books include *Power to the People: The Rise and Fall of the Black Panther Party; Louis Farrakhan and the Nation of Islam; Bayard Rustin: Behind the Scenes of the Civil Rights Movement,* and *I Am Rosa Parks,* written with Rosa Parks, *Hal Jackson: The House That Jack Built, Toni Morrison: The Magic of Words, Conjure Times: Black Magicians in America,* and *Building a New Land: African Americans in Colonial America.* Haskins was born in Demopolis, Alabama, and divides his time between New York and Florida, where he teaches at the University of Florida, Gainesville.

Born in Texas and raised mainly in Alabama, poet ANDREW HUDGINS has published five poetry collections—*Saints and Strangers; After the Lost War: A Narrative* (winner of the Poets' Prize); *The Never-Ending: New Poems* (a finalist for the National Book Award); *The Glass Hammer: A Southern Childhood;* and *Babylon in a Jar*—and an essay collection, *The Glass Anvil.* His poetry and essays appear regularly in literary journals and magazines such as *American Scholar, Atlantic Monthly, Georgia Review, Poetry,* and *Southern Review.* He is currently professor of English at Ohio State University.

ROBERT INMAN grew up in Elba, Alabama. He is an award-winning screenwriter and the author of three novels: *Dairy Queen Days, Home Fires Burning,* and *Old Dogs and Children.* His fourth novel, *Captain Saturday,* will be published by Little, Brown in 2002. His nonfiction collection, *Coming Home: Life, Love, and All Things Southern,* was published in 2000. Recipient of the Writers' Guild of America Award, as well as two awards for outstanding fiction from the Alabama Library Association, Inman was also a longtime columnist for the *Charlotte Observer.*

Born in north Alabama, near Falkville, RODNEY JONES has published poems in every major American poetry magazine and has six collections of poetry, including *The Story They Told Us of Light, The Unborn, Transparent Gestures, Apocalyptic Narrative and Other Poems, Things That Happen Once,* and *Elegy for the Southern Drawl* (runner-up for the 2000 Pulitzer Prize). Among Jones's awards are the National Book Critics Circle Award for Poetry, the Jean Stein Award of the National Institute of Arts and Letters, the Lavan Younger Poets Award from the Academy of American Poets, the *Kenyon Review* Award for Literary Excellence, and a Guggenheim Fellowship. He is professor of English at Southern Illinois University, Carbondale.

NANCI KINCAID grew up in Florida but states that Alabama has always been the constant in her life. She has lived in Alabama three times—during very different chapters in her life. And when living away she has visited Alabama regularly. Her works of fiction include *Crossing Blood, Pretending the Bed Is a Raft,* and *Balls.* Her new novel, *Verbena,* set in Alabama, will be out in May (Algonquin). She has been awarded grants from the National Endowment for the Arts and the Mary Ingraham Bunting Foundation. In 1996 she was awarded a literature fellowship from the Alabama State Council on the Arts.

Born in Athens, Alabama, C. ERIC LINCOLN was William Rand Kenan Jr. Professor Emeritus of Religion and Culture at Duke University. His widely acclaimed publications include *The Black Muslims in America; The Black Church Since Frazier; Race, Religion, and the Continuing American Dilemma;* and with Lawrence H. Mamiya,

The Black Church in the African American Experience. Lincoln was also a novelist *(The Avenue, Clayton City),* a poet *(This Road Since Freedom),* and a writer of acclaimed and widely performed hymns. Founding president of the Black Academy of Arts and Letters and a Fellow of the American Academy of Arts and Sciences, Dr. Lincoln died in June 2000.

ALBERT MURRAY was born in Nokomis, Alabama. He taught literature and directed college theater at Tuskegee Institute and retired as major from the U.S. Air Force. Murray has been O'Connor Professor of Literature at Colgate University, has taught at the University of Massachusetts and Emory University, and has been the Paul Anthony Brick Lecturer at the University of Missouri. He is the author of a trilogy of novels, *South to a Very Old Place, Train Whistle Guitar,* and *The Seven League Boots,* and nonfiction works on aesthetics, literature, race relations, and music, including *The Hero and the Blues, Stomping the Blues, The Omni-Americans,* and *Good Morning Blues: The Autobiography of Count Basie* (as told to Albert Murray). Murray was the first recipient of the Harper Lee Award for the Distinguished Alabama Writer (1998), presented by the Alabama Writers' Forum. He lives in New York City, where he helped found, with musician Winton Marsalis, the Jazz at Lincoln Center Program.

SENA JETER NASLUND was born in Birmingham, Alabama, and attended Alabama public schools before taking a B.A. at Birmingham Southern University and later receiving an M.A. and Ph.D. from the University of Iowa Writers' Workshop. She is the author of the national best-seller *Ahab's Wife, or The Star Gazer; Sherlock in Love;* and *The Animal Way to Love.* Her short-story collections are *The Disobedience of Water* and *Ice Skating at the North Pole.* In 2001 Naslund received the Book of the Year Award from the Alabama Library Association for *Ahab's Wife* and the Harper Lee Award for the Distinguished Alabama Writer. Her work has appeared in *Paris Review, Georgia Review, Michigan Quarterly Review,* and other journals. Naslund teaches creative writing at the University of

Louisville, where she holds the title Distinguished Teaching Professor. She directs the brief-residency MFA in Writing at Spalding University, Louisville.

HELEN NORRIS, a longtime resident of Montgomery, Alabama, has published four novels, *Something More than Earth, For the Glory of God, More than Seven Watchmen,* and *Walk with the Sickle Moon.* Her four short-story collections are *Water into Wine, The Christmas Wife, The Burning Glass,* and *One Day in the Life of a Born Again Loser.* The title story of *The Christmas Wife* was adapted for television, and her short story "The Cracker Man" was made into a PBS film. Norris has received four O. Henry Awards, a Pushcart Prize, and the Pen Women's Biennial Award for best novel. She was a finalist for the PEN/Faulkner Award in 1986 and received the 2000 Harper Lee Award for the Distinguished Alabama Writer. Norris is also the poet laureate of Alabama, 1999–2003. Her poetry collections include *Whatever Is Round* and *Rain Pulse.*

JUDITH HILLMAN PATERSON grew up in Montgomery, Alabama. She is author of several literary studies, including a scholarly work on Sir Thomas More. She has published in *The New York Times Book Review, Los Angeles Times,* and *Village Voice.* Her memoir, *Sweet Mystery: A Book of Remembering,* was published to acclaim by Farrar, Straus & Giroux in 1996 and in paperback by the University of Alabama Press in 2001. Paterson is professor of journalism at the University of Maryland and is currently writing a work of fiction. She also hosts a television program interviewing writers for UMTV cable television in Maryland.

PHYLLIS PERRY was born in Atlanta and grew up in Tuskegee and Perote, Alabama. A Pulitzer Prize–winning newspaper editor, Perry is also author of *Stigmata: A Novel,* which was a selection of both the Book-of-the-Month Club and Quality Paperback Book Club and a finalist of the QPB New Voice Award. Perry lives in Atlanta, where she is at work on a second novel.

Deep South Books

The University of Alabama Press

VICKI COVINGTON
Gathering Home

VICKI COVINGTON
The Last Hotel for Women

NANCI KINCAID
Crossing Blood

PAUL HEMPHILL
Leaving Birmingham: Notes of a Native Son

ROY HOFFMAN
Almost Family

HELEN NORRIS
One Day in the Life of a Born Again Loser and Other Stories

PATRICIA FOSTER
All the Lost Girls: Confessions of a Southern Daughter

SAM HODGES
B–4

HOWELL RAINES
Whiskey Man

3/2004